Beginning Android

Mark L. Murphy

Beginning Android

Copyright © 2009 by Mark L. Murphy

ISBN-13 (pbk): 978-1-4302-2419-8

ISBN-13 (electronic): 978-1-4302-2420-4

Printed and bound in the United States of America (POD)

Trademarked names may appear in this book. Rather than use a trademark symbol with every occurrence of a trademarked name, we use the names only in an editorial fashion and to the benefit of the trademark owner, with no intention of infringement of the trademark.

Java™ and all Java-based marks are trademarks or registered trademarks of Sun Microsystems, Inc., in the US and other countries. Apress, Inc., is not affiliated with Sun Microsystems, Inc., and this book was written without endorsement from Sun Microsystems, Inc.

Lead Editor: Matthew Moodie
Editorial Board: Clay Andres, Steve Anglin, Mark Beckner, Ewan Buckingham, Tony Campbell, Gary Cornell, Jonathan Gennick, Michelle Lowman, Matthew Moodie, Duncan Parkes, Jeffrey Pepper, Douglas Pundick, Frank Pohlmann, Ben Renow-Clarke, Dominic Shakeshaft, Matt Wade, Tom Welsh
Project Manager: Douglas Sulenta
Copy Editors: Candace English and Katie Stence
Associate Production Director: Kari Brooks-Copony
Production Editor: Ellie Fountain
Compositor: Susan Glinert
Proofreader: Lisa Hamilton
Indexer: BIM Indexing & Proofreading Services
Cover Designer: Kurt Krames
Manufacturing Director: Tom Debolski

Distributed to the book trade worldwide by Springer-Verlag New York, Inc., 233 Spring Street, 6th Floor, New York, NY 10013. Phone 1-800-SPRINGER, fax 201-348-4505, e-mail orders-ny@springer-sbm.com, or visit http://www.springeronline.com.

For information on translations, please e-mail info@apress.com, or visit http://www.apress.com.

Apress and friends of ED books may be purchased in bulk for academic, corporate, or promotional use. eBook versions and licenses are also available for most titles. For more information, reference our Special Bulk Sales–eBook Licensing web page at http://www.apress.com/info/bulksales.

The source code for this book is available to readers at http://www.apress.com.

Contents at a Glance

PART 1 ■■■ Core Concepts

PART 2 ■■■ Activities

PART 3 ■■■ Data Stores, Network Services, and APIs

PART 4 ■■■ Intents

PART 5 ■■■ Content Providers and Services

PART 6 ▰▰▰ Other Android Capabilities

Contents

PART 1 ■■■ Core Concepts

PART 2 ■■■ Activities

PART 3 ▪▪▪ Data Stores, Network Services, and APIs

PART 4 ■■■ Intents

PART 5 ■■■ Content Providers and Services

PART 6 ■■■ Other Android Capabilities

xvi CONTENTS

CHAPTER 36 Searching with SearchManager

Hunting Season
Search Yourself
Craft the Search Activity
Update the Manifest
Searching for Meaning in Randomness

CHAPTER 37 Development Tools

Hierarchical Management
Delightful Dalvik Debugging Detailed, Demoed
Logging
File Push and Pull
Screenshots
Location Updates
Placing Calls and Messages
Put it On My Card
Creating a Card Image
Inserting the Card

CHAPTER 38 Where Do We Go from Here?

Questions. Sometimes with Answers.
Heading to the Source
Getting Your News Fix

APPENDIX Introducing Android 1.5

INDEX

xvi CONTENTS

CHAPTER 36 Searching with SearchManager 313

Hunting Season 313
Search Yourself 315
    Craft the Search Activity 315
    Update the Manifest 319
Searching for Meaning in Randomness 320

CHAPTER 37 Development Tools 321

Hierarchical Management 321
Delightful Dalvik Debugging Detailed, Demoed 327
    Logging 328
    File Push and Pull 329
    Screenshots 330
    Location Updates 331
    Placing Calls and Messages 331
Put it On My Card 334
    Creating a Card Image 334
    Inserting the Card 335

CHAPTER 38 Where Do We Go from Here? 337

Questions. Sometimes with Answers. 337
Heading to the Source 338
Getting Your News Fix 338

APPENDIX Introducing Android 1.5 339

INDEX 347

About the Author

MARK MURPHY is the founder of CommonsWare and the author of the Busy Coder's Guide to Android Development. A three-time entrepreneur, his experience ranges from consulting on open source and collaborative development for the Fortune 500 to application development on just about anything smaller than a mainframe. He has been a software developer for over 25 years, from the TRS-80 to the latest crop of mobile devices. A polished speaker, Mr. Murphy has delivered conference presentations and training sessions on a wide array of topics internationally.

Mr. Murphy writes the Building 'Droids column for AndroidGuys and the Android Angle column for NetworkWorld.

Outside of CommonsWare, Mr. Murphy has an avid interest in how the Internet will play a role in citizen involvement with politics and government. He is also a contributor to the Rebooting America essay collection.

Acknowledgments

I would like to thank the Android team, not only for putting out a good product, but for invaluable assistance on the Android Google Groups. In particular, I would like to thank Romain Guy, Justin Mattson, Dianne Hackborn, Jean-Baptiste Queru, Jeff Sharkey, and Xavier Ducrohet.

Icons used in the sample code were provided by the Nuvola[1] icon set.

---

1. http://www.icon-king.com/?p=15

Introduction

Welcome to the Book!

Thanks for your interest in developing applications for Android! Increasingly, people will access Internet-based services using so-called "non-traditional" means, such as mobile devices. The more we do in that space now, the more that people will help invest in that space to make it easier to build more powerful mobile applications in the future. Android is new—Android-powered devices appeared on the scene first in late 2008—but it likely will rapidly grow in importance due to the size and scope of the Open Handset Alliance.

Most of all, thanks for your interest in this book! I sincerely hope you find it useful and at least occasionally entertaining.

Prerequisites

If you are interested in programming for Android, you will need at least basic understanding of how to program in Java. Android programming is done using Java syntax, plus a class library that resembles a subset of the Java SE library (plus Android-specific extensions). If you have not programmed in Java before, you probably should learn how that works before attempting to dive into programming for Android.

The book does not cover in any detail how to download or install the Android development tools, either the Eclipse IDE flavor or the standalone flavor. The Android Web site[2] covers this quite nicely. The material in the book should be relevant whether you use the IDE or not. You should download, install, and test out the Android development tools from the Android Web site before trying any of the examples listed in this book.

Editions of This Book

This book is being produced via a partnership between Apress and CommonsWare. You are reading the Apress edition, which is available in print and in digital form from various digital book services.

CommonsWare continually updates the original material and makes it available to members of its Warescription program, under the title *The Busy Coder's Guide to Android Development*.

CommonsWare maintains a FAQ about this partnership at http://commonsware.com/apress.

---

2. http://code.google.com/android/index.html

Source Code License

The source code samples shown in this book are available for download from the Apress Web site.[3] All of the Android projects are licensed under the Apache 2.0 License[4], in case you have the desire to reuse any of it.

---

3. http://www.apress.com/book/view/1430224193
4. http://www.apache.org/licenses/LICENSE-2.0.html

PART 1

###

Core Concepts

CHAPTER 1

■ ■ ■

The Big Picture

Android devices, by and large, will be mobile phones. While the Android technology is being discussed for use in other areas (e.g., car dashboard "PCs"), for the most part, you can think of Android as being used on phones.

For developers, this has benefits and drawbacks.

On the plus side, circa 2009, Android-style smartphones are sexy. Offering Internet services over mobile devices dates back to the mid-1990s and the Handheld Device Markup Language (HDML). However, only in recent years have phones capable of Internet access taken off. Now, thanks to trends like text messaging and to products like Apple's iPhone, phones that can serve as Internet access devices are rapidly gaining popularity. So, working on Android applications gives you experience with an interesting technology (Android) in a fast-moving market segment (Internet-enabled phones), which is always a good thing.

The problem comes when you actually have to program the darn things.

Anyone with experience in programming for PDAs or phones has felt the pain of phones simply being *small* in all sorts of dimensions:

- Screens are small (you won't get comments like, "Is that a 24-inch LCD in your pocket, or . . .?").

- Keyboards, if they exist, are small.

- Pointing devices, if they exist, are annoying (as anyone who has lost their stylus will tell you) or inexact (large fingers and "multi-touch" LCDs are not a good mix).

- CPU speed and memory are tight compared to desktops and servers you may be used to.

- You can have any programming language and development framework you want, so long as it was what the device manufacturer chose and burned into the phone's silicon.

- And, so on . . .

Moreover, applications running on a phone have to deal with the fact that they're *on a phone*. People with mobile phones tend to get very irritated when their phones don't work, which is why the "Can you hear me now?" ad campaign from Verizon Wireless has been popular for the past few years. Similarly, those same people will get irritated at you if your program "breaks" their phone by

- tying up the CPU so that calls can't be received

- not working properly with the rest of the phone's OS, such that your application doesn't quietly fade to the background when a call comes in or needs to be placed

- crashing the phone's operating system, such as by leaking memory like a sieve

Hence, developing programs for a phone is a different experience than developing desktop applications, Web sites, or back-end server processes. You wind up with different-looking tools, different-behaving frameworks, and "different than you're used to" limitations on what you can do with your program.

What Android tries to do is meet you halfway:

- You get a commonly-used programming language (Java) with some commonly used libraries (e.g., some Apache Commons APIs) along with support for tools you may be used to (Eclipse).

- You get a fairly rigid and separate framework in which your programs need to run so they can be "good citizens" on the phone and not interfere with other programs or the operation of the phone itself.

As you may expect, much of this book deals with that framework and how you write programs that work within its confines and take advantage of its capabilities.

What Androids Are Made Of

When you write a desktop application, you are "master of your own domain." You launch your main window and any child windows—like dialog boxes—that are needed. From your standpoint, you are your own world, leveraging features supported by the operating system, but largely ignorant of any other program that may be running on the computer at the same time. If you do interact with other programs, it is typically through an API, such as using JDBC (or frameworks atop it) to communicate with MySQL or another database.

Android has similar concepts, but packaged differently, and structured to make phones more crash-resistant.

Activities

The building block of the user interface is the **activity**. You can think of an activity as being the Android analogue for the window or dialog in a desktop application.

While it is possible for activities to not have a user interface, most likely your "headless" code will be packaged in the form of content providers or services, like the following described.

Content Providers

Content providers provide a level of abstraction for any data stored on the device that is accessible by multiple applications. The Android development model encourages you to make your own data available to other applications, as well as your own—building a content provider lets you do that, while maintaining complete control over how your data gets accessed.

Intents

Intents are system messages, running around the inside of the device, notifying applications of various events, from hardware state changes (e.g., an SD card was inserted), to incoming data (e.g., an SMS message arrived), to application events (e.g., your activity was launched from the device's main menu). Not only can you respond to intents, but you can create your own, to launch other activities, or to let you know when specific situations arise (e.g., raise such-and-so intent when the user gets within 100 meters of this-and-such location).

Services

Activities, content providers, and intent receivers are all short-lived and can be shut down at any time. Services, on the other hand, are designed to keep running, if needed, independent of any activity. You might use a service for checking for updates to an RSS feed, or to play back music even if the controlling activity is no longer operating.

Stuff at Your Disposal

Android comes with a number of features to help you develop applications.

Storage

You can package data files with your application, for things that do not change, such as icons or help files. You also can carve out a small bit of space on the device itself, for databases or files containing user-entered or retrieved data needed by your application. If the user supplies bulk storage, like an SD card, you can read and write files on there as needed.

Network

Android devices will generally be Internet-ready, through one communications medium or another. You can take advantage of the Internet access at any level you wish, from raw Java sockets all the way up to a built-in WebKit-based Web browser widget you can embed in your application.

Multimedia

Android devices have the ability to play back and record audio and video. While the specifics may vary from device to device, you can query the device to learn its capabilities and then take advantage of the multimedia capabilities as you see fit, whether that is to play back music, take pictures with the camera, or use the microphone for audio note-taking.

GPS

Android devices will frequently have access to location providers, such as GPS, that can tell your applications where the device is on the face of the Earth. In turn, you can display maps or otherwise take advantage of the location data, such as tracking a device's movements if the device has been stolen.

Phone Services

Of course, Android devices are typically phones, allowing your software to initiate calls, send and receive SMS messages, and everything else you expect from a modern bit of telephony technology.

■ ■ ■

CHAPTER 2

Project Structure

$\mathbf{T}$he Android build system is organized around a specific directory tree structure for your Android project, much like any other Java project. The specifics, though, are fairly unique to Android and what it does to prepare the actual application that will run on the device or emulator. Here's a quick primer on the project structure to help you make sense of it all, particularly for the sample code referenced in this book, which can be found in the Source Code area of the Apress Web Site at http://apress.com.

Root Contents

When you create a new Android project (e.g., via the activitycreator script, which you will see in Chapter 4, or an Android-enabled IDE), you get several items in the project's root directory:

- AndroidManifest.xml, an XML file describing the application being built and what components—activities, services, etc.—are being supplied by that application

- build.xml, an Ant[1] script for compiling the application and installing it on the device

- default.properties, a property file used by the Ant build script

- bin/ holds the application once it is compiled

- libs/ holds any third-party Java JARs your application requires

- src/ holds the Java source code for the application

- res/ holds resources, such as icons, GUI layouts, and the like, that get packaged with the compiled Java in the application

- assets/ holds other static files you wish packaged with the application for deployment onto the device

The Sweat of Your Brow

When you create an Android project (e.g., via activitycreator), you supply the fully-qualified class name of the "main" activity for the application (e.g., com.commonsware.android.SomeDemo).

---

1. http://ant.apache.org/

You will then find that your project's src/ tree already has the namespace directory tree in place, plus a stub Activity subclass representing your main activity (e.g., src/com/commonsware/android/SomeDemo.java). You are welcome to modify this file and add others to the src/ tree as needed to implement your application.

The first time you compile the project (e.g., via ant), out in the "main" activity's namespace directory, the Android build chain will create R.java. This contains a number of constants tied to the various resources you placed out in the res/ directory tree. You should not modify R.java yourself, letting the Android tools handle it for you. You will see throughout many of the samples where we reference things in R.java (e.g., referring to a layout's identifier via R.layout.main).

The Rest of the Story

As already mentioned, the res/ directory tree holds resources—static files that are packaged along with your application, either in their original form or, occasionally, in a preprocessed form. Some of the subdirectories you will find or create under res/ include

- res/drawable/ for images (PNG, JPEG, etc.)

- res/layout/ for XML-based UI layout specifications

- res/menu/ for XML-based menu specifications

- res/raw/ for general-purpose files (e.g., a CSV file of account information)

- res/values/ for strings, dimensions, and the like

- res/xml/ for other general-purpose XML files you wish to ship

We will cover all of these and more in later chapters of this book, particularly Chapter 19.

What You Get Out of It

When you compile your project (via ant or the IDE), the results go into the bin/ directory under your project root, specifically:

- bin/classes/ holds the compiled Java classes

- bin/classes.dex holds the executable created from those compiled Java classes

- bin/yourapp.ap_ holds your application's resources, packaged as a ZIP file (where yourapp is the name of your application)

- bin/yourapp-debug.apk or bin/yourapp-unsigned.apk is the actual Android application (where yourapp is the name of your application)

The .apk file is a ZIP archive containing the .dex file, the compiled edition of your resources (resources.arsc), any un-compiled resources (such as what you put in res/raw/) and the AndroidManifest.xml file. It is also digitally signed, with the -debug portion of the filename indicating it has been signed using a debug key that works with the emulator, or -unsigned indicating that you built your application for release (ant release), but the APK still needs to be signed using jarsigner and an official key.

CHAPTER 3

■ ■ ■

Inside the Manifest

The foundation for any Android application is the manifest file: `AndroidManifest.xml` in the root of your project. Here is where you declare what is inside your application—the activities, the services, and so on. You also indicate how these pieces attach themselves to the overall Android system; for example, you indicate which activity (or activities) should appear on the device's main menu (aka the launcher).

When you create your application, you will get a starter manifest generated for you. For a simple application, offering a single activity and nothing else, the auto-generated manifest will probably work out fine, or perhaps require a few minor modifications. On the other end of the spectrum, the manifest file for the Android API demo suite is over 1,000 lines long. Your production Android applications will probably fall somewhere in the middle.

Most of the interesting bits of the manifest will be described in greater detail in the chapters on their associated Android features. For example, the `service` element is described in greater detail in Chapter 30. For now, you just need to understand what the role of the manifest is and its general construction.

In the Beginning There Was the Root, and It Was Good

The root of all manifest files is, not surprisingly, a `manifest` element:

```
<manifest xmlns:android="http://schemas.android.com/apk/res/android"
  package="com.commonsware.android.search">
...
</manifest>
```

Note the namespace declaration. Curiously, the generated manifests apply it only on the attributes, not the elements (e.g., it's `manifest`, not `android:manifest`). However, that pattern works, so unless Android changes, stick with their pattern.

The biggest piece of information you need to supply on the `manifest` element is the `package` attribute (also curiously not namespaced). Here you can provide the name of the Java package that will be considered the "base" of your application. Then, everywhere else in the manifest file that needs a class name, you can just substitute a leading dot as shorthand for the package. For example, if you needed to refer to `com.commonsware.android.search.Snicklefritz` in our example manifest, you could just use `.Snicklefritz` since `com.commonsware.android.search` is defined as the application's package.

Permissions, Instrumentations, and Applications (Oh, My!)

Underneath the manifest element, you will find the following:

- uses-permission elements to indicate what permissions your application will need in order to function properly. See Chapter 29 for more details.

- permission elements to declare permissions that activities or services might require other applications hold in order to use your application's data or logic. Again, more details are forthcoming in Chapter 29.

- instrumentation elements to indicate code that should be invoked on key system events, such as starting up activities, for the purposes of logging or monitoring.

- uses-library elements to hook in optional Android components, such as mapping services

- Possibly a uses-sdk element to indicate what version of the Android SDK the application was built for.

- An application element defining the guts of the application that the manifest describes.

In the following example the manifest has uses-permission elements to indicate some device capabilities the application will need—in this case, permissions to allow the application to determine its current location. And there is the application element, whose contents will describe the activities, services, and whatnot that make up the bulk of the application itself.

```
<manifest xmlns:android="http://schemas.android.com/apk/res/android"
  package="com.commonsware.android">
  <uses-permission
    android:name="android.permission.ACCESS_LOCATION" />
  <uses-permission
    android:name="android.permission.ACCESS_GPS" />
  <uses-permission
    android:name="android.permission.ACCESS_ASSISTED_GPS" />
  <uses-permission
    android:name="android.permission.ACCESS_CELL_ID" />
  <application>
...
  </application>
</manifest>
```

Your Application Does Something, Right?

The real meat of the manifest file is the children of the application element.

By default, when you create a new Android project, you get a single activity element:

```
<manifest xmlns:android="http://schemas.android.com/apk/res/android"
    package="com.commonsware.android.skeleton">
    <application>
        <activity android:name=".Now" android:label="Now">
            <intent-filter>
                <action android:name="android.intent.action.MAIN" />
                <category android:name="android.intent.category.LAUNCHER" />
            </intent-filter>
        </activity>
    </application>
</manifest>
```

This element supplies android:name for the class implementing the activity, android:label for the display name of the activity, and (frequently) an intent-filter child element describing under what conditions this activity will be displayed. The stock activity element sets up your activity to appear in the launcher, so users can choose to run it. As you'll see later in this book, you can have several activities in one project if you so choose.

You may also have one or more receiver elements indicating non-activities that should be triggered under certain conditions, such as when an SMS message comes in. These are called intent receivers and are described in Chapter 23.

You may have one or more provider elements indicating content providers—components that supply data to your activities and, with your permission, other activities in other applications on the device. These wrap up databases or other data stores into a single API that any application can use. Later you'll see how to create content providers and how to use content providers that you or others create.

Finally, you may have one or more service elements describing services—long-running pieces of code that can operate independent of any activity. The quintessential example is the MP3 player, where you want the music to keep playing even if the user pops open other activities and the MP3 player's user interface is "misplaced." Chapters 30 and 31 cover how to create and use services.

Achieving the Minimum

Android, like most operating systems, goes through various revisions, versions, and changes. Some of these affect the Android SDK, meaning there are new classes, methods, or parameters you can use that you could not in previous versions of the SDK.

If you want to ensure your application is run only on devices that have a certain version (or higher) of the Android environment, you will want to add a uses-sdk element as a child of the root manifest element in your AndroidManifest.xml file. The uses-sdk element has one attribute, minSdkVersion, indicating which SDK version your application requires:

```
<manifest xmlns:android="http://schemas.android.com/apk/res/android"
  package="com.commonsware.android.search">
<uses-sdk minSdkVersion="2" />
...
</manifest>
```

At the time of this writing, there are two possible minSdkVersion values:

- 1, indicating the original Android 1.0 SDK

- 2, indicating the Android 1.1 SDK

If you leave the uses-sdk element out entirely, it will behave as though minSdkVersion is set to 1.

If you set uses-sdk, the application will install only on compatible devices. You do not have to specify the latest SDK, but if you choose an older one, it is up to you to ensure your application works on every SDK version you claim is compatible. For example, if you leave off uses-sdk, in effect you are stipulating that your application works on every Android SDK version ever released, and it is up to you to test your application to determine if this is indeed the case.

PART 2

Activities

CHAPTER 4

■■■

Creating a Skeleton Application

Every programming-language or -environment book starts off with the ever-popular "Hello, World!" demonstration: just enough of a program to prove you can build things, not so much that you cannot understand what is going on. However, the typical "Hello, World!" program has no interactivity (that is, it just dumps the words to a console), and so is really boring.

This chapter demonstrates a simple project, but one using Advanced Push-Button Technology and the current time to show you how a simple Android activity works.

Begin at the Beginning

To work with anything in Android, you need a project. With ordinary Java, if you wanted, you could just write a program as a single file, compile it with javac, and run it with java, without any other support structures. Android is more complex, but to help keep it manageable Google has supplied tools to help create the project. If you are using an Android-enabled IDE, such as Eclipse with the Android plugin (available in the Android SDK), you can create a project inside of the IDE (select File ➤ New ➤ Project, then choose Android ➤ Android Project).

If you are using tools that are not Android-enabled, you can use the activitycreator script, found in the tools/ directory in your SDK installation. Just pass activitycreator the package name of the activity you want to create and an --out switch indicating where the project files should be generated. Here's an example:

```
activitycreator --out /path/to/my/project/dir \
com.commonsware.android.Now
```

You will wind up with a handful of pre-generated files, as described in Chapter 2. We'll be using these files for the rest of this chapter.

You can also download the project directories of the samples shown in this book in a ZIP file on the CommonsWare Web site[1]. These projects are ready for use; you do not need to run activitycreator on those unpacked samples.

The Activity

Your project's src/ directory contains the standard Java-style tree of directories based upon the Java package you used when you created the project (i.e., com.commonsware.android resulted

---

1. http://commonsware.com/Android/

in src/com/commonsware/android/). Inside the innermost directory you should find a pre-generated source file named Now.java, which is where your first activity will go. This activity will contain a single button that displays the time the button was last pushed (or the time the application was started if the button hasn't been pushed).

Open Now.java in your editor and paste in the following code:

```
package com.commonsware.android.skeleton;

import android.app.Activity;
import android.os.Bundle;
import android.view.View;
import android.widget.Button;
import java.util.Date;

public class Now extends Activity implements View.OnClickListener {
  Button btn;

  @Override
  public void onCreate(Bundle icicle) {
    super.onCreate(icicle);

    btn = new Button(this);
    btn.setOnClickListener(this);
    updateTime();
    setContentView(btn);
  }

  public void onClick(View view) {
    updateTime();
  }

  private void updateTime() {
    btn.setText(new Date().toString());
  }
}
```

Or, if you download the source files off the CommonsWare Web site, you can just use the Skeleton/Now project directly.

Let's examine this piece-by-piece.

Dissecting the Activity

The package declaration needs to be the same as the one you used when creating the project. And, like in any other Java project, you need to import any classes you reference. Most of the Android-specific classes are in the android package:

```
package com.commonsware.android.skeleton;

import android.app.Activity;
import android.os.Bundle;
import android.view.View;
import android.widget.Button;
import java.util.Date;
```

It's worth noting that not every Java SE class is available to Android programs. Visit the Android class reference[2] to see what is and is not available.

Activities are public classes, inheriting from the android.app.Activity base class. In this case, the activity holds a button (btn):

```
public class Now extends Activity implements View.OnClickListener {
  Button btn;
```

Note A button, as you can see from the package name, is an Android widget, and widgets are the UI elements that you use in your application.

Since, for simplicity, we want to trap all button clicks just within the activity itself, we also have the activity class implement OnClickListener.

```
@Override
public void onCreate(Bundle icicle) {
  super.onCreate(icicle);

  btn = new Button(this);
  btn.setOnClickListener(this);
  updateTime();
  setContentView(btn);
}
```

The onCreate() method is invoked when the activity is started. The first thing you should do is chain upward to the superclass, so the stock Android activity initialization can be done.

In our implementation, we then create the button instance (new Button(this)), tell it to send all button clicks to the activity instance itself (via setOnClickListener()), call a private updateTime() method (discussed in a moment), and then set the activity's content view to be the button itself (via setContentView()).

Note All widgets extend the View base class. We usually build the UI out of a hierarchy of views, but in this example we are using a single view.

---

2. http://code.google.com/android/reference/packages.html

I discuss that magical Bundle icicle in Chapter 16. For the moment, consider it an opaque handle that all activities receive upon creation.

```
public void onClick(View view) {
  updateTime();
}
```

In Swing, a JButton click raises an ActionEvent, which is passed to the ActionListener configured for the button. In Android, a button click causes onClick() to be invoked in the OnClickListener instance configured for the button. The listener is provided the view that triggered the click (in this case, the button). All we do here is call that private updateTime() method:

```
private void updateTime() {
  btn.setText(new Date().toString());
}
```

When we open the activity (onCreate()) or when the button is clicked (onClick()), we update the button's label to be the current time via setText(), which functions much the same in Android as JButton does in Swing.

Building and Running the Activity

To build the activity, either use your IDE's built-in Android packaging tool, or run ant in the base directory of your project. Then, to run the activity do the following:

1. Launch the emulator (e.g., run tools/emulator from your Android SDK installation), as shown in Figure 4-1.

Figure 4-1. *The Android home screen*

2. Install the package (e.g., run `tools/adb install /path/to/this/example/bin/Now.apk` from your Android SDK installation).

3. View the list of installed applications in the emulator and find the Now application (see Figure 4-2).

Figure 4-2. *The Android application "launcher"*

4. Open that application.

You should see an activity screen like the one shown in Figure 4-3.

Figure 4-3. *The Now demonstration activity*

Clicking the button—in other words, clicking pretty much anywhere on the phone's screen—will update the time shown in the button's label.

Note that the label is centered horizontally and vertically, as those are the default styles applied to button captions. We can control that formatting, which Chapter 6 covers.

After you are done gazing at the awesomeness of Advanced Push-Button Technology, you can click the back button on the emulator to return to the launcher.

CHAPTER 5

■ ■ ■

Using XML-Based Layouts

While it is technically possible to create and attach widgets to our activity purely through Java code, the way we did in Chapter 4, the more common approach is to use an XML-based layout file. Dynamic instantiation of widgets is reserved for more complicated scenarios, where the widgets are not known at compile-time (e.g., populating a column of radio buttons based on data retrieved off the Internet).

With that in mind, it's time to break out the XML and learn how to lay out Android activities that way.

What Is an XML-Based Layout?

As the name suggests, an XML-based layout is a specification of widgets' relationships to each other—and to their containers (more on this in Chapter 7)—encoded in XML format. Specifically, Android considers XML-based layouts to be resources, and as such layout files are stored in the res/layout directory inside your Android project.

Each XML file contains a tree of elements specifying a layout of widgets and their containers that make up one view hierarchy. The attributes of the XML elements are properties, describing how a widget should look or how a container should behave. For example, if a Button element has an attribute value of android:textStyle = "bold", that means that the text appearing on the face of the button should be rendered in a boldface font style.

Android's SDK ships with a tool (aapt) which uses the layouts. This tool should be automatically invoked by your Android tool chain (e.g., Eclipse, Ant's build.xml). Of particular importance to you as a developer is that aapt generates the R.java source file within your project, allowing you to access layouts and widgets within those layouts directly from your Java code.

Why Use XML-Based Layouts?

Most everything you do using XML layout files can be achieved through Java code. For example, you could use setTypeface() to have a button render its text in bold, instead of using a property in an XML layout. Since XML layouts are yet another file for you to keep track of, we need good reasons for using such files.

Perhaps the biggest reason is to assist in the creation of tools for view definition, such as a GUI builder in an IDE like Eclipse or a dedicated Android GUI designer like DroidDraw[1]. Such GUI builders could, in principle, generate Java code instead of XML. The challenge is re-reading the UI definition to support edits—that is far simpler if the data is in a structured format like XML than in a programming language. Moreover, keeping generated XML definitions separated from hand-written Java code makes it less likely that somebody's custom-crafted source will get clobbered by accident when the generated bits get re-generated. XML forms a nice middle ground between something that is easy for tool-writers to use and easy for programmers to work with by hand as needed.

Also, XML as a GUI definition format is becoming more commonplace. Microsoft's XAML[2], Adobe's Flex[3], and Mozilla's XUL[4] all take a similar approach to that of Android: put layout details in an XML file and put programming smarts in source files (e.g., JavaScript for XUL). Many less-well-known GUI frameworks, such as ZK[5], also use XML for view definition. While "following the herd" is not necessarily the best policy, it does have the advantage of helping to ease the transition into Android from any other XML-centered view description language.

OK, So What Does It Look Like?

Here is the Button from the previous chapter's sample application, converted into an XML layout file, found in the Layouts/NowRedux sample project. This code sample along with all others in this chapter can be found in the Source Code area of http://apress.com.

```
<?xml version="1.0" encoding="utf-8"?>
<Button xmlns:android="http://schemas.android.com/apk/res/android"
    android:id="@+id/button"
    android:text=""
    android:layout_width="fill_parent"
    android:layout_height="fill_parent"/>
```

The class name of the widget—Button—forms the name of the XML element. Since Button is an Android-supplied widget, we can just use the bare class name. If you create your own widgets as subclasses of android.view.View, you would need to provide a full package declaration as well (e.g., com.commonsware.android.MyWidget).

The root element needs to declare the Android XML namespace:

```
xmlns:android="http://schemas.android.com/apk/res/android"
```

All other elements will be children of the root and will inherit that namespace declaration.

Because we want to reference this button from our Java code, we need to give it an identifier via the android:id attribute. We will cover this concept in greater detail later in this chapter.

---

1. http://droiddraw.org/
2. http://windowssdk.msdn.microsoft.com/en-us/library/ms752059.aspx
3. http://www.adobe.com/products/flex/
4. http://www.mozilla.org/projects/xul/
5. http://www.zkoss.org/

The remaining attributes are properties of this `Button` instance:

- `android:text` indicates the initial text to be displayed on the button face (in this case, an empty string)

- `android:layout_width` and `android:layout_height` tell Android to have the button's width and height fill the "parent", in this case the entire screen—these attributes will be covered in greater detail in Chapter 7.

Since this single widget is the only content in our activity, we only need this single element. Complex UIs will require a whole tree of elements, representing the widgets and containers that control their positioning. All the remaining chapters of this book will use the XML layout form whenever practical, so there are dozens of other examples of more complex layouts for you to peruse from Chapter 7 onward.

What's with the @ Signs?

Many widgets and containers only need to appear in the XML layout file and do not need to be referenced in your Java code. For example, a static label (`TextView`) frequently only needs to be in the layout file to indicate where it should appear. These sorts of elements in the XML file do not need to have the `android:id` attribute to give them a name.

Anything you *do* want to use in your Java source, though, needs an `android:id`.

The convention is to use `@+id/...` as the id value, where the `...` represents your locally-unique name for the widget in question. In the XML layout example in the preceding section, `@+id/button` is the identifier for the `Button` widget.

Android provides a few special `android:id` values, of the form `@android:id/...`. We will see some of these in various chapters of this book, such as Chapters 8 and 10.

We Attach These to the Java . . . How?

Given that you have painstakingly set up the widgets and containers in an XML layout file named `main.xml` stored in `res/layout`, all you need is one statement in your activity's `onCreate()` callback to use that layout:

```
setContentView(R.layout.main);
```

This is the same `setContentView()` we used earlier, passing it an instance of a `View` subclass (in that case, a `Button`). The Android-built view, constructed from our layout, is accessed from that code-generated R class. All of the layouts are accessible under `R.layout`, keyed by the base name of the layout file—`main.xml` results in `R.layout.main`.

To access our identified widgets, use `findViewById()`, passing in the numeric identifier of the widget in question. That numeric identifier was generated by Android in the R class as `R.id.something` (where `something` is the specific widget you are seeking). Those widgets are simply subclasses of `View`, just like the `Button` instance we created in Chapter 4.

The Rest of the Story

In the original Now demo, the button's face would show the current time, which would reflect when the button was last pushed (or when the activity was first shown, if the button had not yet been pushed).

Most of that logic still works, even in this revised demo (NowRedux). However, rather than instantiating the Button in our activity's onCreate() callback, we can reference the one from the XML layout:

```java
package com.commonsware.android.layouts;

import android.app.Activity;
import android.os.Bundle;
import android.view.View;
import android.widget.Button;
import java.util.Date;

public class NowRedux extends Activity
  implements View.OnClickListener {
  Button btn;

  @Override
  public void onCreate(Bundle icicle) {
    super.onCreate(icicle);

    setContentView(R.layout.main);

    btn=(Button)findViewById(R.id.button);
    btn.setOnClickListener(this);
    updateTime();
  }

  public void onClick(View view) {
    updateTime();
  }

  private void updateTime() {
    btn.setText(new Date().toString());
  }
}
```

The first difference is that rather than setting the content view to be a view we created in Java code, we set it to reference the XML layout (setContentView(R.layout.main)). The R.java source file will be updated when we rebuild this project to include a reference to our layout file (stored as main.xml in our project's res/layout directory).

The other difference is that we need to get our hands on our Button instance, for which we use the findViewById() call. Since we identified our button as @+id/button, we can reference the button's identifier as R.id.button. Now, with the Button instance in hand, we can set the callback and set the label as needed.

As you can see in Figure 5-1, the results look the same as with the original Now demo.

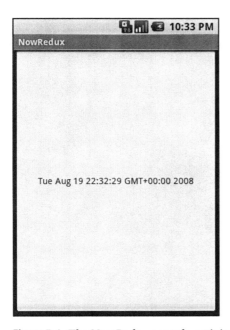

Figure 5-1. *The NowRedux sample activity*

CHAPTER 6

■ ■ ■

Employing Basic Widgets

Every GUI toolkit has some basic widgets: fields, labels, buttons, etc. Android's toolkit is no different in scope, and the basic widgets will provide a good introduction as to how widgets work in Android activities.

Assigning Labels

The simplest widget is the label, referred to in Android as a TextView. Like in most GUI toolkits, labels are bits of text not editable directly by users. Typically, they are used to identify adjacent widgets (e.g., a "Name:" label before a field where one fills in a name).

In Java, you can create a label by creating a TextView instance. More commonly, though, you will create labels in XML layout files by adding a TextView element to the layout, with an android:text property to set the value of the label itself. If you need to swap labels based on certain criteria, such as internationalization, you may wish to use a resource reference in the XML instead, as will be described in Chapter 9. TextView has numerous other properties of relevance for labels, such as:

- android:typeface to set the typeface to use for the label (e.g., monospace)

- android:textStyle to indicate that the typeface should be made bold (bold), italic (italic), or bold and italic (bold_italic)

- android:textColor to set the color of the label's text, in RGB hex format (e.g., #FF0000 for red)

For example, in the Basic/Label project, you will find the following layout file:

```xml
<?xml version="1.0" encoding="utf-8"?>
<TextView xmlns:android="http://schemas.android.com/apk/res/android"
  android:layout_width="fill_parent"
  android:layout_height="wrap_content"
  android:text="You were expecting something profound?"
  />
```

As you can see in Figure 6-1, just that layout alone, with the stub Java source provided by Android's project builder (e.g., activityCreator), gives you the application.

Figure 6-1. *The LabelDemo sample application*

Button, Button, Who's Got the Button?

We've already seen the use of the Button widget in Chapters 4 and 5. As it turns out, Button is a subclass of TextView, so everything discussed in the preceding section in terms of formatting the face of the button still holds.

Fleeting Images

Android has two widgets to help you embed images in your activities: ImageView and ImageButton. As the names suggest, they are image-based analogues to TextView and Button, respectively.

Each widget takes an android:src attribute (in an XML layout) to specify what picture to use. These usually reference a drawable resource, described in greater detail in the chapter on resources. You can also set the image content based on a Uri from a content provider via setImageURI().

ImageButton, a subclass of ImageView, mixes in the standard Button behaviors, for responding to clicks and whatnot.

For example, take a peek at the main.xml layout from the Basic/ImageView sample project which is found along with all other code samples at http://apress.com:

```
<?xml version="1.0" encoding="utf-8"?>
<ImageView xmlns:android="http://schemas.android.com/apk/res/android"
    android:id="@+id/icon"
    android:layout_width="fill_parent"
    android:layout_height="fill_parent"
    android:adjustViewBounds="true"
    android:src="@drawable/molecule"
    />
```

The result, just using the code-generated activity, is shown in Figure 6-2.

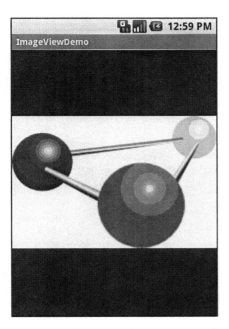

Figure 6-2. *The ImageViewDemo sample application*

Fields of Green. Or Other Colors.

Along with buttons and labels, fields are the third "anchor" of most GUI toolkits. In Android, they are implemented via the EditText widget, which is a subclass of the TextView used for labels.

Along with the standard TextView properties (e.g., android:textStyle), EditText has many others that will be useful for you in constructing fields, including:

- android:autoText, to control if the field should provide automatic spelling assistance

- android:capitalize, to control if the field should automatically capitalize the first letter of entered text (e.g., first name, city)

- android:digits, to configure the field to accept only certain digits

- android:singleLine, to control if the field is for single-line input or multiple-line input (e.g., does <Enter> move you to the next widget or add a newline?)

Beyond those, you can configure fields to use specialized input methods, such as android:numeric for numeric-only input, android:password for shrouded password input, and android:phoneNumber for entering in phone numbers. If you want to create your own input method scheme (e.g., postal codes, Social Security numbers), you need to create your own implementation of the InputMethod interface, then configure the field to use it via android: inputMethod.

For example, from the Basic/Field project, here is an XML layout file showing an EditText:

```xml
<?xml version="1.0" encoding="utf-8"?>
<EditText xmlns:android="http://schemas.android.com/apk/res/android"
  android:id="@+id/field"
  android:layout_width="fill_parent"
  android:layout_height="fill_parent"
  android:singleLine="false"
/>
```

Note that android:singleLine is false, so users will be able to enter in several lines of text. For this project, the FieldDemo.java file populates the input field with some prose:

```java
package com.commonsware.android.basic;

import android.app.Activity;
import android.os.Bundle;
import android.widget.EditText;

public class FieldDemo extends Activity {
  @Override
  public void onCreate(Bundle icicle) {
    super.onCreate(icicle);
    setContentView(R.layout.main);

    EditText fld=(EditText)findViewById(R.id.field);
    fld.setText("Licensed under the Apache License, Version 2.0 " +
            "(the \"License\"); you may not use this file " +
            "except in compliance with the License. You may " +
            "obtain a copy of the License at " +
            "http://www.apache.org/licenses/LICENSE-2.0");
  }
}
```

The result, once built and installed into the emulator, is shown in Figure 6-3.

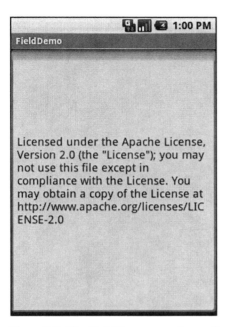

Figure 6-3. *The FieldDemo sample application*

■**Note** Android's emulator only allows one application in the launcher per unique Java package. Since all the demos in this chapter share the `com.commonsware.android.basic` package, you will only see one of these demos in your emulator's launcher at any one time.

Another flavor of field is one that offers auto-completion, to help users supply a value without typing in the whole text. That is provided in Android as the `AutoCompleteTextView` widget and is discussed in Chapter 8.

Just Another Box to Check

The classic checkbox has two states: checked and unchecked. Clicking the checkbox toggles between those states to indicate a choice (e.g., "Add rush delivery to my order").

In Android, there is a `CheckBox` widget to meet this need. It has `TextView` as an ancestor, so you can use `TextView` properties like `android:textColor` to format the widget.

Within Java, you can invoke:

- `isChecked()` to determine if the checkbox has been checked
- `setChecked()` to force the checkbox into a checked or unchecked state
- `toggle()` to toggle the checkbox as if the user checked it

Also, you can register a listener object (in this case, an instance of OnCheckedChangeListener) to be notified when the state of the checkbox changes.

For example, from the Basic/CheckBox project, here is a simple checkbox layout:

```xml
<?xml version="1.0" encoding="utf-8"?>
<CheckBox xmlns:android="http://schemas.android.com/apk/res/android"
    android:id="@+id/check"
    android:layout_width="wrap_content"
    android:layout_height="wrap_content"
    android:text="This checkbox is: unchecked" />
```

The corresponding CheckBoxDemo.java retrieves and configures the behavior of the checkbox:

```java
public class CheckBoxDemo extends Activity
  implements CompoundButton.OnCheckedChangeListener {
  CheckBox cb;

  @Override
  public void onCreate(Bundle icicle) {
    super.onCreate(icicle);
    setContentView(R.layout.main);

    cb=(CheckBox)findViewById(R.id.check);
    cb.setOnCheckedChangeListener(this);
  }

  public void onCheckedChanged(CompoundButton buttonView,
                               boolean isChecked) {
    if (isChecked) {
      cb.setText("This checkbox is: checked");
    }
    else {
      cb.setText("This checkbox is: unchecked");
    }
  }
}
```

Note that the activity serves as its own listener for checkbox state changes since it implements the OnCheckedChangeListener interface (via cb.setOnCheckedChangeListener(this)). The callback for the listener is onCheckedChanged(), which receives the checkbox whose state has changed and what the new state is. In this case, we update the text of the checkbox to reflect what the actual box contains.

The result? Clicking the checkbox immediately updates its text, as you can see in Figures 6-4 and 6-5.

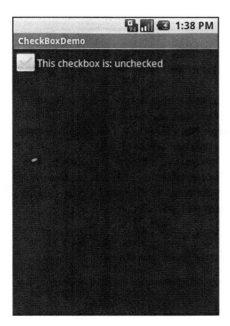

Figure 6-4. *The CheckBoxDemo sample application, with the checkbox unchecked*

Figure 6-5. *The same application, now with the checkbox checked*

Turn the Radio Up

As with other implementations of radio buttons in other toolkits, Android's radio buttons are two-state, like checkboxes, but can be grouped such that only one radio button in the group can be checked at any time.

Like CheckBox, RadioButton inherits from CompoundButton, which in turn inherits from TextView. Hence, all the standard TextView properties for font face, style, color, etc., are available for controlling the look of radio buttons. Similarly, you can call isChecked() on a RadioButton to see if it is selected, toggle() to select it, and so on, like you can with a CheckBox.

Most times, you will want to put your RadioButton widgets inside of a RadioGroup. The RadioGroup indicates a set of radio buttons whose state is tied, meaning only one button out of the group can be selected at any time. If you assign an android:id to your RadioGroup in your XML layout, you can access the group from your Java code and invoke:

- check() to check a specific radio button via its ID (e.g., group.check(R.id.radio1))

- clearCheck() to clear all radio buttons, so none in the group are checked

- getCheckedRadioButtonId() to get the ID of the currently-checked radio button (or -1 if none are checked)

For example, from the Basic/RadioButton sample application, here is an XML layout showing a RadioGroup wrapping a set of RadioButton widgets:

```xml
<?xml version="1.0" encoding="utf-8"?>
<RadioGroup
  xmlns:android="http://schemas.android.com/apk/res/android"
  android:orientation="vertical"
  android:layout_width="fill_parent"
  android:layout_height="fill_parent"
  >
    <RadioButton android:id="@+id/radio1"
      android:layout_width="wrap_content"
      android:layout_height="wrap_content"
      android:text="Rock" />

    <RadioButton android:id="@+id/radio2"
      android:layout_width="wrap_content"
      android:layout_height="wrap_content"
      android:text="Scissors" />

    <RadioButton android:id="@+id/radio3"
      android:layout_width="wrap_content"
      android:layout_height="wrap_content"
      android:text="Paper" />
</RadioGroup>
```

Figure 6-6 shows the result using the stock Android-generated Java for the project and this layout.

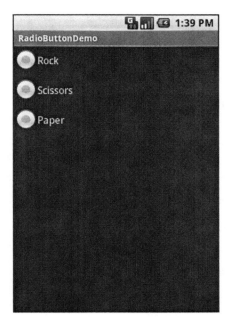

Figure 6-6. *The RadioButtonDemo sample application*

Note that the radio button group is initially set to be completely unchecked at the outset. To pre-set one of the radio buttons to be checked, use either setChecked() on the RadioButton or check() on the RadioGroup from within your onCreate() callback in your activity.

It's Quite a View

All widgets, including the ones previously shown, extend View, and as such give all widgets an array of useful properties and methods beyond those already described.

Useful Properties

Some of the properties on View most likely to be used include:

- Controls the focus sequence:

    - android:nextFocusDown

    - android:nextFocusLeft

    - android:nextFocusRight

    - android:nextFocusUp

- android:visibility, which controls whether the widget is initially visible

- android:background, which typically provides an RGB color value (e.g., #00FF00 for green) to serve as the background for the widget

Useful Methods

You can toggle whether or not a widget is enabled via setEnabled() and see if it is enabled via isEnabled(). One common use pattern for this is to disable some widgets based on a CheckBox or RadioButton selection.

You can give a widget focus via requestFocus() and see if it is focused via isFocused(). You might use this in concert with disabling widgets as previously mentioned, to ensure the proper widget has the focus once your disabling operation is complete.

To help navigate the tree of widgets and containers that make up an activity's overall view, you can use:

- getParent() to find the parent widget or container

- findViewById() to find a child widget with a certain ID

- getRootView() to get the root of the tree (e.g., what you provided to the activity via setContentView())

CHAPTER 7

Working with Containers

Containers pour a collection of widgets (and possibly child containers) into specific layouts you like. If you want a form with labels on the left and fields on the right, you will need a container. If you want OK and Cancel buttons to be beneath the rest of the form, next to one another, and flush to the right side of the screen, you will need a container. From a pure XML perspective, if you have multiple widgets (beyond RadioButton widgets in a RadioGroup), you will need a container just to have a root element to place the widgets inside.

Most GUI toolkits have some notion of layout management, frequently organized into containers. In Java Swing, for example, you have layout managers like BoxLayout and containers that use them (e.g., Box). Some toolkits, such as XUL and Flex, stick strictly to the box model, figuring that any desired layout can be achieved through the right combination of nested boxes.

Android, through LinearLayout, also offers a box model, but in addition it supports a range of containers providing different layout rules. In this chapter we will look at three commonly used containers: LinearLayout (the box model), RelativeLayout (a rule-based model), and TableLayout (the grid model), along with ScrollView, a container designed to assist with implementing scrolling containers. In the next chapter we will examine some more-esoteric containers.

Thinking Linearly

As noted already, LinearLayout is a box model—widgets or child containers are lined up in a column or row, one after the next. This works similarly to FlowLayout in Java Swing, vbox and hbox in Flex and XUL, etc.

Flex and XUL use the box as their primary unit of layout. If you want, you can use LinearLayout in much the same way, eschewing some of the other containers. Getting the visual representation you want is mostly a matter of identifying where boxes should nest and what properties those boxes should have, such as alignment vis-à-vis other boxes.

Concepts and Properties

To configure a LinearLayout, you have five main areas of control besides the container's contents: the orientation, the fill model, the weight, the gravity, and the padding.

Orientation

Orientation indicates whether the LinearLayout represents a row or a column. Just add the android:orientation property to your LinearLayout element in your XML layout, setting the value to be horizontal for a row or vertical for a column.

The orientation can be modified at runtime by invoking setOrientation() on the LinearLayout, supplying it with either HORIZONTAL or VERTICAL.

Fill Model

Let's imagine a row of widgets, such as a pair of radio buttons. These widgets have a "natural" size based on their text. Their combined sizes probably do not exactly match the width of the Android device's screen—particularly since screens come in various sizes. We then have the issue of what to do with the remaining space.

All widgets inside a LinearLayout must supply android:layout_width and android:layout_height properties to help address this issue. These properties' values have three flavors:

- You can provide a specific dimension, such as 125px, to indicate the widget should take up exactly 125 pixels.

- You can provide wrap_content, which means the widget should fill up its natural space unless that is too big, in which case Android can use word wrap as needed to make it fit.

- You can provide fill_parent, which means the widget should fill up all available space in its enclosing container after all other widgets are taken care of.

The latter two flavors are the most common, as they are independent of screen size, allowing Android to adjust your view to fit the available space.

Weight

What happens if we have two widgets that should split the available free space? For example, suppose we have two multi-line fields in a column, and we want them to take up the remaining space in the column after all other widgets have been allocated their space.

To make this work, in addition to setting android:layout_width (for rows) or android:layout_height (for columns) to fill_parent, you must also set android:layout_weight. This property indicates what proportion of the free space should go to that widget. If you set android:layout_weight to be the same value for a pair of widgets (e.g., 1), the free space will be split evenly between them. If you set it to be 1 for one widget and 2 for another widget, the second widget will use up twice the free space that the first widget does, and so on.

Gravity

By default, everything is left- and top-aligned. So if you create a row of widgets via a horizontal LinearLayout, the row will start flush on the left side of the screen.

If that is not what you want, you need to specify a gravity. Using android:layout_gravity on a widget (or calling setGravity() at runtime on the widget's Java object), you can tell the widget and its container how to align it vis-à-vis the screen.

For a column of widgets, common gravity values are left, center_horizontal, and right for left-aligned, centered, and right-aligned widgets, respectively.

For a row of widgets, the default is for them to be aligned so their text is aligned on the baseline (the invisible line that letters seem to "sit on"), though you may wish to specify a gravity of center_vertical to center the widgets along the row's vertical midpoint.

Padding

By default, widgets are tightly packed next to each other. If you want to increase the whitespace between widgets, you will want to use the android:padding property (or call setPadding() at runtime on the widget's Java object).

The padding specifies how much space there is between the boundaries of the widget's "cell" and the actual widget contents. Padding is analogous to the margins on a word-processing document—the page size might be 8.5"×11", but 1" margins would leave the actual text to reside within a 6.5"×9" area.

The android:padding property allows you to set the same padding on all four sides of the widget, with the widget's contents centered within that padded-out area. If you want the padding to differ on different sides, use android:paddingLeft, android:paddingRight, android:paddingTop, and android:paddingBottom (see Figure 7-1).

The value of the padding is a dimension, such as 5px for 5 pixels' worth of padding.

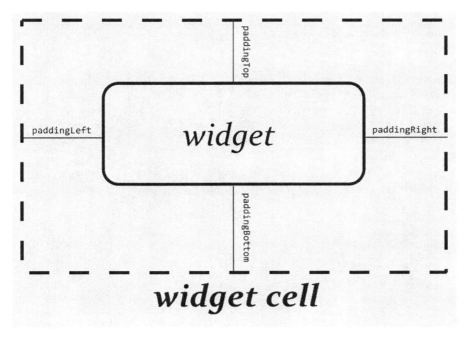

Figure 7-1. *The relationship between a widget, its cell, and the padding values*

LinearLayout Example

Let's look at an example (Containers/Linear) that shows LinearLayout properties set both in the XML layout file and at runtime.

```
<?xml version="1.0" encoding="utf-8"?>
<LinearLayout
  xmlns:android="http://schemas.android.com/apk/res/android"
  android:orientation="vertical"
  android:layout_width="fill_parent"
  android:layout_height="fill_parent"
  >
  <RadioGroup android:id="@+id/orientation"
    android:orientation="horizontal"
    android:layout_width="wrap_content"
    android:layout_height="wrap_content"
    android:padding="5px">
    <RadioButton
      android:id="@+id/horizontal"
      android:text="horizontal" />
    <RadioButton
      android:id="@+id/vertical"
      android:text="vertical" />
  </RadioGroup>
  <RadioGroup android:id="@+id/gravity"
    android:orientation="vertical"
    android:layout_width="fill_parent"
    android:layout_height="wrap_content"
    android:padding="5px">
    <RadioButton
      android:id="@+id/left"
      android:text="left" />
    <RadioButton
      android:id="@+id/center"
      android:text="center" />
    <RadioButton
      android:id="@+id/right"
      android:text="right" />
  </RadioGroup>
</LinearLayout>
```

Note that we have a LinearLayout wrapping two RadioGroup sets. RadioGroup is a subclass of LinearLayout, so our example demonstrates nested boxes as if they were all LinearLayout containers.

The top RadioGroup sets up a row (android:orientation = "horizontal") of RadioButton widgets. The RadioGroup has 5px of padding on all sides, separating it from the other RadioGroup. The width and height are both set to wrap_content, so the radio buttons will take up only the space that they need.

The bottom RadioGroup is a column (android:orientation = "vertical") of three RadioButton widgets. Again, we have 5px of padding on all sides and a "natural" height (android:layout_height = "wrap_content"). However, we have set android:layout_width to be fill_parent, meaning the column of radio buttons "claims" the entire width of the screen.

To adjust these settings at runtime based on user input, we need some Java code:

```java
package com.commonsware.android.containers;

import android.app.Activity;
import android.os.Bundle;
import android.view.Gravity;
import android.text.TextWatcher;
import android.widget.LinearLayout;
import android.widget.RadioGroup;
import android.widget.EditText;

public class LinearLayoutDemo extends Activity
  implements RadioGroup.OnCheckedChangeListener {
  RadioGroup orientation;
  RadioGroup gravity;

  @Override
  public void onCreate(Bundle icicle) {
    super.onCreate(icicle);
    setContentView(R.layout.main);

    orientation=(RadioGroup)findViewById(R.id.orientation);
    orientation.setOnCheckedChangeListener(this);
    gravity=(RadioGroup)findViewById(R.id.gravity);
    gravity.setOnCheckedChangeListener(this);
  }

  public void onCheckedChanged(RadioGroup group, int checkedId) {
    if (group==orientation) {
      if (checkedId==R.id.horizontal) {
        orientation.setOrientation(LinearLayout.HORIZONTAL);
      }
      else {
        orientation.setOrientation(LinearLayout.VERTICAL);
      }
    }
```

```
      else if (group==gravity) {
        if (checkedId==R.id.left) {
          gravity.setGravity(Gravity.LEFT);
        }
        else if (checkedId==R.id.center) {
          gravity.setGravity(Gravity.CENTER_HORIZONTAL);
        }
        else if (checkedId==R.id.right) {
          gravity.setGravity(Gravity.RIGHT);
        }
      }
    }
  }
```

In onCreate(), we look up our two RadioGroup containers and register a listener on each, so we are notified when the radio buttons change state (setOnCheckedChangeListener(this)). Since the activity implements OnCheckedChangeListener, the activity itself is the listener.

In onCheckedChanged() (the callback for the listener), we see which RadioGroup had a state change. If it was the orientation group, we adjust the orientation based on the user's selection. If it was the gravity group, we adjust the gravity based on the user's selection.

Figure 7-2 shows the result when the sample application is first launched inside the emulator.

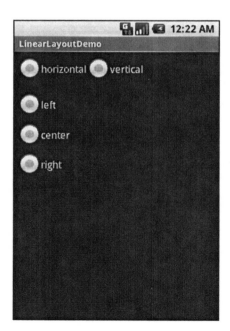

Figure 7-2. *The LinearLayoutDemo sample application, as initially launched*

If we toggle on the Vertical radio button, the top RadioGroup adjusts to match (see Figure 7-3).

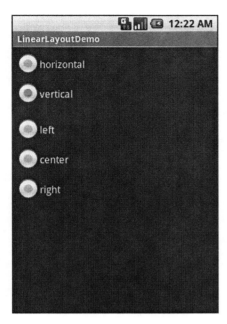

Figure 7-3. *The same application, with the Vertical radio button selected*

If we toggle the Center or Right radio button, the bottom RadioGroup adjusts to match (see Figures 7-4 and 7-5).

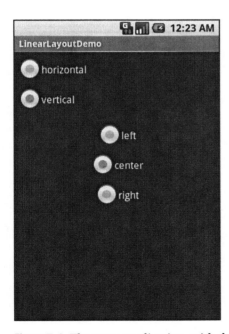

Figure 7-4. *The same application, with the Vertical and Center radio buttons selected*

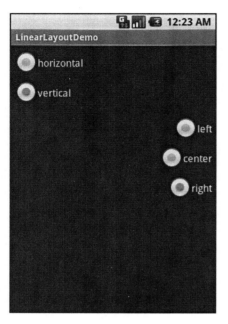

Figure 7-5. *The same application, with the Vertical and Right radio buttons selected*

All Things Are Relative

RelativeLayout, as the name suggests, lays out widgets based upon their relationship to other widgets in the container and in the parent container. You can place Widget X below and to the left of Widget Y, or have Widget Z's bottom edge align with the bottom of the container, and so on.

This is reminiscent of James Elliott's RelativeLayout[1] for use with Java Swing.

Concepts and Properties

To make all this work, we need ways to reference other widgets within an XML layout file, plus ways to indicate the relative positions of those widgets.

Positions Relative to a Container

The easiest relations to set up tie a widget's position to that of its container:

- android:layout_alignParentTop says the widget's top should align with the top of the container.

- android:layout_alignParentBottom says the widget's bottom should align with the bottom of the container.

---

1. http://www.onjava.com/pub/a/onjava/2002/09/18/relativelayout.html

- `android:layout_alignParentLeft` says the widget's left side should align with the left side of the container.

- `android:layout_alignParentRight` says the widget's right side should align with the right side of the container.

- `android:layout_centerHorizontal` says the widget should be positioned horizontally at the center of the container.

- `android:layout_centerVertical` says the widget should be positioned vertically at the center of the container.

- `android:layout_centerInParent` says the widget should be positioned both horizontally and vertically at the center of the container.

All of these properties take a simple Boolean value (`true` or `false`).

Note that the padding of the widget is taken into account when performing these various alignments. The alignments are based on the widget's overall cell (a combination of its natural space plus the padding).

Relative Notation in Properties

The remaining properties of relevance to `RelativeLayout` take as a value the identity of a widget in the container. To identify and reference widgets this way, follow these steps:

1. Put identifiers (`android:id` attributes) on all elements that you will need to address, of the form `@+id/....`

2. Reference other widgets using the same identifier value without the plus sign (`@id/...`).

For example, if Widget A is identified as `@+id/widget_a`, Widget B can refer to Widget A in one of its own properties via the identifier `@id/widget_a`.

Positions Relative to Other Widgets

There are four properties that control position of a widget in relation to other widgets:

- `android:layout_above` indicates that the widget should be placed above the widget referenced in the property.

- `android:layout_below` indicates that the widget should be placed below the widget referenced in the property.

- `android:layout_toLeftOf` indicates that the widget should be placed to the left of the widget referenced in the property.

- `android:layout_toRightOf` indicates that the widget should be placed to the right of the widget referenced in the property.

There are five additional properties that can control one widget's alignment relative to another:

- `android:layout_alignTop` indicates that the widget's top should be aligned with the top of the widget referenced in the property.

- `android:layout_alignBottom` indicates that the widget's bottom should be aligned with the bottom of the widget referenced in the property.

- `android:layout_alignLeft` indicates that the widget's left side should be aligned with the left side of the widget referenced in the property.

- `android:layout_alignRight` indicates that the widget's right side should be aligned with the right side of the widget referenced in the property.

- `android:layout_alignBaseline` indicates that the baselines of the two widgets should be aligned.

The last property in the list is useful for aligning labels and fields so that the text appears "natural." Since fields have a box around them and labels do not, `android:layout_alignTop` will align the top of the field's box with the top of the label, which will cause the text of the label to be higher on-screen than the text entered into the field.

So, if we want Widget B to be positioned to the right of Widget A, in the XML element for Widget B we need to include `android:layout_toRight = "@id/widget_a"` (assuming `@id/widget_a` is the identity of Widget A).

Order of Evaluation

What makes this even more complicated is the order of evaluation. Android makes a single pass through your XML layout and computes the size and position of each widget in sequence. This has a couple of ramifications:

- You cannot reference a widget that has not yet been defined in the file.

- You must be careful that any uses of `fill_parent` in `android:layout_width` or `android:layout_height` do not "eat up" all the space before subsequent widgets have been defined.

RelativeLayout Example

With all that in mind, let's examine a typical "form" with a field, a label, plus a pair of buttons labeled "OK" and "Cancel."

Here is the XML layout, pulled from the `Containers/Relative` sample project:

```
<?xml version="1.0" encoding="utf-8"?>
<RelativeLayout
  xmlns:android="http://schemas.android.com/apk/res/android"
  android:layout_width="fill_parent"
  android:layout_height="wrap_content"
  android:padding="5px">
```

```
    <TextView android:id="@+id/label"
      android:layout_width="wrap_content"
      android:layout_height="wrap_content"
      android:text="URL:"
      android:paddingTop="15px"/>
    <EditText
      android:id="@+id/entry"
      android:layout_width="fill_parent"
      android:layout_height="wrap_content"
      android:layout_toRightOf="@id/label"
      android:layout_alignBaseline="@id/label"/>
    <Button
      android:id="@+id/ok"
      android:layout_width="wrap_content"
      android:layout_height="wrap_content"
      android:layout_below="@id/entry"
      android:layout_alignRight="@id/entry"
      android:text="OK" />
    <Button
      android:id="@+id/cancel"
      android:layout_width="wrap_content"
      android:layout_height="wrap_content"
      android:layout_toLeftOf="@id/ok"
      android:layout_alignTop="@id/ok"
      android:text="Cancel" />
</RelativeLayout>
```

First we open up the RelativeLayout. In this case, we want to use the full width of the screen (android:layout_width = "fill_parent"), use only as much height as we need (android: layout_height = "wrap_content"), and have a 5-pixel pad between the boundaries of the container and its contents (android:padding = "5px").

Next we define the label, which is fairly basic, except for its own 15-pixel padding (android:padding = "15px"). More on that in a moment.

After that we add in the field. We want the field to be to the right of the label, have both the field and label text aligned along the baseline, and for the field to take up the rest of this "row" in the layout. Those components are handled by three properties:

- android:layout_toRight = "@id/label"

- android:layout_alignBaseline = "@id/label"

- android:layout_width = "fill_parent"

If we were to skip the 15-pixel padding on the label, we would find that the top of the field is clipped off. That's because of the 5-pixel padding on the container itself. The android: layout_alignBaseline = "@id/label" property simply aligns the baselines of the label and field. The label, by default, has its top aligned with the top of the parent. But the label is shorter than the field because of the field's box. Since the field is dependent on the label's position and the label's position is already defined (because it appeared first in the XML), the field winds up being too high and has the top of its box clipped off by the container's padding.

You may find yourself running into these sorts of problems as you try to get your RelativeLayout to behave the way you want it to.

The solution to this conundrum, used in the XML layout shown earlier in this section, is to give the label 15 pixels' worth of padding on the top. This pushes the label down far enough that the field will not get clipped.

Here are some points of note:

- You cannot use android:layout_alignParentTop on the field, because you cannot have two properties that both attempt to set the vertical position of the field. In this case, android:layout_alignParentTop conflicts with the later android:layout_alignBaseline = "@id/label" property, and the last one in wins. So, you either have the top aligned properly or the baselines aligned properly, but not both.

- You cannot define the field first, then put the label to the left of the field, because you cannot "forward-reference" labeled widgets—you must define the widget before you can reference it by its ID.

Going back to the example, the OK button is set to be below the field (android:layout_below = "@id/entry") and have its right side align with the right side of the field (android:layout_alignRight = "@id/entry"). The Cancel button is set to be to the left of the OK button (android:layout_toLeft = "@id/ok") and have its top aligned with the OK button (android:layout_alignTop = "@id/ok").

With no changes to the auto-generated Java code, the emulator gives us the result shown in Figure 7-6.

Figure 7-6. *The RelativeLayoutDemo sample application*

Tabula Rasa

If you like HTML tables, spreadsheet grids, and the like, you will like Android's `TableLayout`—it allows you to position your widgets in a grid to your specifications. You control the number of rows and columns, which columns might shrink or stretch to accommodate their contents, and so on.

`TableLayout` works in conjunction with `TableRow`. `TableLayout` controls the overall behavior of the container, with the widgets themselves poured into one or more `TableRow` containers, one per row in the grid.

Concepts and Properties

For all this to work, we need to know how widgets work with rows and columns, plus how to handle widgets that live outside of rows.

Putting Cells in Rows

Rows are declared by you, the developer, by putting widgets as children of a `TableRow` inside the overall `TableLayout`. You, therefore, control directly how many rows appear in the table.

The number of columns is determined by Android; you control the number of columns in an indirect fashion.

There will be at least one column per widget in your longest row. So if you have three rows—one with two widgets, one with three widgets, and one with four widgets—there will be at least four columns.

However, a widget can take up more than one column if you include the `android:layout_span` property, indicating the number of columns the widget spans. This is akin to the `colspan` attribute one finds in table cells in HTML:

```
<TableRow>
  <TextView android:text="URL:" />
  <EditText
    android:id="@+id/entry"
    android:layout_span="3"/>
</TableRow>
```

In this XML layout fragment, the field spans three columns.

Ordinarily, widgets are put into the first available column. In the preceding fragment, the label would go in the first column (column 0, as columns are counted starting from 0), and the field would go into a spanned set of three columns (columns 1 through 3). However, you can put a widget into a different column via the `android:layout_column` property, specifying the 0-based column the widget belongs to:

```
<TableRow>
  <Button
    android:id="@+id/cancel"
    android:layout_column="2"
    android:text="Cancel" />
  <Button android:id="@+id/ok" android:text="OK" />
</TableRow>
```

In this XML layout fragment, the Cancel button goes in the third column (column 2). The OK button then goes into the next available column, which is the fourth column.

Non-Row Children of TableLayout

Normally, `TableLayout` contains only `TableRow` elements as immediate children. However, it is possible to put other widgets in between rows. For those widgets, `TableLayout` behaves a bit like `LinearLayout` with vertical orientation. The widgets automatically have their width set to `fill_parent`, so they will fill the same space that the longest row does.

One pattern for this is to use a plain `View` as a divider (e.g., `<View android:layout_height = "2px" android:background = "#0000FF" />` as a two-pixel-high blue bar across the width of the table).

Stretch, Shrink, and Collapse

By default, each column will be sized according to the "natural" size of the widest widget in that column (taking spanned columns into account). Sometimes, though, that does not work out very well, and you need more control over column behavior.

You can place an `android:stretchColumns` property on the `TableLayout`. The value should be a single column number (again, 0-based) or a comma-delimited list of column numbers. Those columns will be stretched to take up any available space on the row. This helps if your content is narrower than the available space.

Conversely, you can place an `android:shrinkColumns` property on the `TableLayout`. Again, this should be a single column number or a comma-delimited list of column numbers. The columns listed in this property will try to word-wrap their contents to reduce the effective width of the column; by default, widgets are not word-wrapped. This helps if you have columns with potentially wordy content that might cause some columns to be pushed off the right side of the screen.

You can also leverage an `android:collapseColumns` property on the `TableLayout`, again with a column number or a comma-delimited list of column numbers. These columns will start out "collapsed," meaning they will be part of the table information but will be invisible. Programmatically, you can collapse and un-collapse columns by calling `setColumnCollapsed()` on the `TableLayout`. You might use this to allow users to control which columns are of importance to them and should be shown, versus which ones are less important and can be hidden.

You can also control stretching and shrinking at runtime via `setColumnStretchable()` and `setColumnShrinkable()`.

TableLayout Example

The XML layout fragments shown previously, when combined, give us a `TableLayout` rendition of the "form" we created for `RelativeLayout`, with the addition of a divider line between the label/field and the two buttons (found in the `Containers/Table` demo in the Source Code area of `http://apress.com`):

```
<?xml version="1.0" encoding="utf-8"?>
<TableLayout
  xmlns:android="http://schemas.android.com/apk/res/android"
  android:layout_width="fill_parent"
```

```
android:layout_height="fill_parent"
android:stretchColumns="1">
<TableRow>
  <TextView
      android:text="URL:" />
  <EditText android:id="@+id/entry"
    android:layout_span="3"/>
</TableRow>
<View
  android:layout_height="2px"
  android:background="#0000FF" />
<TableRow>
  <Button android:id="@+id/cancel"
    android:layout_column="2"
    android:text="Cancel" />
  <Button android:id="@+id/ok"
    android:text="OK" />
</TableRow>
</TableLayout>
```

When compiled against the generated Java code and run on the emulator, we get the result shown in Figure 7-7.

Figure 7-7. *The TableLayoutDemo sample application*

Scrollwork

Phone screens tend to be small, which requires developers to use some tricks to present a lot of information in the limited available space. One trick for doing this is to use scrolling, so only part of the information is visible at one time, and the rest is available via scrolling up or down.

ScrollView is a container that provides scrolling for its contents. You can take a layout that might be too big for some screens, wrap it in a ScrollView, and still use your existing layout logic. It just so happens that the user can see only part of your layout at one time; the rest is available via scrolling.

For example, here is a ScrollView used in an XML layout file (from the Containers/Scroll demo in the Source Code area of http://apress.com):

```xml
<?xml version="1.0" encoding="utf-8"?>
<ScrollView
  xmlns:android="http://schemas.android.com/apk/res/android"
  android:layout_width="fill_parent"
  android:layout_height="wrap_content">
  <TableLayout
    android:layout_width="fill_parent"
    android:layout_height="fill_parent"
    android:stretchColumns="0">
    <TableRow>
      <View
        android:layout_height="80px"
        android:background="#000000"/>
      <TextView android:text="#000000"
        android:paddingLeft="4px"
        android:layout_gravity="center_vertical" />
    </TableRow>
    <TableRow>
      <View
        android:layout_height="80px"
        android:background="#440000" />
      <TextView android:text="#440000"
        android:paddingLeft="4px"
        android:layout_gravity="center_vertical" />
    </TableRow>
    <TableRow>
      <View
        android:layout_height="80px"
        android:background="#884400" />
      <TextView android:text="#884400"
        android:paddingLeft="4px"
        android:layout_gravity="center_vertical" />
    </TableRow>
```

```
    <TableRow>
      <View
        android:layout_height="80px"
        android:background="#aa8844" />
      <TextView android:text="#aa8844"
        android:paddingLeft="4px"
        android:layout_gravity="center_vertical" />
    </TableRow>
    <TableRow>
      <View
        android:layout_height="80px"
        android:background="#ffaa88" />
      <TextView android:text="#ffaa88"
        android:paddingLeft="4px"
        android:layout_gravity="center_vertical" />
    </TableRow>
    <TableRow>
      <View
        android:layout_height="80px"
        android:background="#ffffaa" />
      <TextView android:text="#ffffaa"
        android:paddingLeft="4px"
        android:layout_gravity="center_vertical" />
    </TableRow>
    <TableRow>
      <View
        android:layout_height="80px"
        android:background="#ffffff" />
      <TextView android:text="#ffffff"
        android:paddingLeft="4px"
        android:layout_gravity="center_vertical" />
    </TableRow>
  </TableLayout>
</ScrollView>
```

Without the ScrollView, the table would take up at least 560 pixels (7 rows at 80 pixels each, based on the View declarations). There may be some devices with screens capable of showing that much information, but many will be smaller. The ScrollView lets us keep the table as is, but present only part of it at a time.

On the stock Android emulator, when the activity is first viewed, you see what's shown in Figure 7-8.

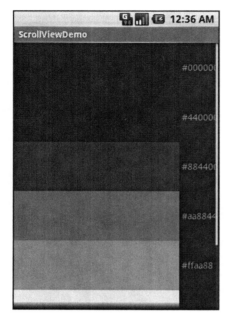

Figure 7-8. *The ScrollViewDemo sample application*

Notice how only five rows and part of the sixth are visible. By pressing the up/down buttons on the directional pad, you can scroll up and down to see the remaining rows. Also note how the right side of the content gets clipped by the scrollbar—be sure to put some padding on that side or otherwise ensure your own content does not get clipped in that fashion.

■■■

CHAPTER 8

Using Selection Widgets

In Chapter 6, you saw how fields could have constraints placed upon them to limit possible input, such as numeric-only or phone-number-only. These sorts of constraints help users "get it right" when entering information, particularly on a mobile device with cramped keyboards.

Of course, the ultimate in constrained input is to select a choice from a set of items, such as the radio buttons seen earlier. Classic UI toolkits have listboxes, comboboxes, drop-down lists, and the like for that very purpose. Android has many of the same sorts of widgets, plus others of particular interest for mobile devices (e.g., the Gallery for examining saved photos).

Moreover, Android offers a flexible framework for determining what choices are available in these widgets. Specifically, Android offers a framework of data adapters that provide a common interface to selection lists ranging from static arrays to database contents. Selection views—widgets for presenting lists of choices—are handed an adapter to supply the actual choices.

Adapting to the Circumstances

In the abstract, adapters provide a common interface to multiple disparate APIs. More specifically, in Android's case, adapters provide a common interface to the data model behind a selection-style widget, such as a listbox. This use of Java interfaces is fairly common (e.g., Java/Swing's model adapters for JTable), and Java is far from the only environment offering this sort of abstraction (e.g., Flex's XML data-binding framework accepts XML inlined as static data or retrieved from the Internet).

Android's adapters are responsible for providing the roster of data for a selection widget plus converting individual elements of data into specific views to be displayed inside the selection widget. The latter facet of the adapter system may sound a little odd, but in reality it is not that different from other GUI toolkits' ways of overriding default display behavior. For example, in Java/Swing, if you want a JList-backed listbox to actually be a checklist (where individual rows are a checkbox plus label, and clicks adjust the state of the checkbox), you inevitably wind up calling setCellRenderer() to supply your own ListCellRenderer, which in turn converts strings for the list into JCheckBox-plus-JLabel composite widgets.

Using ArrayAdapter

The easiest adapter to use is ArrayAdapter—all you need to do is wrap one of these around a Java array or java.util.List instance, and you have a fully-functioning adapter:

```
String[] items={"this", "is", "a",
                "really", "silly", "list"};
new ArrayAdapter<String>(this,
  android.R.layout.simple_list_item_1, items);
```

The `ArrayAdapter` constructor takes three parameters:

- The `Context` to use (typically this will be your activity instance)

- The resource ID of a view to use (such as a built-in system resource ID, as previously shown)

- The actual array or list of items to show

By default, the `ArrayAdapter` will invoke `toString()` on the objects in the list and wrap each of those strings in the view designated by the supplied resource. `android.R.layout.simple_list_item_1` simply turns those strings into `TextView` objects. Those `TextView` widgets, in turn, will be shown the list or spinner or whatever widget uses this `ArrayAdapter`.

You can subclass `ArrayAdapter` and override `getView()` to "roll your own" views:

```
public View getView(int position, View convertView,
                        ViewGroup parent) {
  if (convertView==null) {
    convertView=new TextView(this);
  }

  convertView.setText(buildStringFor(position));

  return(convertView);
}
```

Here, `getView()` receives three parameters:

- The index of the item in the array to show in the view

- An existing view to update with the data for this position (if one already existed, such as from scrolling—if `null`, you need to instantiate your own)

- The widget that will contain this view, if needed for instantiating the view

In the previous example, the adapter still returns a `TextView`, but uses a different behavior for determining the string that goes in the view. Chapter 9 will cover fancier `ListViews`.

Other Key Adapters

Here are some other adapters in Android that you will likely use:

- `CursorAdapter` converts a `Cursor`, typically from a content provider, into something that can be displayed in a selection view

- `SimpleAdapter` converts data found in XML resources

- `ActivityAdapter` and `ActivityIconAdapter` provide you with the names or icons of activities that can be invoked upon a particular intent

Lists of Naughty and Nice

The classic listbox widget in Android is known as `ListView`. Include one of these in your layout, invoke `setAdapter()` to supply your data and child views, and attach a listener via `setOnItemSelectedListener()` to find out when the selection has changed. With that, you have a fully-functioning listbox.

However, if your activity is dominated by a single list, you might well consider creating your activity as a subclass of `ListActivity`, rather than the regular `Activity` base class. If your main view is just the list, you do not even need to supply a layout—`ListActivity` will construct a full-screen list for you. If you do want to customize the layout, you can, so long as you identify your `ListView` as `@android:id/list`, so `ListActivity` knows which widget is the main list for the activity.

For example, here is a layout pulled from the `Selection/List` sample project. This sample along with all others in this chapter can be found in the Source Code area of `http://apress.com`.

```xml
<?xml version="1.0" encoding="utf-8"?>
<LinearLayout
  xmlns:android="http://schemas.android.com/apk/res/android"
  android:orientation="vertical"
  android:layout_width="fill_parent"
  android:layout_height="fill_parent" >
  <TextView
    android:id="@+id/selection"
    android:layout_width="fill_parent"
    android:layout_height="wrap_content"/>
  <ListView
    android:id="@android:id/list"
    android:layout_width="fill_parent"
    android:layout_height="fill_parent"
    android:drawSelectorOnTop="false"
    />
</LinearLayout>
```

It is just a list with a label on top to show the current selection.

The Java code to configure the list and connect the list with the label is:

```java
public class ListViewDemo extends ListActivity {
  TextView selection;
  String[] items={"lorem", "ipsum", "dolor", "sit", "amet",
          "consectetuer", "adipiscing", "elit", "morbi", "vel",
          "ligula", "vitae", "arcu", "aliquet", "mollis",
          "etiam", "vel", "erat", "placerat", "ante",
          "porttitor", "sodales", "pellentesque", "augue", "purus"};

  @Override
  public void onCreate(Bundle icicle) {
    super.onCreate(icicle);
    setContentView(R.layout.main);
```

```
    setListAdapter(new ArrayAdapter<String>(this,
                        android.R.layout.simple_list_item_1,
                        items));
    selection=(TextView)findViewById(R.id.selection);
  }

  public void onListItemClick(ListView parent, View v, int position,
                                long id) {
    selection.setText(items[position]);
  }
}
```

With ListActivity, you can set the list adapter via setListAdapter()—in this case, providing an ArrayAdapter wrapping an array of nonsense strings. To find out when the list selection changes, override onListItemClick() and take appropriate steps based on the supplied child view and position (in this case, updating the label with the text for that position).

The results are shown in Figure 8-1.

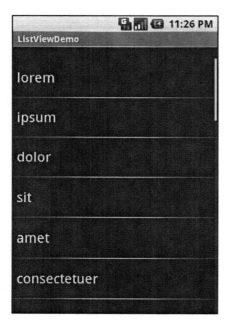

Figure 8-1. *The ListViewDemo sample application*

Spin Control

In Android, the Spinner is the equivalent of the drop-down selector you might find in other toolkits (e.g., JComboBox in Java/Swing). Pressing the center button on the D-pad pops up a selection dialog for the user to choose an item from. You basically get the ability to select from a list without taking up all the screen space of a ListView, at the cost of an extra click or screen tap to make a change.

As with ListView, you provide the adapter for data and child views via setAdapter() and hook in a listener object for selections via setOnItemSelectedListener().

If you want to tailor the view used when displaying the drop-down perspective, you need to configure the adapter, not the Spinner widget. Use the setDropDownViewResource() method to supply the resource ID of the view to use.

For example, culled from the Selection/Spinner sample project, here is an XML layout for a simple view with a Spinner:

```
<?xml version="1.0" encoding="utf-8"?>
<LinearLayout
  xmlns:android="http://schemas.android.com/apk/res/android"
  android:orientation="vertical"
  android:layout_width="fill_parent"
  android:layout_height="fill_parent"
  >
  <TextView
    android:id="@+id/selection"
    android:layout_width="fill_parent"
    android:layout_height="wrap_content"
    />
  <Spinner android:id="@+id/spinner"
    android:layout_width="fill_parent"
    android:layout_height="wrap_content"
    android:drawSelectorOnTop="true"
  />
</LinearLayout>
```

This is the same view as shown in the previous section, just with a Spinner instead of a ListView. The Spinner property android:drawSelectorOnTop controls whether the arrows are drawn on the selector button on the right side of the Spinner UI.

To populate and use the Spinner, we need some Java code:

```java
public class SpinnerDemo extends Activity
  implements AdapterView.OnItemSelectedListener {
  TextView selection;
  String[] items={"lorem", "ipsum", "dolor", "sit", "amet",
          "consectetuer", "adipiscing", "elit", "morbi", "vel",
          "ligula", "vitae", "arcu", "aliquet", "mollis",
          "etiam", "vel", "erat", "placerat", "ante",
          "porttitor", "sodales", "pellentesque", "augue", "purus"};

  @Override
  public void onCreate(Bundle icicle) {
    super.onCreate(icicle);
    setContentView(R.layout.main);
    selection=(TextView)findViewById(R.id.selection);

    Spinner spin=(Spinner)findViewById(R.id.spinner);
    spin.setOnItemSelectedListener(this);

    ArrayAdapter<String> aa=new ArrayAdapter<String>(this,
                            android.R.layout.simple_spinner_item,
                            items);

    aa.setDropDownViewResource(
      android.R.layout.simple_spinner_dropdown_item);
    spin.setAdapter(aa);
  }

  public void onItemSelected(AdapterView<?> parent,
                              View v, int position, long id) {
    selection.setText(items[position]);
  }

  public void onNothingSelected(AdapterView<?> parent) {
    selection.setText("");
  }
}
```

Here, we attach the activity itself as the selection listener
(spin.setOnItemSelectedListener(this)). This works because the activity implements the
OnItemSelectedListener interface. We configure the adapter not only with the list of fake words,
but also with a specific resource to use for the drop-down view (via
aa.setDropDownViewResource()). Also note the use of android.R.layout.simple_spinner_item as
the built-in View for showing items in the spinner itself. Finally, we implement the callbacks
required by OnItemSelectedListener to adjust the selection label based on user input.

The resulting application is shown in Figures 8-2 and 8-3.

Figure 8-2. *The SpinnerDemo sample application, as initially launched*

Figure 8-3. *The same application, with the spinner drop-down list displayed*

Grid Your Lions (or Something Like That . . .)

As the name suggests, GridView gives you a two-dimensional grid of items to choose from. You have moderate control over the number and size of the columns; the number of rows is dynamically determined based on the number of items the supplied adapter says are available for viewing.

There are a few properties which, when combined, determine the number of columns and their sizes:

- android:numColumns spells out how many columns there are, or, if you supply a value of auto_fit, Android will compute the number of columns based on available space and the following properties.

- android:verticalSpacing and its counterpart android:horizontalSpacing indicate how much whitespace there should be between items in the grid.

- android:columnWidth indicates how many pixels wide each column should be.

- android:stretchMode indicates, for grids with auto_fit for android:numColumns, what should happen for any available space not taken up by columns or spacing—this should be columnWidth to have the columns take up available space or spacingWidth to have the whitespace between columns absorb extra space. For example, suppose the screen is 320 pixels wide, and we have android:columnWidth set to 100px and android:horizontalSpacing set to 5px. Three columns would use 310 pixels (three columns of 100 pixels and two whitespaces of 5 pixels). With android:stretchMode set to columnWidth, the three columns will each expand by 3–4 pixels to use up the remaining 10 pixels. With android:stretchMode set to spacingWidth, the two whitespaces will each grow by 5 pixels to consume the remaining 10 pixels.

Otherwise, the GridView works much like any other selection widget—use setAdapter() to provide the data and child views, invoke setOnItemSelectedListener() to register a selection listener, etc.

For example, here is a XML layout from the Selection/Grid sample project, showing a GridView configuration:

```
<?xml version="1.0" encoding="utf-8"?>
<LinearLayout
  xmlns:android="http://schemas.android.com/apk/res/android"
  android:orientation="vertical"
  android:layout_width="fill_parent"
  android:layout_height="fill_parent"
  >
  <TextView
    android:id="@+id/selection"
    android:layout_width="fill_parent"
    android:layout_height="wrap_content"
    />
```

```
<GridView
  android:id="@+id/grid"
  android:layout_width="fill_parent"
  android:layout_height="fill_parent"
  android:verticalSpacing="35px"
  android:horizontalSpacing="5px"
  android:numColumns="auto_fit"
  android:columnWidth="100px"
  android:stretchMode="columnWidth"
  android:gravity="center"
  />
</LinearLayout>
```

For this grid, we take up the entire screen except for what our selection label requires. The number of columns is computed by Android (android:numColumns = "auto_fit") based on 5-pixel horizontal spacing (android:horizontalSpacing = "5px"), 100-pixel columns (android:columnWidth = "100px"), with the columns absorbing any "slop" width left over (android:stretchMode = "columnWidth").

The Java code to configure the GridView is:

```
public class GridDemo extends Activity
  implements AdapterView.OnItemSelectedListener {
  TextView selection;
  String[] items={"lorem", "ipsum", "dolor", "sit", "amet",
          "consectetuer", "adipiscing", "elit", "morbi", "vel",
          "ligula", "vitae", "arcu", "aliquet", "mollis",
          "etiam", "vel", "erat", "placerat", "ante",
          "porttitor", "sodales", "pellentesque", "augue", "purus"};

  @Override
  public void onCreate(Bundle icicle) {
    super.onCreate(icicle);
    setContentView(R.layout.main);
    selection=(TextView)findViewById(R.id.selection);

    GridView g=(GridView) findViewById(R.id.grid);
    g.setAdapter(new FunnyLookingAdapter(this,
                      android.R.layout.simple_list_item_1,
                      items));
    g.setOnItemSelectedListener(this);
  }
```

```
    public void onItemSelected(AdapterView<?> parent, View v,
                               int position, long id) {
      selection.setText(items[position]);
    }

    public void onNothingSelected(AdapterView<?> parent) {
      selection.setText("");
    }

    private class FunnyLookingAdapter extends ArrayAdapter {
      Context ctxt;

      FunnyLookingAdapter(Context ctxt, int resource,
                          String[] items) {
        super(ctxt, resource, items);

        this.ctxt=ctxt;
      }

      public View getView(int position, View convertView,
                          ViewGroup parent) {
        TextView label=(TextView)convertView;

        if (convertView==null) {
          convertView=new TextView(ctxt);
          label=(TextView)convertView;
        }

        label.setText(items[position]);

        return(convertView);
      }
    }
  }
}
```

For the grid cells, rather than using auto-generated TextView widgets as in the previous sections, we create our own views, by subclassing ArrayAdapter and overriding getView(). In this case, we wrap the funny-looking strings in our own TextView widgets, just to be different. If getView() receives a TextView, we just reset its text; otherwise, we create a new TextView instance and populate it.

With the 35-pixel vertical spacing from the XML layout (android:verticalSpacing = "35"), the grid overflows the boundaries of the emulator's screen as shown in Figures 8-4 and 8-5.

Figure 8-4. *The GridDemo sample application, as initially launched*

Figure 8-5. *The same application, scrolled to the bottom of the grid*

Fields: Now with 35% Less Typing!

The AutoCompleteTextView is sort of a hybrid between the EditText (field) and the Spinner. With auto-completion, as the user types, the text is treated as a prefix filter, comparing the entered text as a prefix against a list of candidates. Matches are shown in a selection list that, like with Spinner, folds down from the field. The user can either type out an entry (e.g., something not in the list) or choose an entry from the list to be the value of the field.

AutoCompleteTextView subclasses EditText, so you can configure all the standard look-and-feel aspects, such as font face and color.

In addition, AutoCompleteTextView has a android:completionThreshold property, to indicate the minimum number of characters a user must enter before the list filtering begins.

You can give AutoCompleteTextView an adapter containing the list of candidate values via setAdapter(). However, since the user could type something not in the list, AutoCompleteTextView does not support selection listeners. Instead, you can register a TextWatcher, like you can with any EditText, to be notified when the text changes. These events will occur either because of manual typing or from a selection from the drop-down list.

The following is a familiar-looking XML layout, this time containing an AutoCompleteTextView (pulled from the Selection/AutoComplete sample application):

```xml
<?xml version="1.0" encoding="utf-8"?>
<LinearLayout
  xmlns:android="http://schemas.android.com/apk/res/android"
  android:orientation="vertical"
  android:layout_width="fill_parent"
  android:layout_height="fill_parent"
  >
  <TextView
    android:id="@+id/selection"
    android:layout_width="fill_parent"
    android:layout_height="wrap_content"
    />
  <AutoCompleteTextView android:id="@+id/edit"
      android:layout_width="fill_parent"
      android:layout_height="wrap_content"
      android:completionThreshold="3"/>
</LinearLayout>
```

The corresponding Java code is:

```java
public class AutoCompleteDemo extends Activity
  implements TextWatcher {
  TextView selection;
  AutoCompleteTextView edit;
```

```
  String[] items={"lorem", "ipsum", "dolor", "sit", "amet",
          "consectetuer", "adipiscing", "elit", "morbi", "vel",
          "ligula", "vitae", "arcu", "aliquet", "mollis",
          "etiam", "vel", "erat", "placerat", "ante",
          "porttitor", "sodales", "pellentesque", "augue", "purus"};

  @Override
  public void onCreate(Bundle icicle) {
    super.onCreate(icicle);
    setContentView(R.layout.main);
    selection=(TextView)findViewById(R.id.selection);
    edit=(AutoCompleteTextView)findViewById(R.id.edit);
    edit.addTextChangedListener(this);

    edit.setAdapter(new ArrayAdapter<String>(this,
                        android.R.layout.simple_dropdown_item_1line,
                        items));
  }

  public void onTextChanged(CharSequence s, int start, int before,
                            int count) {
    selection.setText(edit.getText());
  }

  public void beforeTextChanged(CharSequence s, int start,
                                int count, int after) {
    // needed for interface, but not used
  }

  public void afterTextChanged(Editable s) {
    // needed for interface, but not used
  }
}
```

This time, our activity implements TextWatcher, which means our callbacks are onTextChanged() and beforeTextChanged(). In this case, we are only interested in the former, and we update the selection label to match the AutoCompleteTextView's current contents.

Figures 8-6, 8-7, and 8-8 show the application results.

Figure 8-6. *The AutoCompleteDemo sample application, as initially launched*

Figure 8-7. *The same application, after a few matching letters were entered, showing the auto-complete drop-down*

Figure 8-8. *The same application, after the auto-complete value was selected*

Galleries, Give or Take the Art

The Gallery widget is not one ordinarily found in GUI toolkits. It is, in effect, a horizontally-laid-out listbox. One choice follows the next across the horizontal plane, with the currently-selected item highlighted. On an Android device, one rotates through the options through the left and right D-pad buttons.

Compared to the ListView, the Gallery takes up less screen space while still showing multiple choices at one time (assuming they are short enough). Compared to the Spinner, the Gallery always shows more than one choice at a time.

The quintessential example use for the Gallery is image preview—given a collection of photos or icons, the Gallery lets people preview the pictures in the process of choosing one.

Code-wise, the Gallery works much like a Spinner or GridView. In your XML layout, you have a few properties at your disposal:

- android:spacing controls the number of pixels between entries in the list.

- android:spinnerSelector controls what is used to indicate a selection—this can either be a reference to a Drawable (see the resources chapter) or an RGB value in #AARRGGBB or similar notation.

- android:drawSelectorOnTop indicates if the selection bar (or Drawable) should be drawn before (false) or after (true) drawing the selected child—if you choose true, be sure that your selector has sufficient transparency to show the child through the selector, otherwise users will not be able to read the selection.

■ ■ ■

CHAPTER 9

Getting Fancy with Lists

The humble ListView is one of the most important widgets in all of Android, simply because it is used so frequently. Whether choosing a contact to call or an email message to forward or an ebook to read, ListView widgets are employed in a wide range of activities. Of course, it would be nice if they were more than just plain text.

The good news is that they can be as fancy as you want, within the limitations of a mobile device's screen, of course. However, making them fancy takes some work and some features of Android that I will cover in this chapter.

Getting to First Base

The classic Android ListView is a plain list of text—solid but uninspiring. This is because all we hand to the ListView is a bunch of words in an array, and we tell Android to use a simple built-in layout for pouring those words into a list.

However, you can have a list whose rows are made up of icons, or icons and text, or checkboxes and text, or whatever you want. It is merely a matter of supplying enough data to the adapter and helping the adapter to create a richer set of View objects for each row.

For example, suppose you want a ListView whose entries are made up of an icon, followed by some text. You could construct a layout for the row that looks like this, found in the FancyLists/Static sample project available in the Source Code section of the Apress Web site:

```xml
<?xml version="1.0" encoding="utf-8"?>
<LinearLayout xmlns:android="http://schemas.android.com/apk/res/android"
  android:layout_width="fill_parent"
  android:layout_height="wrap_content"
  android:orientation="horizontal"
>
  <ImageView
    android:id="@+id/icon"
    android:layout_width="22px"
    android:paddingLeft="2px"
    android:paddingRight="2px"
    android:paddingTop="2px"
    android:layout_height="wrap_content"
    android:src="@drawable/ok"
  />
```

```
<TextView
  android:id="@+id/label"
  android:layout_width="wrap_content"
  android:layout_height="wrap_content"
  android:textSize="44sp"
/>
</LinearLayout>
```

This layout uses a LinearLayout to set up a row, with the icon on the left and the text (in a nice big font) on the right.

By default, though, Android has no idea that you want to use this layout with your ListView. To make the connection, you need to supply your Adapter with the resource ID of the custom layout shown in the preceding code:

```
public class StaticDemo extends ListActivity {
  TextView selection;
  String[] items={"lorem", "ipsum", "dolor", "sit", "amet",
        "consectetuer", "adipiscing", "elit", "morbi", "vel",
        "ligula", "vitae", "arcu", "aliquet", "mollis",
        "etiam", "vel", "erat", "placerat", "ante",
        "porttitor", "sodales", "pellentesque", "augue",
        "purus"};

  @Override
  public void onCreate(Bundle icicle) {
    super.onCreate(icicle);
    setContentView(R.layout.main);
    setListAdapter(new ArrayAdapter<String>(this,
                        R.layout.row, R.id.label,
                        items));
    selection=(TextView)findViewById(R.id.selection);
  }

  public void onListItemClick(ListView parent, View v,
                        int position,  long id) {
   selection.setText(items[position]);
  }
}
```

This follows the general structure for the previous ListView sample.

The key in this example is that you have told ArrayAdapter that you want to use your custom layout (R.layout.row) and that the TextView where the word should go is known as R.id.label within that custom layout. Remember: to reference a layout (row.xml), use R.layout as a prefix on the base name of the layout XML file (R.layout.row).

The result is a ListView with icons down the left side. In particular, all the icons are the same, as Figure 9-1 shows.

Figure 9-1. *The StaticDemo application*

A Dynamic Presentation

This technique—supplying an alternate layout to use for rows—handles simple cases very nicely. However, it isn't sufficient when you have more-complicated scenarios for your rows, such as the following:

- Not every row uses the same layout (e.g., some have one line of text, others have two).

- You need to configure the widgets in the rows (e.g., different icons for different cases).

In those cases, the better option is to create your own subclass of your desired Adapter, override getView(), and construct your rows yourself. The getView() method is responsible for returning a View, representing the row for the supplied position in the adapter data.

For example, let's rework the preceding code to use getView() so we can have different icons for different rows—in this case, one icon for short words and one for long words (from the FancyLists/Dynamic sample project at http://apress.com/):

```
public class DynamicDemo extends ListActivity {
  TextView selection;
  String[] items={"lorem", "ipsum", "dolor", "sit", "amet",
          "consectetuer", "adipiscing", "elit", "morbi", "vel",
          "ligula", "vitae", "arcu", "aliquet", "mollis",
          "etiam", "vel", "erat", "placerat", "ante",
          "porttitor", "sodales", "pellentesque", "augue",
          "purus"};
```

```
  @Override
  public void onCreate(Bundle icicle) {
    super.onCreate(icicle);
    setContentView(R.layout.main);
    setListAdapter(new IconicAdapter(this));
    selection=(TextView)findViewById(R.id.selection);
  }

  public void onListItemClick(ListView parent, View v,
                              int position, long id) {
   selection.setText(items[position]);
  }

  class IconicAdapter extends ArrayAdapter {
    Activity context;

    IconicAdapter(Activity context) {
      super(context, R.layout.row, items);

      this.context=context;
    }

    public View getView(int position, View convertView,
                        ViewGroup parent) {
      LayoutInflater inflater=context.getLayoutInflater();
      View row=inflater.inflate(R.layout.row, null);
      TextView label=(TextView)row.findViewById(R.id.label);

      label.setText(items[position]);

      if (items[position].length()>4) {
        ImageView icon=(ImageView)row.findViewById(R.id.icon);

        icon.setImageResource(R.drawable.delete);
      }

      return(row);
    }
  }
}
```

The theory is that we override getView() and return rows based on which object is being displayed, where the object is indicated by a position index into the Adapter. However, if you look at the implementation shown in the code here, you will see a reference to a LayoutInflater class—and that concept takes a little bit of an explanation.

A Bit About Inflation

In this case, "inflation" means the act of converting an XML layout specification into the actual tree of View objects the XML represents. This is undoubtedly a tedious bit of code: take an element, create an instance of the specified View class, walk the attributes, convert those into property setter calls, iterate over all child elements, lather, rinse, repeat.

The good news is that the fine folk on the Android team wrapped all that up into a class called LayoutInflater that we can use ourselves. When it comes to fancy lists, for example, we will want to inflate Views for each row shown in the list, so we can use the convenient short-hand of the XML layout to describe what the rows are supposed to look like.

In the preceding example, we inflate the R.layout.row layout we created in the previous section. This gives us a View object that, in reality, is our LinearLayout with an ImageView and a TextView, just as R.layout.row specifies. However, rather than having to create all those objects ourselves and wire them together, the XML and LayoutInflater handle the "heavy lifting" for us.

And Now, Back to Our Story

So we have used LayoutInflater to get a View representing the row. This row is "empty" since the static layout file has no idea what actual data goes into the row. It is our job to customize and populate the row as we see fit before returning it. So, we do the following:

- Put the text label into our label widget, using the word at the supplied position.

- See if the word is longer than four characters and, if so, find our ImageView icon widget and replace the stock resource with a different one.

Now we have a ListView with different icons based upon context of that specific entry in the list (see Figure 9-2).

Figure 9-2. *The DynamicDemo application*

This was a fairly contrived example, but you can see where this technique could be used to customize rows based on any sort of criteria, such as other columns in a returned Cursor.

Better. Stronger. Faster.

The getView() implementation shown previously works, but it is inefficient. Every time the user scrolls, we have to create a bunch of new View objects to accommodate the newly shown rows. And since the Android framework does not cache existing View objects itself, we wind up making new row View objects even for rows we just created a second or two ago. This is bad.

It might be bad for the immediate user experience, if the list appears to be sluggish. More likely, though, it will be bad due to battery usage—every bit of CPU that is used eats up the battery. This is compounded by the extra work the garbage collector needs to do to get rid of all those extra objects you create. So the less efficient your code, the more quickly the phone's battery will be drained, and the less happy the user will be. And you want happy users, right?

So, let us take a look at a few tricks to make your fancy ListView widgets more efficient.

Using convertView

The getView() method receives, as one of its parameters, a View named, by convention, convertView. Sometimes convertView will be null. In those cases, you have to create a new row View from scratch (e.g., via inflation), just as we did before.

However, if convertView is not null, then it is actually one of your previously created Views. This will be the case primarily when the user scrolls the ListView—as new rows appear, Android will attempt to recycle the views of the rows that scrolled off the other end of the list, to save you having to rebuild them from scratch.

Assuming that each of your rows has the same basic structure, you can use findViewById() to get at the individual widgets that make up your row and change their contents, then return convertView from getView() rather than create a whole new row.

For example, here is the getView() implementation from last time, now optimized via convertView (from the FancyLists/Recycling project at http://apress.com/):

```
public class RecyclingDemo extends ListActivity {
  TextView selection;
  String[] items={"lorem", "ipsum", "dolor", "sit", "amet",
          "consectetuer", "adipiscing", "elit", "morbi", "vel",
          "ligula", "vitae", "arcu", "aliquet", "mollis",
          "etiam", "vel", "erat", "placerat", "ante",
          "porttitor", "sodales", "pellentesque", "augue",
          "purus"};

  @Override
  public void onCreate(Bundle icicle) {
    super.onCreate(icicle);
    setContentView(R.layout.main);
    setListAdapter(new IconicAdapter(this));
    selection=(TextView)findViewById(R.id.selection);
  }
```

```java
public void onListItemClick(ListView parent, View v,
                            int position, long id) {
  selection.setText(items[position]);
}

class IconicAdapter extends ArrayAdapter {
  Activity context;

  IconicAdapter(Activity context) {
    super(context, R.layout.row, items);

    this.context=context;
  }

  public View getView(int position, View convertView,
                      ViewGroup parent) {
    View row=convertView;

    if (row==null) {
      LayoutInflater inflater=context.getLayoutInflater();

      row=inflater.inflate(R.layout.row, null);
    }

    TextView label=(TextView)row.findViewById(R.id.label);

    label.setText(items[position]);

    ImageView icon=(ImageView)row.findViewById(R.id.icon);

    if (items[position].length()>4) {
      icon.setImageResource(R.drawable.delete);
    }
    else {
      icon.setImageResource(R.drawable.ok);
    }

    return(row);
  }
}
}
```

Here we check to see if the convertView is null and, if so we then inflate our row—but if it is not null, we just reuse it. The work to fill in the contents (icon image, text) is the same in either case. The advantage is that if the convertView is not null, we avoid the potentially expensive inflation step.

This approach will not work in every case, though. For example, it may be that you have a ListView for which some rows will have one line of text and others will have two. In this case, recycling existing rows becomes tricky, as the layouts may differ significantly. For example, if the row we need to create a View for requires two lines of text, we cannot just use a View with one line of text as is. We either need to tinker with the innards of that View, or ignore it and inflate a new View.

Of course, there are ways to deal with this, such as making the second line of text visible or invisible depending on whether it is needed. And on a phone every millisecond of CPU time is precious, possibly for the user experience, but always for battery life—more CPU utilization means a more quickly drained battery.

That being said, particularly if you are a rookie to Android, focus on getting the functionality right first, then looking to optimize performance on a second pass through your code rather than getting lost in a sea of Views, trying to tackle it all in one shot.

Using the Holder Pattern

Another somewhat expensive operation we do a lot with fancy views is call findViewById(). This dives into our inflated row and pulls out widgets by their assigned identifiers so we can customize the widget contents (e.g., change the text of a TextView, change the icon in an ImageView). Since findViewById() can find widgets anywhere in the tree of children of the row's root View, this could take a fair number of instructions to execute, particularly if we keep having to re-find widgets we had found once before.

In some GUI toolkits, this problem is avoided by having the composite Views, like our rows, be declared totally in program code (in this case, Java). Then accessing individual widgets is merely a matter of calling a getter or accessing a field. And you can certainly do that with Android, but the code gets rather verbose. We need a way that lets us use the layout XML yet cache our row's key child widgets so we have to find them only once. That's where the holder pattern comes into play, in a class we'll call ViewWrapper.

All View objects have getTag() and setTag() methods. These allow you to associate an arbitrary object with the widget. That holder pattern uses that "tag" to hold an object that, in turn, holds each of the child widgets of interest. By attaching that holder to the row View, every time we use the row, we already have access to the child widgets we care about, without having to call findViewById() again.

So, let's take a look at one of these holder classes (taken from the FancyLists/ViewWrapper sample project at http://apress.com/):

```java
class ViewWrapper {
  View base;
  TextView label=null;
  ImageView icon=null;

  ViewWrapper(View base) {
    this.base=base;
  }

  TextView getLabel() {
    if (label==null) {
      label=(TextView)base.findViewById(R.id.label);
    }
```

```
      return(label);
    }

    ImageView getIcon() {
      if (icon==null) {
        icon=(ImageView)base.findViewById(R.id.icon);
      }

      return(icon);
    }
  }
```

ViewWrapper not only holds onto the child widgets, but also lazy-finds the child widgets. If you create a wrapper and never need a specific child, you never go through the findViewById() operation for it and never have to pay for those CPU cycles.

The holder pattern also allows us to do the following:

- Consolidate all our per-widget type casting in one place, rather than having to cast it everywhere we call findViewById()

- Perhaps track other information about the row, such as state information we are not yet ready to "flush" to the underlying model

Using ViewWrapper is a matter of creating an instance whenever we inflate a row and attaching said instance to the row View via setTag(), as shown in this rewrite of getView():

```
public class ViewWrapperDemo extends ListActivity {
  TextView selection;
  String[] items={"lorem", "ipsum", "dolor", "sit", "amet",
          "consectetuer", "adipiscing", "elit", "morbi", "vel",
          "ligula", "vitae", "arcu", "aliquet", "mollis",
          "etiam", "vel", "erat", "placerat", "ante",
          "porttitor", "sodales", "pellentesque", "augue",
          "purus"};

  @Override
  public void onCreate(Bundle icicle) {
    super.onCreate(icicle);
    setContentView(R.layout.main);
    setListAdapter(new IconicAdapter(this));
    selection=(TextView)findViewById(R.id.selection);
  }

  private String getModel(int position) {
    return(((IconicAdapter)getListAdapter()).getItem(position));
  }
```

```java
  public void onListItemClick(ListView parent, View v,
                             int position, long id) {
    selection.setText(getModel(position));
  }

  class IconicAdapter extends ArrayAdapter<String> {
    Activity context;

    IconicAdapter(Activity context) {
      super(context, R.layout.row, items);

      this.context=context;
    }

    public View getView(int position, View convertView,
                        ViewGroup parent) {
      View row=convertView;
      ViewWrapper wrapper=null;

      if (row==null) {
        LayoutInflater inflater=context.getLayoutInflater();

        row=inflater.inflate(R.layout.row, null);
        wrapper=new ViewWrapper(row);
        row.setTag(wrapper);
      }
      else {
        wrapper=(ViewWrapper)row.getTag();
      }

      wrapper.getLabel().setText(getModel(position));

      if (getModel(position).length()>4) {
        wrapper.getIcon().setImageResource(R.drawable.delete);
      }
      else {
        wrapper.getIcon().setImageResource(R.drawable.ok);
      }

      return(row);
    }
  }
}
```

Just as we check convertView to see if it is null in order to create the row Views as needed, we also pull out (or create) the corresponding row's ViewWrapper. Then accessing the child widgets is merely a matter of calling their associated methods on the wrapper.

Making a List . . .

Lists with pretty icons next to them are all fine and well. But can we create ListView widgets whose rows contain interactive child widgets instead of just passive widgets like TextView and ImageView? For example, could we combine the RatingBar with text in order to allow people to scroll a list of, say, songs and rate them right inside the list?

There is good news and bad news.

The good news is that interactive widgets in rows work just fine. The bad news is that it is a little tricky, specifically when it comes to taking action when the interactive widget's state changes (e.g., a value is typed into a field). We need to store that state somewhere, since our RatingBar widget will be recycled when the ListView is scrolled. We need to be able to set the RatingBar state based upon the actual word we are viewing as the RatingBar is recycled, and we need to save the state when it changes so it can be restored when this particular row is scrolled back into view.

What makes this interesting is that, by default, the RatingBar has absolutely no idea what model in the ArrayAdapter it is looking at. After all, the RatingBar is just a widget, used in a row of a ListView. We need to teach the rows which model they are currently displaying, so when their checkbox is checked they know which model's state to modify.

So, let's see how this is done, using the activity in the FancyLists/RateList sample project at http://apress.com/. We'll use the same basic classes as our previous demo—we're showing a list of nonsense words, which you can then rate. In addition, words given a top rating will appear in all caps.

```java
public class RateListDemo extends ListActivity {
  TextView selection;
  String[] items={"lorem", "ipsum", "dolor", "sit", "amet",
        "consectetuer", "adipiscing", "elit", "morbi", "vel",
        "ligula", "vitae", "arcu", "aliquet", "mollis",
        "etiam", "vel", "erat", "placerat", "ante",
        "porttitor", "sodales", "pellentesque", "augue",
        "purus"};

  @Override
  public void onCreate(Bundle icicle) {
    super.onCreate(icicle);
    setContentView(R.layout.main);

    ArrayList<RowModel> list=new ArrayList<RowModel>();

    for (String s : items) {
      list.add(new RowModel(s));
    }

    setListAdapter(new CheckAdapter(this, list));
    selection=(TextView)findViewById(R.id.selection);
  }
```

```
  private RowModel getModel(int position) {
    return(((CheckAdapter)getListAdapter()).getItem(position));
  }

  public void onListItemClick(ListView parent, View v,
                              int position, long id) {
   selection.setText(getModel(position).toString());
  }

  class CheckAdapter extends ArrayAdapter<RowModel> {
    Activity context;

    CheckAdapter(Activity context, ArrayList<RowModel> list) {
      super(context, R.layout.row, list);

      this.context=context;
    }

    public View getView(int position, View convertView,
                        ViewGroup parent) {
      View row=convertView;
      ViewWrapper wrapper;
      RatingBar rate;

      if (row==null) {
        LayoutInflater inflater=context.getLayoutInflater();

        row=inflater.inflate(R.layout.row, null);
        wrapper=new ViewWrapper(row);
        row.setTag(wrapper);
        rate=wrapper.getRatingBar();

        RatingBar.OnRatingBarChangeListener l=
                  new RatingBar.OnRatingBarChangeListener() {
          public void onRatingChanged(RatingBar ratingBar,
                                      float rating,
                                      boolean fromTouch)  {
            Integer myPosition=(Integer)ratingBar.getTag();
            RowModel model=getModel(myPosition);

            model.rating=rating;

            LinearLayout parent=(LinearLayout)ratingBar.getParent();
            TextView label=(TextView)parent.findViewById(R.id.label);

            label.setText(model.toString());
          }
        };
```

```
        rate.setOnRatingBarChangeListener(l);
      }
      else {
        wrapper=(ViewWrapper)row.getTag();
        rate=wrapper.getRatingBar();
      }

      RowModel model=getModel(position);

      wrapper.getLabel().setText(model.toString());
      rate.setTag(new Integer(position));
      rate.setRating(model.rating);

      return(row);
    }
  }

  class RowModel {
    String label;
    float rating=2.0f;

    RowModel(String label) {
      this.label=label;
    }

    public String toString() {
      if (rating>=3.0) {
        return(label.toUpperCase());
      }

      return(label);
    }
  }
}
```

Here is what is different between our earlier code and this activity and getView()
implementation:

- While we are still using String[] items as the list of nonsense words, but rather than
  pouring that String array straight into an ArrayAdapter, we turn it into a list of RowModel
  objects. RowModel is this demo's poor excuse for a mutable model; it holds the nonsense
  word plus the current checked state. In a real system, these might be objects populated
  from a Cursor, and the properties would have more business meaning.

- Utility methods like onListItemClick() had to be updated to reflect the change from a
  pure String model to use a RowModel.

- The ArrayAdapter subclass (CheckAdapter) in getView() looks to see if convertView is null. If so, we create a new row by inflating a simple layout (see the following code) and also attach a ViewWrapper (also in the following code). For the row's RatingBar, we add an anonymous onRatingChanged() listener that looks at the row's tag (getTag()) and converts that into an Integer, representing the position within the ArrayAdapter that this row is displaying. Using that, the checkbox can get the actual RowModel for the row and update the model based upon the new state of the rating bar. It also updates the text adjacent to the RatingBar when checked to match the rating-bar state.

- We always make sure that the RatingBar has the proper contents and has a tag (via setTag()) pointing to the position in the adapter the row is displaying.

The row layout is very simple: just a RatingBar and a TextView inside a LinearLayout:

```xml
<?xml version="1.0" encoding="utf-8"?>
<LinearLayout xmlns:android="http://schemas.android.com/apk/res/android"
  android:layout_width="fill_parent"
  android:layout_height="wrap_content"
  android:orientation="horizontal"
>
  <RatingBar
    android:id="@+id/rate"
    android:layout_width="wrap_content"
    android:layout_height="wrap_content"
    android:numStars="3"
    android:stepSize="1"
    android:rating="2" />
  <TextView
    android:id="@+id/label"
    android:paddingLeft="2px"
    android:paddingRight="2px"
    android:paddingTop="2px"
    android:textSize="40sp"
    android:layout_width="fill_parent"
    android:layout_height="wrap_content"/>
</LinearLayout>
```

The ViewWrapper is similarly simple, just extracting the RatingBar and the TextView out of the row View:

```java
class ViewWrapper {
  View base;
  RatingBar rate=null;
  TextView label=null;
```

```
  ViewWrapper(View base) {
    this.base=base;
  }

  RatingBar getRatingBar() {
    if (rate==null) {
      rate=(RatingBar)base.findViewById(R.id.rate);
    }

    return(rate);
  }

  TextView getLabel() {
    if (label==null) {
      label=(TextView)base.findViewById(R.id.label);
    }

    return(label);
  }
}
```

And the result (Figure 9-3) is what you would expect, visually.

Figure 9-3. *The RateListDemo application, as initially launched*

This includes the toggled checkboxes turning their words into all caps (Figure 9-4).

Figure 9-4. *The same application, showing a top-rated word*

. . . And Checking It Twice

The rating list in the previous section works, but implementing it is very tedious. Worse, much of that tedium would not be reusable except in very limited circumstances. We can do better.

What we'd really like is to be able to create a layout like this:

```xml
<?xml version="1.0" encoding="utf-8"?>
<LinearLayout
  xmlns:android="http://schemas.android.com/apk/res/android"
  android:orientation="vertical"
  android:layout_width="fill_parent"
  android:layout_height="fill_parent" >
<TextView
  android:id="@+id/selection"
  android:layout_width="fill_parent"
  android:layout_height="wrap_content"/>
<com.commonsware.android.fancylists.seven.RateListView
  android:id="@android:id/list"
  android:layout_width="fill_parent"
  android:layout_height="fill_parent"
  android:drawSelectorOnTop="false"
  />
</LinearLayout>
```

where, in our code, almost all of the logic that might have referred to a ListView before "just works" with the RateListView we put in the layout:

```
public class RateListViewDemo extends ListActivity {
  TextView selection;
  String[] items={"lorem", "ipsum", "dolor", "sit", "amet",
          "consectetuer", "adipiscing", "elit", "morbi", "vel",
          "ligula", "vitae", "arcu", "aliquet", "mollis",
          "etiam", "vel", "erat", "placerat", "ante",
          "porttitor", "sodales", "pellentesque", "augue",
          "purus"};

  @Override
  public void onCreate(Bundle icicle) {
    super.onCreate(icicle);
    setContentView(R.layout.main);

    setListAdapter(new ArrayAdapter<String>(this,
                      android.R.layout.simple_list_item_1,
                      items));
    selection=(TextView)findViewById(R.id.selection);
  }

  public void onListItemClick(ListView parent, View v,
                              int position, long id) {
  selection.setText(items[position]);
  }
}
```

Things get a wee bit challenging when you realize that in everything up to this point in this chapter, never were we actually changing the ListView itself. All our work was with the adapters, overriding getView() and inflating our own rows and whatnot.

So if we want RateListView to take in any ordinary ListAdapter and "just work," putting checkboxes on the rows as needed, we are going to need to do some fancy footwork. Specifically, we are going to need to wrap the "raw" ListAdapter in some other ListAdapter that knows how to put the checkboxes on the rows and track the state of those checkboxes.

First we need to establish the pattern of one ListAdapter augmenting another. Here is the code for AdapterWrapper, which takes a ListAdapter and delegates all of the interface's methods to the delegate (from the FancyLists/RateListView sample project at http://apress.com/):

```
public class AdapterWrapper implements ListAdapter {
  ListAdapter delegate=null;

  public AdapterWrapper(ListAdapter delegate) {
    this.delegate=delegate;
  }

  public int getCount() {
    return(delegate.getCount());
  }
```

```java
  public Object getItem(int position) {
    return(delegate.getItem(position));
  }

  public long getItemId(int position) {
    return(delegate.getItemId(position));
  }

  public View getView(int position, View convertView,
                      ViewGroup parent) {
    return(delegate.getView(position, convertView, parent));
  }

  public void registerDataSetObserver(DataSetObserver observer) {
    delegate.registerDataSetObserver(observer);
  }

  public boolean hasStableIds() {
    return(delegate.hasStableIds());
  }

  public boolean isEmpty() {
    return(delegate.isEmpty());
  }

  public int getViewTypeCount() {
    return(delegate.getViewTypeCount());
  }

  public int getItemViewType(int position) {
    return(delegate.getItemViewType(position));
  }

  public void unregisterDataSetObserver(DataSetObserver observer) {
    delegate.unregisterDataSetObserver(observer);
  }

  public boolean areAllItemsEnabled() {
    return(delegate.areAllItemsEnabled());
  }

  public boolean isEnabled(int position) {
    return(delegate.isEnabled(position));
  }
}
```

We can then subclass AdapterWrapper to create RateableWrapper, overriding the default getView() but otherwise allowing the delegated ListAdapter to do the "real work:"

```
public class RateableWrapper extends AdapterWrapper {
  Context ctxt=null;
  float[] rates=null;

  public RateableWrapper(Context ctxt, ListAdapter delegate) {
    super(delegate);

    this.ctxt=ctxt;
    this.rates=new float[delegate.getCount()];

    for (int i=0;i<delegate.getCount();i++) {
      this.rates[i]=2.0f;
    }
  }

  public View getView(int position, View convertView,
                      ViewGroup parent) {
    ViewWrapper wrap=null;
    View row=convertView;

    if (convertView==null) {
      LinearLayout layout=new LinearLayout(ctxt);
      RatingBar rate=new RatingBar(ctxt);

      rate.setNumStars(3);
      rate.setStepSize(1.0f);

      View guts=delegate.getView(position, null, parent);

      layout.setOrientation(LinearLayout.HORIZONTAL);

      rate.setLayoutParams(new LinearLayout.LayoutParams(
          LinearLayout.LayoutParams.WRAP_CONTENT,
          LinearLayout.LayoutParams.FILL_PARENT));
      guts.setLayoutParams(new LinearLayout.LayoutParams(
          LinearLayout.LayoutParams.FILL_PARENT,
          LinearLayout.LayoutParams.FILL_PARENT));

      RatingBar.OnRatingBarChangeListener l=
                  new RatingBar.OnRatingBarChangeListener() {
        public void onRatingChanged(RatingBar ratingBar,
                                    float rating,
                                    boolean fromTouch)  {
          rates[(Integer)ratingBar.getTag()]=rating;
        }
      };
```

```
      rate.setOnRatingBarChangeListener(1);

      layout.addView(rate);
      layout.addView(guts);

      wrap=new ViewWrapper(layout);
      wrap.setGuts(guts);
      layout.setTag(wrap);

      rate.setTag(new Integer(position));
      rate.setRating(rates[position]);

      row=layout;
    }
    else {
      wrap=(ViewWrapper)convertView.getTag();
      wrap.setGuts(delegate.getView(position, wrap.getGuts(),
                                    parent));
      wrap.getRatingBar().setTag(new Integer(position));
      wrap.getRatingBar().setRating(rates[position]);
    }

    return(row);
  }
}
```

The idea is that RateableWrapper is where most of our rate-list logic resides. It puts the rating bars on the rows and it tracks the rating bars' states as they are adjusted by the user. For the states, it has a float[] sized to fit the number of rows that the delegate says are in the list.

RateableWrapper's implementation of getView() is reminiscent of the one from RateListDemo, except that rather than use LayoutInflater, we need to manually construct a LinearLayout to hold our RatingBar and the "guts" (that is, whatever view the delegate created that we are decorating with the checkbox). LayoutInflater is designed to construct a View from raw widgets; in our case, we don't know in advance what the rows will look like, other than that we need to add a checkbox to them. However, the rest is similar to what we saw in RateListDemo:

```
class ViewWrapper {
  ViewGroup base;
  View guts=null;
  RatingBar rate=null;

  ViewWrapper(ViewGroup base) {
    this.base=base;
  }
```

```
  RatingBar getRatingBar() {
    if (rate==null) {
      rate=(RatingBar)base.getChildAt(0);
    }

    return(rate);
  }

  void setRatingBar(RatingBar rate) {
    this.rate=rate;
  }

  View getGuts() {
    if (guts==null) {
      guts=base.getChildAt(1);
    }

    return(guts);
  }

  void setGuts(View guts) {
    this.guts=guts;
  }
}
```

With all that in place, RateListView is comparatively simple:

```
public class RateListView extends ListView {
  public RateListView(Context context) {
    super(context);
  }

  public RateListView(Context context, AttributeSet attrs) {
    super(context, attrs);
  }

  public RateListView(Context context, AttributeSet attrs,
                      int defStyle) {
    super(context, attrs, defStyle);
  }

  public void setAdapter(ListAdapter adapter) {
    super.setAdapter(new RateableWrapper(getContext(), adapter));
  }
}
```

We simply subclass ListView and override setAdapter() so we can wrap the supplied ListAdapter in our own RateableWrapper.

Visually, the results are similar to the RateListDemo, albeit without top-rated words appearing in all caps (see Figure 9-5).

Figure 9-5. *The RateListViewDemo sample application*

The difference is in reusability. We could package RateListView in its own JAR and plop it into any Android project where we need it. So while RateListView is somewhat complicated to write, we have to write it only once, and the rest of the application code is blissfully simple.

Of course, this RateListView could use some more features, such as programmatically changing states (updating both the float[] and the actual RatingBar itself), allowing other application logic to be invoked when a RatingBar state is toggled (via some sort of callback), etc.

CHAPTER 10

■ ■ ■

Employing Fancy Widgets and Containers

The widgets and containers covered to date are not only found in many GUI toolkits (in one form or fashion), but also are widely used in building GUI applications, whether Web-based, desktop, or mobile. The widgets and containers in this chapter are a little less widely used, though you will likely find many to be quite useful.

Pick and Choose

With limited-input devices like phones, having widgets and dialogs that are aware of the type of stuff somebody is supposed to be entering is very helpful. It minimizes keystrokes and screen taps, plus reduces the chance of making some sort of error (e.g., entering a letter someplace where only numbers are expected).

As previously shown, EditText has content-aware flavors for entering in numbers, phone numbers, etc. Android also supports widgets (DatePicker, TimePicker) and dialogs (DatePickerDialog, TimePickerDialog) for helping users enter dates and times.

The DatePicker and DatePickerDialog allow you to set the starting date for the selection, in the form of a year, month, and day of month value. Note that the month runs from 0 for January through 11 for December. Most importantly, each let you provide a callback object (OnDateChangedListener or OnDateSetListener) where you are informed of a new date selected by the user. It is up to you to store that date someplace, particularly if you are using the dialog, since there is no other way for you to get at the chosen date later on.

Similarly, TimePicker and TimePickerDialog let you:

- set the initial time the user can adjust, in the form of an hour (0 through 23) and a minute (0 through 59)

- indicate if the selection should be in 12-hour mode with an AM/PM toggle, or in 24-hour mode (what in the US is thought of as "military time" and in the rest of the world is thought of as "the way times are supposed to be")

- provide a callback object (OnTimeChangedListener or OnTimeSetListener) to be notified of when the user has chosen a new time, which is supplied to you in the form of an hour and minute

The Fancy/Chrono sample project, found along with all other code samples in this chapter in the Source Code area of http://apress.com, shows a trivial layout containing a label and two buttons—the buttons will pop up the dialog flavors of the date and time pickers:

```xml
<?xml version="1.0" encoding="utf-8"?>
<LinearLayout
  xmlns:android="http://schemas.android.com/apk/res/android"
  android:orientation="vertical"
  android:layout_width="fill_parent"
  android:layout_height="fill_parent"
  >
  <TextView android:id="@+id/dateAndTime"
    android:layout_width="fill_parent"
    android:layout_height="wrap_content"
    />
  <Button android:id="@+id/dateBtn"
    android:layout_width="fill_parent"
    android:layout_height="wrap_content"
    android:text="Set the Date"
    />
  <Button android:id="@+id/timeBtn"
    android:layout_width="fill_parent"
    android:layout_height="wrap_content"
    android:text="Set the Time"
    />
</LinearLayout>
```

The more interesting stuff comes in the Java source:

```java
public class ChronoDemo extends Activity {
  DateFormat fmtDateAndTime=DateFormat.getDateTimeInstance();
  TextView dateAndTimeLabel;
  Calendar dateAndTime=Calendar.getInstance();
  DatePickerDialog.OnDateSetListener d=new DatePickerDialog.OnDateSetListener() {
    public void onDateSet(DatePicker view, int year, int monthOfYear,
              int dayOfMonth) {
      dateAndTime.set(Calendar.YEAR, year);
      dateAndTime.set(Calendar.MONTH, monthOfYear);
      dateAndTime.set(Calendar.DAY_OF_MONTH, dayOfMonth);
      updateLabel();
    }
  };
```

```
TimePickerDialog.OnTimeSetListener t=new TimePickerDialog.OnTimeSetListener() {
  public void onTimeSet(TimePicker view, int hourOfDay,
                        int minute) {
    dateAndTime.set(Calendar.HOUR_OF_DAY, hourOfDay);
    dateAndTime.set(Calendar.MINUTE, minute);
    updateLabel();
  }
};

@Override
public void onCreate(Bundle icicle) {
  super.onCreate(icicle);
  setContentView(R.layout.main);

  Button btn=(Button)findViewById(R.id.dateBtn);

  btn.setOnClickListener(new View.OnClickListener() {
    public void onClick(View v) {
      new DatePickerDialog(ChronoDemo.this,
          d,
          dateAndTime.get(Calendar.YEAR),
          dateAndTime.get(Calendar.MONTH),
          dateAndTime.get(Calendar.DAY_OF_MONTH)).show();
    }
  });

  btn=(Button)findViewById(R.id.timeBtn);

  btn.setOnClickListener(new View.OnClickListener() {
    public void onClick(View v) {
      new TimePickerDialog(ChronoDemo.this,
                  t,
                  dateAndTime.get(Calendar.HOUR_OF_DAY),
                  dateAndTime.get(Calendar.MINUTE),
                  true).show();
    }
  });

  dateAndTimeLabel=(TextView)findViewById(R.id.dateAndTime);

  updateLabel();
}
```

```
    private void updateLabel() {
      dateAndTimeLabel.setText(fmtDateAndTime
                              .format(dateAndTime.getTime()));
    }
}
```

The "model" for this activity is just a Calendar instance, initially set to be the current date and time. We pour it into the view via a DateFormat formatter. In the updateLabel() method, we take the current Calendar, format it, and put it in the TextView.

Each button is given a OnClickListener callback object. When the button is clicked, either a DatePickerDialog or a TimePickerDialog is shown. In the case of the DatePickerDialog, we give it a OnDateSetListener callback that updates the Calendar with the new date (year, month, day of month). We also give the dialog the last-selected date, getting the values out of the Calendar. In the case of the TimePickerDialog, it gets a OnTimeSetListener callback to update the time portion of the Calendar, the last-selected time, and a true indicating we want 24-hour mode on the time selector.

With all this wired together, the resulting activity is shown in Figures 10-1, 10-2, and 10-3.

Figure 10-1. *The ChronoDemo sample application, as initially launched*

Figure 10-2. *The same application, showing the date picker dialog*

Figure 10-3. *The same application, showing the time picker dialog*

Time Keeps Flowing Like a River

If you want to display the time, rather than have users enter the time, you may wish to use the DigitalClock or AnalogClock widgets. These are extremely easy to use, as they automatically update with the passage of time. All you need to do is put them in your layout and let them do their thing.

For example, from the Fancy/Clocks sample application, here is an XML layout containing both DigitalClock and AnalogClock:

```xml
<?xml version="1.0" encoding="utf-8"?>
<RelativeLayout xmlns:android="http://schemas.android.com/apk/res/android"
  android:orientation="vertical"
  android:layout_width="fill_parent"
  android:layout_height="fill_parent"
  >
  <AnalogClock android:id="@+id/analog"
    android:layout_width="fill_parent"
    android:layout_height="wrap_content"
    android:layout_centerHorizontal="true"
    android:layout_alignParentTop="true"
    />
  <DigitalClock android:id="@+id/digital"
    android:layout_width="wrap_content"
    android:layout_height="wrap_content"
    android:layout_centerHorizontal="true"
    android:layout_below="@id/analog"
    />
</RelativeLayout>
```

Without any Java code other than the generated stub, we can build this project (see Figure 10-4).

Figure 10-4. *The ClocksDemo sample application*

Making Progress

If you need to be doing something for a long period of time, you owe it to your users to do two things:

- Use a background thread, which will be covered in Chapter 15

- Keep them apprised of your progress, or else they think your activity has wandered away and will never come back

The typical approach to keeping users informed of progress is some form of progress bar or "throbber" (think the animated graphic towards the upper-right corner of many Web browsers). Android supports this through the ProgressBar widget.

A ProgressBar keeps track of progress, defined as an integer, with 0 indicating no progress has been made. You can define the maximum end of the range—what value indicates progress is complete—via setMax(). By default, a ProgressBar starts with a progress of 0, though you can start from some other position via setProgress().

If you prefer your progress bar to be indeterminate, use setIndeterminate(), setting it to true.

In your Java code, you can either positively set the amount of progress that has been made (via setProgress()) or increment the progress from its current amount (via incrementProgressBy()). You can find out how much progress has been made via getProgress().

Since the ProgressBar is tied closely to the use of threads—a background thread doing work, updating the UI thread with new progress information—we will hold off demonstrating the use of ProgressBar until Chapter 15.

Putting It on My Tab

The general Android philosophy is to keep activities short and sweet. If there is more information than can reasonably fit on one screen, albeit perhaps with scrolling, then it most likely belongs in another activity kicked off via an Intent, as will be described Chapter 24. However, that can be complicated to set up. Moreover, sometimes there legitimately is a lot of information that needs to be collected to be processed as an atomic operation.

In a traditional UI, you might use tabs to accomplish this end, such as a JTabbedPane in Java/Swing. In Android, you now have an option of using a TabHost container in much the same way—a portion of your activity's screen is taken up with tabs which, when clicked, swap out part of the view and replace it with something else. For example, you might have an activity with a tab for entering a location and a second tab for showing a map of that location.

Some GUI toolkits refer to "tabs" as being just the things a user clicks on to toggle from one view to another. Some toolkits refer to "tabs" as being the combination of the clickable button-ish element and the content that appears when that tab is chosen. Android treats the tab buttons and contents as discrete entities, so we will call them "tab buttons" and "tab contents" in this section.

The Pieces

There are a few widgets and containers you need to use in order to set up a tabbed portion of a view:

- TabHost is the overarching container for the tab buttons and tab contents.

- TabWidget implements the row of tab buttons, which contain text labels and optionally contain icons.

- FrameLayout is the container for the tab contents; each tab content is a child of the FrameLayout.

This is similar to the approach that Mozilla's XUL takes. In XUL's case, the tabbox element corresponds to Android's TabHost, the tabs element corresponds to TabWidget, and tabpanels corresponds to the FrameLayout.

The Idiosyncrasies

There are a few rules to follow, at least in this milestone edition of the Android toolkit, in order to make these three work together:

- You must give the TabWidget an android:id of @android:id/tabs.

- You must set aside some padding in the FrameLayout for the tab buttons.

- If you wish to use the TabActivity, you must give the TabHost an android:id of @android:id/tabhost.

TabActivity, like ListActivity, wraps a common UI pattern (activity made up entirely of tabs) into a pattern-aware activity subclass. You do not necessarily have to use TabActivity—a plain activity can use tabs as well.

With respect to the FrameLayout padding issue, for whatever reason, the TabWidget does not seem to allocate its own space inside the TabHost container. In other words, no matter what you specify for android:layout_height for the TabWidget, the FrameLayout ignores it and draws at the top of the overall TabHost. Your tab contents obscure your tab buttons. Hence, you need to leave enough padding (via android:paddingTop) in FrameLayout to "shove" the actual tab contents down beneath the tab buttons.

In addition, the TabWidget seems to always draw itself with room for icons, even if you do not supply icons. Hence, for this version of the toolkit, you need to supply at least 62 pixels of padding, perhaps more depending on the icons you supply.

For example, here is a layout definition for a tabbed activity, from Fancy/Tab:

```
<?xml version="1.0" encoding="utf-8"?>
<LinearLayout xmlns:android="http://schemas.android.com/apk/res/android"
  android:orientation="vertical"
  android:layout_width="fill_parent"
  android:layout_height="fill_parent">
  <TabHost android:id="@+id/tabhost"
    android:layout_width="fill_parent"
    android:layout_height="fill_parent">
    <TabWidget android:id="@android:id/tabs"
      android:layout_width="fill_parent"
      android:layout_height="wrap_content"
    />
    <FrameLayout android:id="@android:id/tabcontent"
      android:layout_width="fill_parent"
      android:layout_height="fill_parent"
      android:paddingTop="62px">
      <AnalogClock android:id="@+id/tab1"
        android:layout_width="fill_parent"
        android:layout_height="fill_parent"
        android:layout_centerHorizontal="true"
      />
```

```
      <Button android:id="@+id/tab2"
        android:layout_width="fill_parent"
        android:layout_height="fill_parent"
        android:text="A semi-random button"
      />
    </FrameLayout>
  </TabHost>
</LinearLayout>
```

Note that the TabWidget and FrameLayout are immediate children of the TabHost, and the FrameLayout itself has children representing the various tabs. In this case, there are two tabs: a clock and a button. In a more complicated scenario, the tabs are probably some form of container (e.g., LinearLayout) with their own contents.

Wiring It Together

The Java code needs to tell the TabHost what views represent the tab contents and what the tab buttons should look like. This is all wrapped up in TabSpec objects. You get a TabSpec instance from the host via newTabSpec(), fill it out, then add it to the host in the proper sequence.

The two key methods on TabSpec are:

- setContent(), where you indicate what goes in the tab content for this tab, typically the android:id of the view you want shown when this tab is selected

- setIndicator(), where you provide the caption for the tab button and, in some flavors of this method, supply a Drawable to represent the icon for the tab

Note that tab "indicators" can actually be views in their own right, if you need more control than a simple label and optional icon.

Also note that you must call setup() on the TabHost before configuring any of these TabSpec objects. The call to setup() is not needed if you are using the TabActivity base class for your activity.

For example, here is the Java code to wire together the tabs from the preceding layout example:

```
package com.commonsware.android.fancy;

import android.app.Activity;
import android.os.Bundle;
import android.widget.TabHost;

public class TabDemo extends Activity {
  @Override
  public void onCreate(Bundle icicle) {
    super.onCreate(icicle);
    setContentView(R.layout.main);
```

```
    TabHost tabs=(TabHost)findViewById(R.id.tabhost);

    tabs.setup();

    TabHost.TabSpec spec=tabs.newTabSpec("tag1");

    spec.setContent(R.id.tab1);
    spec.setIndicator("Clock");
    tabs.addTab(spec);

    spec=tabs.newTabSpec("tag2");
    spec.setContent(R.id.tab2);
    spec.setIndicator("Button");
    tabs.addTab(spec);

    tabs.setCurrentTab(0);
  }
}
```

We find our TabHost via the familiar findViewById() method, then have it call setup().
After that, we get a TabSpec via newTabSpec(), supplying a tag whose purpose is unknown at this
time. Given the spec, you call setContent() and setIndicator(), then call addTab() back on the
TabHost to register the tab as available for use. Finally, you can choose which tab is the one to
show via setCurrentTab(), providing the 0-based index of the tab.

The results can be seen in Figures 10-5 and 10-6.

Figure 10-5. *The TabDemo sample application, showing the first tab*

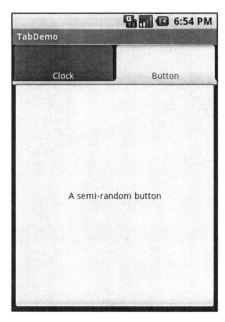

Figure 10-6. *The same application, showing the second tab*

Adding Them Up

TabWidget is set up to allow you to easily define tabs at compile time. However, sometimes, you want to add tabs to your activity during runtime. For example, imagine an email client where individual emails get opened in their own tab for easy toggling between messages. In this case, you don't know how many tabs or what their contents will be until runtime, when the user chooses to open a message.

Fortunately, Android also supports adding tabs dynamically at runtime.

Adding tabs dynamically at runtime works much like the compile-time tabs previously shown, except you use a different flavor of setContent(), one that takes a TabHost. TabContentFactory instance. This is just a callback that will be invoked—you provide an implementation of createTabContent() and use it to build and return the Let's take a look at an example (Fancy/DynamicTab).

First, here is some layout XML for an activity that sets up the tabs and defines one tab, containing a single button:

```xml
<?xml version="1.0" encoding="utf-8"?>
<LinearLayout xmlns:android="http://schemas.android.com/apk/res/android"
  android:orientation="vertical"
  android:layout_width="fill_parent"
  android:layout_height="fill_parent">
```

```xml
<TabHost android:id="@+id/tabhost"
  android:layout_width="fill_parent"
  android:layout_height="fill_parent">
  <TabWidget android:id="@android:id/tabs"
    android:layout_width="fill_parent"
    android:layout_height="wrap_content"
  />
  <FrameLayout android:id="@android:id/tabcontent"
    android:layout_width="fill_parent"
    android:layout_height="fill_parent"
    android:paddingTop="62px">
    <Button android:id="@+id/buttontab"
      android:layout_width="fill_parent"
      android:layout_height="fill_parent"
      android:text="A semi-random button"
    />
  </FrameLayout>
</TabHost>
</LinearLayout>
```

What we want to do is add new tabs whenever the button is clicked. That can be accomplished in just a few lines of code:

```java
public class DynamicTabDemo extends Activity {
  @Override
  public void onCreate(Bundle icicle) {
    super.onCreate(icicle);
    setContentView(R.layout.main);

    final TabHost tabs=(TabHost)findViewById(R.id.tabhost);

    tabs.setup();

    TabHost.TabSpec spec=tabs.newTabSpec("buttontab");
    spec.setContent(R.id.buttontab);
    spec.setIndicator("Button");
    tabs.addTab(spec);

    tabs.setCurrentTab(0);

    Button btn=(Button)tabs.getCurrentView().findViewById(R.id.buttontab);
```

```
btn.setOnClickListener(new View.OnClickListener() {
  public void onClick(View view) {
    TabHost.TabSpec spec=tabs.newTabSpec("tag1");

    spec.setContent(new TabHost.TabContentFactory() {
      public View createTabContent(String tag) {
        return(new AnalogClock(DynamicTabDemo.this));
      }
    });
    spec.setIndicator("Clock");
    tabs.addTab(spec);
  }
});
  }
}
```

In our button's setOnClickListener() callback, we create a TabHost.TabSpec object and give it an anonymous TabHost.TabContentFactory. The factory, in turn, returns the View to be used for the tab—in this case, just an AnalogClock. The logic for constructing the tab's View could be much more elaborate, such as using LayoutInflater to construct a view from layout XML.

In Figure 10-7 you can see that initially, when the activity is launched, we just have the one tab whereas Figure 10-8 shows multiple tabs.

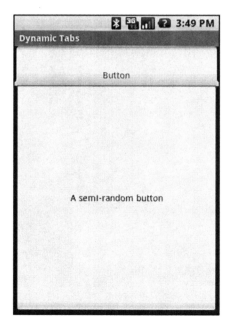

Figure 10-7. *The DynamicTab application, with the single initial tab*

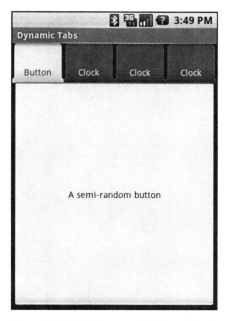

Figure 10-8. *The DynamicTab application, with three dynamically-created tabs*

Intents and Views

In the preceding examples, the contents of each tab were set to be a View, such as a Button. This is easy and straight-forward, but it is not the only option. You can also integrate another activity from your application via an Intent.

Intents are ways of specifying something you want accomplished, then telling Android to go find something to accomplish it. Frequently, these are used to cause activities to spawn. For example, whenever you launch an application from the main Android application launcher, the launcher creates an Intent and has Android open up the activity associated with that Intent. This whole concept, and how activities can be placed in tabs, will be described in greater detail in Chapter 25.

Flipping Them Off

Sometimes, you want the overall effect of tabs (only some Views visible at a time), but you do not want the actual UI implementation of tabs. Maybe the tabs take up too much screen space. Maybe you want to switch between perspectives based on a gesture or a device shake. Or maybe you just like being different.

The good news is that the guts of the view-flipping logic from tabs can be found in the ViewFlipper container, which can be used in other ways than the traditional tab.

ViewFlipper inherits from FrameLayout, just like we used to describe the innards of a TabWidget. However, initially, it just shows the first child view. It is up to you to arrange for the views to flip, either manually by user interaction, or automatically via a timer.

For example, here is a layout for a simple activity (Fancy/Flipper1) using a Button and a ViewFlipper:

```xml
<?xml version="1.0" encoding="utf-8"?>
<LinearLayout xmlns:android="http://schemas.android.com/apk/res/android"
    android:orientation="vertical"
    android:layout_width="fill_parent"
    android:layout_height="fill_parent"
    >
  <Button android:id="@+id/flip_me"
      android:layout_width="fill_parent"
      android:layout_height="wrap_content"
      android:text="Flip Me!"
      />
  <ViewFlipper android:id="@+id/details"
      android:layout_width="fill_parent"
      android:layout_height="fill_parent"
      >
      <TextView
        android:layout_width="fill_parent"
        android:layout_height="wrap_content"
        android:textStyle="bold"
        android:textColor="#FF00FF00"
        android:text="This is the first panel"
      />
      <TextView
        android:layout_width="fill_parent"
        android:layout_height="wrap_content"
        android:textStyle="bold"
        android:textColor="#FFFF0000"
        android:text="This is the second panel"
      />
      <TextView
        android:layout_width="fill_parent"
        android:layout_height="wrap_content"
        android:textStyle="bold"
        android:textColor="#FFFFFF00"
        android:text="This is the third panel"
      />
  </ViewFlipper>
</LinearLayout>
```

Notice that the layout defines three child views for the ViewFlipper, each a TextView with a simple message. Of course, you could have very complicated child views, if you so chose.

To manually flip the views, we need to hook into the Button and flip them ourselves when the button is clicked:

```java
public class FlipperDemo extends Activity {
  ViewFlipper flipper;

  @Override
  public void onCreate(Bundle icicle) {
    super.onCreate(icicle);
    setContentView(R.layout.main);

    flipper=(ViewFlipper)findViewById(R.id.details);

    Button btn=(Button)findViewById(R.id.flip_me);

    btn.setOnClickListener(new View.OnClickListener() {
      public void onClick(View view) {
        flipper.showNext();
      }
    });
  }
}
```

This is just a matter of calling showNext() on the ViewFlipper, like you can on any ViewAnimator class.

The result is a trivial activity: click the button, and the next TextView in sequence is displayed, wrapping around to the first after viewing the last (see Figures 10-9 and 10-10).

Figure 10-9. *The Flipper1 application, showing the first panel*

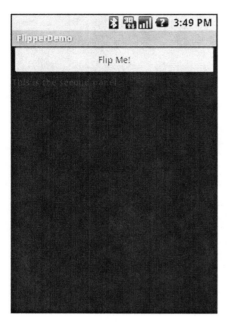

Figure 10-10. *The same application, after switching to the second panel*

This, of course, could be handled more simply by having a single TextView and changing the text and color on each click. However, you can imagine that the ViewFlipper contents could be much more complicated, like the contents you might put into a TabView.

As with the TabWidget, sometimes, your ViewFlipper contents may not be known at compile time. As with TabWidget, though, you can add new contents on the fly with ease.

For example, let's look at another sample activity (Fancy/Flipper2), using this layout:

```
<?xml version="1.0" encoding="utf-8"?>
<LinearLayout xmlns:android="http://schemas.android.com/apk/res/android"
    android:orientation="vertical"
    android:layout_width="fill_parent"
    android:layout_height="fill_parent"
    >
  <ViewFlipper android:id="@+id/details"
    android:layout_width="fill_parent"
    android:layout_height="fill_parent"
    >
  </ViewFlipper>
</LinearLayout>
```

Notice that the ViewFlipper has no contents at compile time. Also note that there is no Button for flipping between the contents—more on this in a moment.

For the ViewFlipper contents, we will create large Button widgets, each containing one of a set of random words. And, we will set up the ViewFlipper to automatically rotate between the Button widgets, using an animation for transition:

```
public class FlipperDemo2 extends Activity {
  static String[] items={"lorem", "ipsum", "dolor", "sit", "amet",
                         "consectetuer", "adipiscing", "elit",
                         "morbi", "vel", "ligula", "vitae",
                         "arcu", "aliquet", "mollis", "etiam",
                         "vel", "erat", "placerat", "ante",
                         "porttitor", "sodales", "pellentesque",
                         "augue", "purus"};
  ViewFlipper flipper;

  @Override
  public void onCreate(Bundle icicle) {
    super.onCreate(icicle);
    setContentView(R.layout.main);

    flipper=(ViewFlipper)findViewById(R.id.details);

    flipper.setInAnimation(AnimationUtils.loadAnimation(this,
                                   R.anim.push_left_in));
    flipper.setOutAnimation(AnimationUtils.loadAnimation(this,
                                   R.anim.push_left_out));

    for (String item : items) {
      Button btn=new Button(this);

      btn.setText(item);

      flipper.addView(btn,
                  new ViewGroup.LayoutParams(
                          ViewGroup.LayoutParams.FILL_PARENT,
                          ViewGroup.LayoutParams.FILL_PARENT));
    }

    flipper.setFlipInterval(2000);
    flipper.startFlipping();
  }
}
```

After getting our ViewFlipper widget from the layout, we first set up the "in" and "out" animations. In Android terms, an animation is a description of how a widget leaves ("out") or enters ("in") the viewable area. Animations are a complex beast, eventually worthy of their own chapter but not covered in this text. For now, realize that animations are resources, stored in res/anim/ in your project. For this example, we are using a pair of animations supplied by the SDK samples, available under the Apache 2.0 License. As their names suggest, widgets are "pushed" to the left, either to enter or leave the viewable area.

After iterating over the funky words, turning each into a Button, and adding the Button as a child of the ViewFlipper, we set up the flipper to automatically flip between children (flipper.setFlipInterval(2000);) and to start flipping (flipper.startFlipping();).

The result is an endless series of buttons, each appearing, then sliding out to the left after 2 seconds, being replaced by the next button in sequence, wrapping around to the first after the last has been shown (see Figure 10-11).

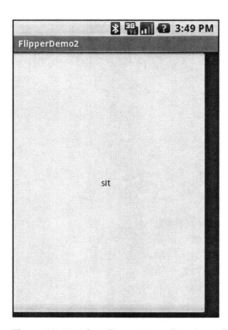

Figure 10-11. *The Flipper2 application, showing an animated transition*

The auto-flipping `ViewFlipper` is useful for status panels or other situations where you have a lot of information to display, but not much room. The key is that, since it automatically flips between views, expecting users to interact with individual views is dicey —the view might switch away part-way through their interaction.

Other Containers of Note

Android offers `AbsoluteLayout`, where the contents are laid out based on specific coordinate positions. You tell `AbsoluteLayout` where to place a child in precise X,Y coordinates, and Android puts it there, no questions asked. On the plus side, this gives you precise positioning. On the minus side, it means your views will only look "right" on screens of a certain dimension, or it requires you to write a bunch of code to adjust the coordinates based on screen size. Since Android screens might run the gamut of sizes, plus have new sizes crop up periodically, using `AbsoluteLayout` could get quite annoying.

Android also has a new flavor of list, the `ExpandableListView`. This provides a simplified tree representation, supporting two levels of depth: groups and children. Groups contain children; children are "leaves" of the tree. This requires a new set of adapters, since the `ListAdapter` family does not provide any sort of group information for the items in the list.

CHAPTER 11

■ ■ ■

Applying Menus

Like applications for the desktop and some mobile operating systems, such as Palm OS and Windows Mobile, Android supports activities with application menus. Some Android phones will have a dedicated menu key for popping up the menu; others will offer alternate means for triggering the menu to appear.

Also, as with many GUI toolkits, you can create context menus. On a traditional GUI, this might be triggered by the right mouse button. On mobile devices, context menus typically appear when the user taps-and-holds over a particular widget. For example, if a TextView had a context menu and the device was designed for finger-based touch input, you could push the TextView with your finger, hold it for a second or two, and a pop-up menu would appear for you to choose from.

Android differs from most other GUI toolkits in terms of menu construction. While you can add items to the menu, you do not have full control over the menu's contents, nor of the timing of when the menu is built. Part of the menu is system-defined, and that portion is managed by the Android framework itself.

Flavors of Menu

Android considers application menus and context menus to be the options menu and the context menu, respectively. The options menu is triggered by pressing the hardware Menu button on the device, while the context menu is raised by a tap-and-hold on the widget sporting the menu.

In addition, the options menu operates in one of two modes: icon and expanded. When the user first presses the Menu button, the icon mode will appear, showing up to the first six menu choices as large, finger-friendly buttons in a grid at the bottom of the screen. If the menu has more than six choices, the sixth button will become More—clicking that option will bring up the expanded mode, showing the remaining choices not visible in the regular menu. The menu is scrollable, so the user can get to any of the menu choices.

Menus of Options

Rather than building your activity's options menu during onCreate(), the way you wire up the rest of your UI, you instead need to implement onCreateOptionsMenu(). This callback receives an instance of Menu.

The first thing you should do is chain upward to the superclass (super.
onCreateOptionsMenu(menu)) so the Android framework can add in any menu choices it feels
are necessary. Then you can go about adding your own options, described momentarily.

If you will need to adjust the menu during your activity's use (e.g., disable a now-invalid
menu choice), just hold onto the Menu instance you receive in onCreateOptionsMenu() or implement onPrepareOptionsMenu(), which is called just before displaying the menu each time it
is requested.

Given that you have received a Menu object via onCreateOptionsMenu(), you add menu
choices by calling add(). There are many flavors of this method, which require some combination of the following parameters:

- A group identifier (int), which should be NONE unless you are creating a specific grouped
  set of menu choices for use with setGroupCheckable() (see the following list).

- A choice identifier (also an int) for use in identifying this choice in the
  onOptionsItemSelected() callback when a menu choice is selected.

- An order identifier (yet another int), for indicating where this menu choice should be
  slotted if the menu has Android-supplied choices alongside your own—for now, just
  use NONE.

- The text of the menu choice, as a String or a resource ID.

The add() family of methods all return an instance of MenuItem, where you can adjust
any of the menu-item settings you have already set (e.g., the text of the menu choice). You
can also set the shortcuts for the menu choice—single-character mnemonics that select that
menu choice when the menu is visible. Android supports both an alphabetic (or QWERTY)
set of shortcuts and a numeric set of shortcuts. These are set individually by calling
setAlphabeticShortcut() and setNumericShortcut(), respectively. The menu is placed into
alphabetic shortcut mode by calling setQwertyMode() on the menu with a true parameter.

The choice and group identifiers are keys used to unlock additional menu features, such
as these:

- Calling MenuItem#setCheckable() with a choice identifier to control if the menu choice
  has a two-state checkbox alongside the title, where the checkbox value gets toggled
  when the user chooses that menu choice

- Calling Menu#setGroupCheckable() with a group identifier to turn a set of menu choices
  into ones with a mutual-exclusion radio button between them, so one out of the group
  can be in the "checked" state at any time

You can also call addIntentOptions() to populate the menu with menu choices corresponding
to the available activities for an intent (see Chapter 25).

Finally, you can create fly-out sub-menus by calling addSubMenu() and supplying the same
parameters as addMenu(). Android will eventually call onCreatePanelMenu(), passing it the choice
identifier of your sub-menu, along with another Menu instance representing the sub-menu
itself. As with onCreateOptionsMenu(), you should chain upward to the superclass, then add

menu choices to the sub-menu. One limitation is that you cannot indefinitely nest sub-menus—a menu can have a sub-menu, but a sub-menu cannot itself have a sub-sub-menu.

If the user makes a menu choice, your activity will be notified via the onOptionsItemSelected() callback that a menu choice was selected. You are given the MenuItem object corresponding to the selected menu choice. A typical pattern is to switch() on the menu ID (item.getItemId()) and take appropriate action. Note that onOptionsItemSelected() is used regardless of whether the chosen menu item was in the base menu or in a sub-menu.

Menus in Context

By and large, context menus use the same guts as option menus. The two main differences are how you populate the menu and how you are informed of menu choices.

First you need to indicate which widget(s) on your activity have context menus. To do this, call registerForContextMenu() from your activity, supplying the View that is the widget in need of a context menu.

Next you need to implement onCreateContextMenu(), which, among other things, is passed the View you supplied in registerForContextMenu(). You can use that to determine which menu to build, assuming your activity has more than one.

The onCreateContextMenu() method gets the ContextMenu itself, the View the context menu is associated with, and a ContextMenu.ContextMenuInfo, which tells you which item in the list the user did the tap-and-hold over, in case you want to customize the context menu based on that information. For example, you could toggle a checkable menu choice based on the current state of the item.

It is also important to note that onCreateContextMenu() gets called each time the context menu is requested. Unlike the options menu (which is built only once per activity), context menus are discarded once they are used or dismissed. Hence, you do not want to hold onto the supplied ContextMenu object; just rely on getting the chance to rebuild the menu to suit your activity's needs on demand based on user actions.

To find out when a context-menu choice was selected, implement onContextItemSelected() on the activity. Note that you get only the MenuItem instance that was chosen in this callback. As a result, if your activity has two or more context menus, you may want to ensure they have unique menu-item identifiers for all their choices so you can tell them apart in this callback. Also, you can call getMenuInfo() on the MenuItem to get the ContextMenu.ContextMenuInfo you received in onCreateContextMenu(). Otherwise, this callback behaves the same as onOptionsItemSelected(), described in the previous section.

Taking a Peek

In the sample project Menus/Menus at http://apress.com/, you will find an amended version of the ListView sample (List) with an associated menu. Since the menus are defined in Java code, the XML layout need not change and is not reprinted here.

However, the Java code has a few new behaviors, as shown here:

```java
public class MenuDemo extends ListActivity {
  TextView selection;
  String[] items={"lorem", "ipsum", "dolor", "sit", "amet",
          "consectetuer", "adipiscing", "elit", "morbi", "vel",
          "ligula", "vitae", "arcu", "aliquet", "mollis",
          "etiam", "vel", "erat", "placerat", "ante",
          "porttitor", "sodales", "pellentesque", "augue", "purus"};
  public static final int EIGHT_ID = Menu.FIRST+1;
  public static final int SIXTEEN_ID = Menu.FIRST+2;
  public static final int TWENTY_FOUR_ID = Menu.FIRST+3;
  public static final int TWO_ID = Menu.FIRST+4;
  public static final int THIRTY_TWO_ID = Menu.FIRST+5;
  public static final int FORTY_ID = Menu.FIRST+6;
  public static final int ONE_ID = Menu.FIRST+7;

  @Override
  public void onCreate(Bundle icicle) {
    super.onCreate(icicle);
    setContentView(R.layout.main);
    setListAdapter(new ArrayAdapter<String>(this,
                android.R.layout.simple_list_item_1, items));
    selection=(TextView)findViewById(R.id.selection);

    registerForContextMenu(getListView());
  }

  public void onListItemClick(ListView parent, View v,
                                  int position, long id) {
   selection.setText(items[position]);
  }

  @Override
  public void onCreateContextMenu(ContextMenu menu, View v,
                                    ContextMenu.ContextMenuInfo menuInfo) {
    populateMenu(menu);
  }

  @Override
  public boolean onCreateOptionsMenu(Menu menu) {
    populateMenu(menu);

    return(super.onCreateOptionsMenu(menu));
  }
```

```java
@Override
public boolean onOptionsItemSelected(MenuItem item) {
  return(applyMenuChoice(item) ||
          super.onOptionsItemSelected(item));
}

@Override
public boolean onContextItemSelected(MenuItem item) {
  return(applyMenuChoice(item) ||
          super.onContextItemSelected(item));
}

private void populateMenu(Menu menu) {
  menu.add(Menu.NONE, ONE_ID, Menu.NONE, "1 Pixel");
  menu.add(Menu.NONE, TWO_ID, Menu.NONE, "2 Pixels");
  menu.add(Menu.NONE, EIGHT_ID, Menu.NONE, "8 Pixels");
  menu.add(Menu.NONE, SIXTEEN_ID, Menu.NONE, "16 Pixels");
  menu.add(Menu.NONE, TWENTY_FOUR_ID, Menu.NONE, "24 Pixels");
  menu.add(Menu.NONE, THIRTY_TWO_ID, Menu.NONE, "32 Pixels");
  menu.add(Menu.NONE, FORTY_ID, Menu.NONE, "40 Pixels");
}

private boolean applyMenuChoice(MenuItem item) {
  switch (item.getItemId()) {
    case ONE_ID:
      getListView().setDividerHeight(1);
      return(true);

    case EIGHT_ID:
      getListView().setDividerHeight(8);
      return(true);

    case SIXTEEN_ID:
      getListView().setDividerHeight(16);
      return(true);

    case TWENTY_FOUR_ID:
      getListView().setDividerHeight(24);
      return(true);

    case TWO_ID:
      getListView().setDividerHeight(2);
      return(true);

    case THIRTY_TWO_ID:
      getListView().setDividerHeight(32);
      return(true);
```

```
    case FORTY_ID:
      getListView().setDividerHeight(40);
      return(true);
  }

  return(false);
 }
}
```

In onCreate(), we register our list widget as having a context menu, which we fill in via our populateMenu() private method, by way of onCreateContextMenu(). We also implement the onCreateOptionsMenu() callback, indicating that our activity also has an options menu. Once again, we delegate to populateMenu() to fill in the menu.

Our implementations of onOptionsItemSelected() (for options-menu selections) and onContextItemSelected() (for context-menu selections) both delegate to a private applyMenuChoice() method, plus chaining upwards to the superclass if none of our menu choices was the one selected by the user.

In populateMenu() we add seven menu choices, each with a unique identifier. Being lazy, we eschew the icons.

In applyMenuChoice() we see if any of our menu choices were chosen; if so, we set the list's divider size to be the user-selected width.

Initially the activity looks the same in the emulator as it did for ListDemo (see Figure 11-1).

Figure 11-1. *The MenuDemo sample application, as initially launched*

But if you press the Menu button, you will get our options menu (Figure 11-2).

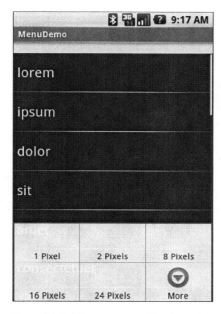

Figure 11-2. *The same application, showing the options menu*

Clicking the More button shows the remaining two menu choices (Figure 11-3).

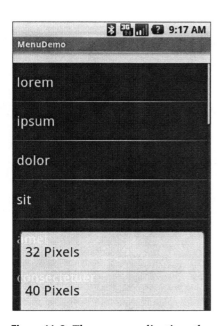

Figure 11-3. *The same application, the remaining menu choices*

Choosing a height (say, 16 pixels) then changes the divider height of the list to something garish (Figure 11-4).

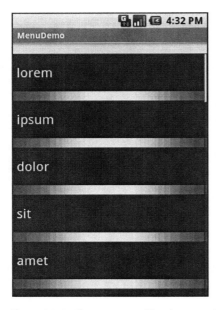

Figure 11-4. *The same application, made ugly*

You can trigger the context menu by doing a tap-and-hold on any item in the list (Figure 11-5).

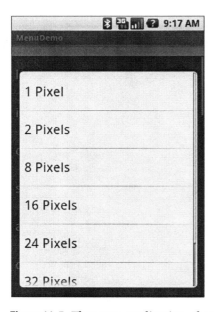

Figure 11-5. *The same application, showing a context menu*

Once again, choosing an option sets the divider height.

Yet More Inflation

You saw in Chapter 9 that you can describe Views via XML files and inflate them into actual View objects at runtime. Android also allows you to describe menus via XML files and inflate them when a menu is called for. This helps you keep your menu structure separate from the implementation of menu-handling logic, and it provides easier ways to develop menu-authoring tools.

Menu XML Structure

Menu XML goes in res/menu/ in your project tree, alongside the other types of resources that your project might employ. As with layouts, you can have several menu XML files in your project, each with their own filename and the .xml extension.

For example, from the Menus/Inflation sample project at http://apress.com/, here is a menu called sample.xml:

```xml
<?xml version="1.0" encoding="utf-8"?>
<menu xmlns:android="http://schemas.android.com/apk/res/android">
  <item android:id="@+id/close"
    android:title="Close"
    android:orderInCategory="3"
    android:icon="@drawable/eject" />
  <item android:id="@+id/no_icon"
    android:orderInCategory="2"
    android:title="Sans Icon" />
  <item android:id="@+id/disabled"
    android:orderInCategory="4"
    android:enabled="false"
    android:title="Disabled" />
  <group android:id="@+id/other_stuff"
    android:menuCategory="secondary"
    android:visible="false">
    <item android:id="@+id/later"
      android:orderInCategory="0"
      android:title="2nd-To-Last" />
    <item android:id="@+id/last"
      android:orderInCategory="1"
      android:title="Last" />
  </group>
  <item android:id="@+id/submenu"
    android:orderInCategory="3"
    android:title="A Submenu">
    <menu>
      <item android:id="@+id/non_ghost"
        android:title="Non-Ghost"
        android:visible="true"
        android:alphabeticShortcut="n" />
```

```
        <item android:id="@+id/ghost"
          android:title="A Ghost"
          android:visible="false"
          android:alphabeticShortcut="g" />
      </menu>
   </item>
</menu>
```

Note the following about menu XML definitions:

- You must start with a menu root element.

- Inside a menu are item elements and group elements, the latter representing a collection of menu items that can be operated upon as a group.

- Sub-menus are specified by adding a menu element as a child of an item element, using this new menu element to describe the contents of the sub-menu.

- If you want to detect when an item is chosen or to reference an item or group from your Java code, be sure to apply an android:id, just as you do with View layout XML.

Menu Options and XML

Inside the item and group elements you can specify various options, matching up with corresponding methods on Menu or MenuItem.

Title

The title of a menu item is provided via the android:title attribute on an item element. This can be either a literal string or a reference to a string resource (e.g., @string/foo).

Icon

Menu items can have icons. To provide an icon—in the form of a reference to a drawable resource (e.g., @drawable/eject), use the android:icon attribute on the item element.

Order

By default, the order of the items in the menu is determined by the order they appear in the menu XML. If you want, you can change that default by specifying the android:orderInCategory attribute on the item element. This is a 0-based index of the order for the items associated with the current category. There is an implicit default category; groups can provide an android:menuCategory attribute to specify a different category to use for items in that group.

Generally, though, it is simplest just to put the items in the XML in the order you want them to appear.

Enabled

Items and groups can be enabled or disabled, controlled in the XML via the android:enabled attribute on the item or group element. By default, items and groups are enabled. Disabled items and groups appear in the menu but cannot be selected. You can change an item's status at runtime via the setEnabled() method on MenuItem, or change a group's status via setGroupEnabled() on Menu.

Visible

Similarly, items and groups can be visible or invisible, controlled in the XML via the android: visible attribute on the item or group element. By default, items and groups are visible. Invisible items and groups do not appear in the menu at all. You can change an item's status at runtime via the setVisible() method on MenuItem, or change a group's status via setGroupVisible() on Menu.

In the layout XML shown earlier, the other_stuff group is initially invisible. If we make it visible in our Java code, the two menu items in the group will "magically" appear.

Shortcut

Items can have shortcuts—single letters (android:alphabeticShortcut) or numbers (android: numericShortcut) that can be pressed to choose the item without having to use the touch screen, D-pad, or trackball to navigate the full menu.

Inflating a Menu

Actually using a menu, once it's defined in XML, is easy. Just create a MenuInflater and tell it to inflate your menu:

```
@Override
public boolean onCreateOptionsMenu(Menu menu) {
  theMenu=menu;

  new MenuInflater(getApplication())
                        .inflate(R.menu.sample, menu);

  return(super.onCreateOptionsMenu(menu));
}
```

■■■

CHAPTER 12

Fonts

Inevitably, you'll get the question "Hey, can we change this font?" when doing application development. The answer depends on what fonts come with the platform, whether you can add other fonts, and how to apply them to the widget or whatever needs the font change.

Android is no different. It comes with some fonts plus a means for adding new fonts. Though, as with any new environment, there are a few idiosyncrasies to deal with.

Love the One You're With

Android natively knows three fonts, by the shorthand names of "sans", "serif", and "monospace". These fonts are actually the Droid series of fonts, created for the Open Handset Alliance by Ascender.[1]

For those fonts, you can just reference them in your layout XML, if you so choose. The following layout from the Fonts/FontSampler sample project shows example code, and can also be found in the Source Code area at http://apress.com:

```
<?xml version="1.0" encoding="utf-8"?>
<TableLayout
  xmlns:android="http://schemas.android.com/apk/res/android"
  android:layout_width="fill_parent"
  android:layout_height="fill_parent"
  android:stretchColumns="1">
  <TableRow>
    <TextView
      android:text="sans:"
      android:layout_marginRight="4px"
      android:textSize="20sp"
    />
```

---

1. http://www.ascendercorp.com/oha.html

```
    <TextView
      android:id="@+id/sans"
      android:text="Hello, world!"
      android:typeface="sans"
      android:textSize="20sp"
    />
  </TableRow>
  <TableRow>
    <TextView
      android:text="serif:"
      android:layout_marginRight="4px"
      android:textSize="20sp"
    />
    <TextView
      android:id="@+id/serif"
      android:text="Hello, world!"
      android:typeface="serif"
      android:textSize="20sp"
    />
  </TableRow>
  <TableRow>
    <TextView
      android:text="monospace:"
      android:layout_marginRight="4px"
      android:textSize="20sp"
    />
    <TextView
      android:id="@+id/monospace"
      android:text="Hello, world!"
      android:typeface="monospace"
      android:textSize="20sp"
    />
  </TableRow>
  <TableRow>
    <TextView
      android:text="Custom:"
      android:layout_marginRight="4px"
      android:textSize="20sp"
    />
```

```
    <TextView
      android:id="@+id/custom"
      android:text="Hello, world!"
      android:textSize="20sp"
    />
  </TableRow>
</TableLayout>
```

This layout builds a table showing short samples of four fonts. Notice how the first three have the android:typeface attribute, whose value is one of the three built-in font faces (e.g., "sans").

The three built-in fonts are very nice. However, it may be that a designer, or a manager, or a customer wants a different font than one of those three. Or perhaps you want to use a font for specialized purposes, such as a "dingbats" font instead of a series of PNG graphics.

The easiest way to accomplish this is to package the desired font(s) with your application. To do this, simply create an assets/ folder in the project root, and put your TrueType (TTF) fonts in the assets. You might, for example, create assets/fonts/ and put your TTF files in there.

Then, you need to tell your widgets to use that font. Unfortunately, you can no longer use layout XML for this, since the XML does not know about any fonts you may have tucked away as an application asset. Instead, you need to make the change in Java code:

```
public class FontSampler extends Activity {
  @Override
  public void onCreate(Bundle icicle) {
    super.onCreate(icicle);
    setContentView(R.layout.main);

    TextView tv=(TextView)findViewById(R.id.custom);
    Typeface face=Typeface.createFromAsset(getAssets(),
                                "fonts/HandmadeTypewriter.ttf");

    tv.setTypeface(face);
  }
}
```

Here we grab the TextView for our "custom" sample, then create a Typeface object via the static createFromAsset() builder method. This takes the application's AssetManager (from getAssets()) and a path within your assets/ directory to the font you want.

Then, it is just a matter of telling the TextView to setTypeface(), providing the Typeface you just created. In this case, we are using the Handmade Typewriter[2] font (see Figure 12-1).

---

2. http://moorstation.org/typoasis/designers/klein07/text01/handmade.htm

Figure 12-1. *The FontSampler application*

Note that Android does not seem to like all TrueType fonts. When Android dislikes a custom font, rather than raise an `Exception`, it seems to substitute Droid Sans ("sans") quietly. So, if you try to use a different font and it does not seem to be working, it may be that the font in question is incompatible with Android, for whatever reason.

Also, you are probably best served by changing the case of your font filenames to be all lowercase, to match the naming convention used in the rest of your resources.

Also note that TrueType fonts can be rather pudgy, particularly if they support an extensive subset of the available Unicode characters. The Handmade Typewriter font used here runs over 70KB; the DejaVu free fonts can run upwards of 500KB apiece. Even compressed, these add bulk to your application, so be careful not to go overboard with custom fonts, or your application could take up too much room on your users' phones.

■ ■ ■

CHAPTER 13

Embedding the WebKit Browser

Other GUI toolkits let you use HTML for presenting information, from limited HTML renderers (e.g., Java/Swing, wxWidgets) to embedding Internet Explorer into .NET applications. Android is much the same, in that you can embed the built-in Web browser as a widget in your own activities, for displaying HTML or full-fledged browsing. The Android browser is based on WebKit, the same engine that powers Apple's Safari Web browser.

The Android browser is sufficiently complex that it gets its own Java package (`android.webkit`), though using the `WebView` widget itself can be simple or powerful, based upon your requirements.

A Browser, Writ Small

For simple stuff, `WebView` is not significantly different than any other widget in Android—pop it into a layout, tell it what URL to navigate to via Java code, and you're done.

For example, `WebKit/Browser1` is a simple layout with a `WebView`. You can find `WebKit/Browser1` along with all the code samples for this chapter in the Source Code area at `http://apress.com`.

```xml
<?xml version="1.0" encoding="utf-8"?>
<LinearLayout xmlns:android="http://schemas.android.com/apk/res/android"
  android:orientation="vertical"
  android:layout_width="fill_parent"
  android:layout_height="fill_parent"
  >
  <WebView android:id="@+id/webkit"
    android:layout_width="fill_parent"
    android:layout_height="fill_parent"
  />
</LinearLayout>
```

As with any other widget, you need to tell it how it should fill up the space in the layout (in this case, it fills all remaining space).

The Java code is equally simple:

```
package com.commonsware.android.webkit;

import android.app.Activity;
import android.os.Bundle;
import android.webkit.WebView;

public class BrowserDemo1 extends Activity {
  WebView browser;

  @Override
  public void onCreate(Bundle icicle) {
    super.onCreate(icicle);
    setContentView(R.layout.main);
    browser=(WebView)findViewById(R.id.webkit);

    browser.loadUrl("http://commonsware.com");
  }
}
```

The only unusual bit with this edition of onCreate() is that we invoke loadUrl() on the WebView widget, to tell it to load a Web page (in this case, the home page of some random firm).

However, we also have to make one change to AndroidManifest.xml, requesting permission to access the Internet:

```
<manifest xmlns:android="http://schemas.android.com/apk/res/android"
  package="com.commonsware.android.webkit">
  <uses-permission android:name="android.permission.INTERNET" />
  <application>
    <activity android:name=".BrowserDemo1" android:label="BrowserDemo1">
      <intent-filter>
        <action android:name="android.intent.action.MAIN" />
        <category android:name="android.intent.category.LAUNCHER" />
      </intent-filter>
    </activity>
  </application>
</manifest>
```

If we fail to add this permission, the browser will refuse to load pages.

The resulting activity looks like a Web browser, just with hidden scrollbars (see Figure 13-1).

Figure 13-1. *The Browser1 sample application*

As with the regular Android browser, you can pan around the page by dragging it, while the directional pad moves you around all the focusable elements on the page.

What is missing is all the extra accouterments that make up a Web browser, such as a navigational toolbar.

Now, you may be tempted to replace the URL in that source code with something else, such as Google's home page or another page that relies upon Javascript. By default Javascript is turned off in WebView widgets. If you want to enable Javascript, call getSettings(). setJavaScriptEnabled(true); on the WebView instance.

Loading It Up

There are two main ways to get content into the WebView. One, shown earlier, is to provide the browser with a URL and have the browser display that page via loadUrl(). The browser will access the Internet through whatever means are available to that specific device at the present time (WiFi, cellular network, Bluetooth-tethered phone, well-trained tiny carrier pigeons, etc.).

The alternative is to use loadData(). Here, you supply the HTML for the browser to view. You might use this to

- display a manual that was installed as a file with your application package

- display snippets of HTML you retrieved as part of other processing, such as the description of an entry in an Atom feed

- generate a whole user interface using HTML, instead of using the Android widget set

There are two flavors of loadData(). The simpler one allows you to provide the content, the MIME type, and the encoding, all as strings. Typically, your MIME type will be text/html and your encoding will be UTF-8 for ordinary HTML.

For instance, if you replace the loadUrl() invocation in the previous example with the following code, you get the result shown in Figure 13-2.

```
browser.loadData("<html><body>Hello, world!</body></html>",
                 "text/html", "UTF-8");
```

Figure 13-2. *The Browser2 sample application*

This is also available as a fully-buildable sample, as WebKit/Browser2.

Navigating the Waters

As previously mentioned, there is no navigation toolbar with the WebView widget. This allows you to use it in places where such a toolbar would be pointless and a waste of screen real estate. That being said, if you want to offer navigational capabilities, you can, but you have to supply the UI.

WebView offers ways to perform garden-variety browser navigation, including the following:

- reload() to refresh the currently-viewed Web page

- goBack() to go back one step in the browser history, and canGoBack() to determine if there is any history to go back to

- goForward() to go forward one step in the browser history, and canGoForward() to determine if there is any history to go forward to

- goBackOrForward() to go backward or forward in the browser history, where a negative number as an argument represents a count of steps to go backward, and a positive number represents how many steps to go forward

- canGoBackOrForward() to see if the browser can go backward or forward the stated number of steps (following the same positive/negative convention as goBackOrForward())

- clearCache() to clear the browser resource cache and clearHistory() to clear the browsing history

Entertaining the Client

If you are going to use the WebView as a local user interface (vs. browsing the Web), you will want to be able to get control at key times, particularly when users click on links. You will want to make sure those links are handled properly, either by loading your own content back into the WebView, by submitting an Intent to Android to open the URL in a full browser, or by some other means (see Chapter 25).

Your hook into the WebView activity is via setWebViewClient(), which takes an instance of a WebViewClient implementation as a parameter. The supplied callback object will be notified of a wide range of activities, ranging from when parts of a page have been retrieved (onPageStarted(), etc.) to when you, as the host application, need to handle certain user- or circumstance-initiated events, such as onTooManyRedirects() and onReceivedHttpAuthRequest(), etc.

A common hook will be shouldOverrideUrlLoading(), where your callback is passed a URL (plus the WebView itself) and you return true if you will handle the request or false if you want default handling (e.g., actually fetch the Web page referenced by the URL). In the case of a feed reader application, for example, you will probably not have a full browser with navigation built into your reader, so if the user clicks a URL, you probably want to use an Intent to ask Android to load that page in a full browser. But, if you have inserted a "fake" URL into the HTML, representing a link to some activity-provided content, you can update the WebView yourself.

For example, let's amend the first browser example to be a browser-based equivalent of our original example: an application that, upon a click, shows the current time.

From WebKit/Browser3, here is the revised Java:

```java
public class BrowserDemo3 extends Activity {
  WebView browser;

  @Override
  public void onCreate(Bundle icicle) {
    super.onCreate(icicle);
    setContentView(R.layout.main);
    browser=(WebView)findViewById(R.id.webkit);
    browser.setWebViewClient(new Callback());

    loadTime();
  }
```

```
void loadTime() {
  String page="<html><body><a href=\"clock\">"
          +new Date().toString()
          +"</a></body></html>";

          browser.loadDataWithBaseURL("x-data://base", page,
                                      "text/html", "UTF-8",
                                      null);
}

private class Callback extends WebViewClient {
  public boolean shouldOverrideUrlLoading(WebView view, String url) {
    loadTime();

    return(true);
  }
}
}
```

Here, we load a simple Web page into the browser (loadTime()) that consists of the current time, made into a hyperlink to the /clock URL. We also attach an instance of a WebViewClient subclass, providing our implementation of shouldOverrideUrlLoading(). In this case, no matter what the URL, we want to just reload the WebView via loadTime().

Running this activity gives the result shown in Figure 13-3.

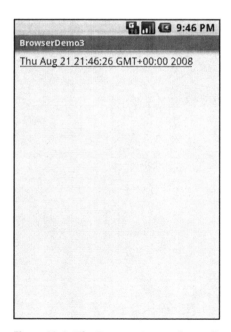

Figure 13-3. *The Browser3 sample application*

Selecting the link and clicking the D-pad center button will "click" the link, causing us to rebuild the page with the new time.

Settings, Preferences, and Options (Oh, My!)

With your favorite desktop Web browser, you have some sort of "settings" or "preferences" or "options" window. Between that and the toolbar controls, you can tweak and twiddle the behavior of your browser, from preferred fonts to the behavior of Javascript.

Similarly, you can adjust the settings of your WebView widget as you see fit, via the WebSettings instance returned from calling the widget's getSettings() method.

There are lots of options on WebSettings to play with. Most appear fairly esoteric (e.g., setFantasyFontFamily()). However, here are some that you may find more useful:

- Control the font sizing via setDefaultFontSize() (to use a point size) or setTextSize() (to use constants indicating relative sizes like LARGER and SMALLEST)

- Control Javascript via setJavaScriptEnabled() (to disable it outright) and setJavaScriptCanOpenWindowsAutomatically() (to merely stop it from opening pop-up windows)

- Control Web site rendering via setUserAgent() – 0 means the WebView gives the Web site a user-agent string that indicates it is a mobile browser, while 1 results in a user-agent string that suggests it is a desktop browser

The settings you change are not persistent, so you should store them somewhere (such as via the Android preferences engine) if you are allowing your users to determine the settings, versus hard-wiring the settings in your application.

CHAPTER 14

■■■

Showing Pop-Up Messages

Sometimes your activity (or other piece of Android code) will need to speak up.

Not every interaction with Android users will be neat, tidy, and containable in activities composed of views. Errors will crop up. Background tasks may take way longer than expected. Something asynchronous may occur, such as an incoming message. In these and other cases, you may need to communicate with the user outside the bounds of the traditional user interface.

Of course, this is nothing new. Error messages in the form of dialog boxes have been around for a very long time. More-subtle indicators also exist, from task-tray icons to bouncing dock icons to a vibrating cell phone.

Android has quite a few systems for letting you alert your users outside the bounds of an Activity-based UI. One, notifications, is tied heavily into intents and services and, as such, is covered in Chapter 32. In this chapter, you will see two means of raising pop-up messages: toasts and alerts.

Raising Toasts

A Toast is a transient message, meaning that it displays and disappears on its own without user interaction. Moreover, it does not take focus away from the currently active Activity, so if the user is busy writing the next Great American Programming Guide, they will not have keystrokes be "eaten" by the message.

Since a Toast is transient, you have no way of knowing if the user even notices it. You get no acknowledgment from them, nor does the message stick around for a long time to pester the user. Hence, the Toast is mostly for advisory messages, such as indicating a long-running background task is completed, the battery has dropped to a low-but-not-too-low level, etc.

Making a Toast is fairly easy. The Toast class offers a static makeText() that accepts a String (or string resource ID) and returns a Toast instance. The makeText() method also needs the Activity (or other Context) plus a duration. The duration is expressed in the form of the LENGTH_SHORT or LENGTH_LONG constants to indicate, on a relative basis, how long the message should remain visible.

If you would prefer your Toast be made out of some other View, rather than be a boring old piece of text, simply create a new Toast instance via the constructor (which takes a Context), then call setView() to supply it with the view to use and setDuration() to set the duration.

Once your Toast is configured, call its show() method, and the message will be displayed.

Alert! Alert!

If you would prefer something in the more classic dialog-box style, what you want is an AlertDialog. As with any other modal dialog box, an AlertDialog pops up, grabs the focus, and stays there until closed by the user. You might use this for a critical error, a validation message that cannot be effectively displayed in the base activity UI, or something else where you are sure that the user needs to see the message and needs to see it now.

The simplest way to construct an AlertDialog is to use the Builder class. Following in true builder style, Builder offers a series of methods to configure an AlertDialog, each method returning the Builder for easy chaining. At the end, you call show() on the builder to display the dialog box.

Commonly used configuration methods on Builder include the following:

- setMessage() if you want the "body" of the dialog to be a simple textual message, from either a supplied String or a supplied string resource ID

- setTitle() and setIcon() to configure the text and/or icon to appear in the title bar of the dialog box

- setPositiveButton(),setNeutralButton(), and setNegativeButton() to indicate which button(s) should appear across the bottom of the dialog, where they should be positioned (left, center, or right, respectively), what their captions should be, and what logic should be invoked when the button is clicked (besides dismissing the dialog)

If you need to configure the AlertDialog beyond what the builder allows, instead of calling show(), call create() to get the partially built AlertDialog instance, configure it the rest of the way, then call one of the flavors of show() on the AlertDialog itself.

Once show() is called, the dialog box will appear and await user input.

Checking Them Out

To see how these work in practice, take a peek at Messages/Message (available from the Source Code section of the Apress Web site), containing the following layout:

```xml
<?xml version="1.0" encoding="utf-8"?>
<LinearLayout xmlns:android="http://schemas.android.com/apk/res/android"
  android:orientation="vertical"
  android:layout_width="fill_parent"
  android:layout_height="fill_parent" >
  <Button
    android:id="@+id/alert"
    android:text="Raise an alert"
    android:layout_width="fill_parent"
    android:layout_height="wrap_content"/>
  <Button
    android:id="@+id/toast"
    android:text="Make a toast"
    android:layout_width="fill_parent"
    android:layout_height="wrap_content"/>
</LinearLayout>
```

and the following Java code:

```java
public class MessageDemo extends Activity implements View.OnClickListener {
  Button alert;
  Button toast;

  @Override
  public void onCreate(Bundle icicle) {
    super.onCreate(icicle);

    setContentView(R.layout.main);

    alert=(Button)findViewById(R.id.alert);
    alert.setOnClickListener(this);
    toast=(Button)findViewById(R.id.toast);
    toast.setOnClickListener(this);
  }

  public void onClick(View view) {
    if (view==alert) {
      new AlertDialog.Builder(this)
        .setTitle("MessageDemo")
        .setMessage("eek!")
        .setNeutralButton("Close", new DialogInterface.OnClickListener() {
          public void onClick(DialogInterface dlg, int sumthin) {
            // do nothing - it will close on its own
          }
        })
        .show();
    }
    else {
      Toast
        .makeText(this, "<clink, clink>", Toast.LENGTH_SHORT)
        .show();
    }
  }
}
```

The layout is unremarkable—just a pair of buttons to trigger the alert and the Toast.

When the Raise an Alert button is clicked, we use a builder (new Builder(this)) to set the title (setTitle("MessageDemo")), message (setMessage("eek!")), and neutral button (setNeutralButton("Close", new OnClickListener() ...) before showing the dialog. When the button is clicked, the OnClickListener callback does nothing; the mere fact the button was pressed causes the dialog to be dismissed. However, you could update information in your activity based upon the user action, particularly if you have multiple buttons for the user to choose from. The result is a typical dialog box like the one in Figure 14-1.

Figure 14-1. *The MessageDemo sample application, after clicking the Raise an Alert button*

When you click the Make a Toast button, the Toast class makes us a text-based Toast (makeText(this, "<clink, clink>", LENGTH_SHORT)), which we then show(). The result is a short-lived, non-interrupting message (see Figure 14-2).

Figure 14-2. *The same application, after clicking the Make a Toast button*

■ ■ ■

CHAPTER 15

Dealing with Threads

Ideally, you want your activities to be downright snappy, so your users don't feel that your application is sluggish. Responding to user input quickly (e.g., 200ms) is a fine goal. At minimum, though, you need to make sure you respond within 5 seconds, or the ActivityManager could decide to play the role of the Grim Reaper and kill off your activity as being non-responsive.

Of course, your activity might have real work to do, which takes non-negligible amounts of time. There are two ways of dealing with this:

- Do expensive operations in a background service, relying on notifications to prompt users to go back to your activity

- Do expensive work in a background thread

Android provides a veritable cornucopia of means to set up background threads yet allow them to safely interact with the UI on the UI thread. These include Handler objects and posting Runnable objects to the View.

Getting Through the Handlers

The most flexible means of making an Android-friendly background thread is to create an instance of a Handler subclass. You only need one Handler object per activity, and you do not need to manually register it or anything—merely creating the instance is sufficient to register it with the Android threading subsystem.

Your background thread can communicate with the Handler, which will do all of its work on the activity's UI thread. This is important because UI changes, such as updating widgets, should only occur on the activity's UI thread.

You have two options for communicating with the Handler: messages and Runnable objects.

Messages

To send a Message to a Handler, first invoke obtainMessage() to get the Message object out of the pool. There are a few flavors of obtainMessage(), allowing you to just create empty Message objects, or ones populated with message identifiers and arguments. The more complicated your Handler processing needs to be, the more likely it is you will need to put data into the Message to help the Handler distinguish different events.

Then, you send the Message to the Handler via its message queue, using one of the following sendMessage...() family of methods:

- sendMessage() puts the message on the queue immediately

- sendMessageAtFrontOfQueue() puts the message on the queue immediately, and more-over puts it at the front of the message queue (versus the back, as is the default), so your message takes priority over all others

- sendMessageAtTime() puts the message on the queue at the stated time, expressed in the form of milliseconds based on system uptime (SystemClock.uptimeMillis())

- sendMessageDelayed() puts the message on the queue after a delay, expressed in milliseconds

To process these messages, your Handler needs to implement handleMessage(), which will be called with each message that appears on the message queue. There, the handler can update the UI as needed. However, it should still do that work quickly, as other UI work is suspended until the Handler is done.

For example, let's create a ProgressBar and update it via a Handler. Here is the layout from the Threads/Handler sample project. This sample code along with all others in this chapter can be found in the Source Code section at http://apress.com.

```xml
<?xml version="1.0" encoding="utf-8"?>
<LinearLayout xmlns:android="http://schemas.android.com/apk/res/android"
  android:orientation="vertical"
  android:layout_width="fill_parent"
  android:layout_height="fill_parent"
  >
  <ProgressBar android:id="@+id/progress"
    style="?android:attr/progressBarStyleHorizontal"
    android:layout_width="fill_parent"
    android:layout_height="wrap_content" />
</LinearLayout>
```

The ProgressBar, in addition to setting the width and height as normal, also employs the style property, which I won't cover in detail in this book. Suffice it to say, style property indicates this ProgressBar should be drawn as the traditional horizontal bar showing the amount of work that has been completed.

Here is the Java:

```java
package com.commonsware.android.threads;

import android.app.Activity;
import android.os.Bundle;
import android.os.Handler;
import android.os.Message;
import android.widget.ProgressBar;

public class HandlerDemo extends Activity {
  ProgressBar bar;
  Handler handler=new Handler() {
    @Override
```

```
      public void handleMessage(Message msg) {
        bar.incrementProgressBy(5);
      }
   };
   boolean isRunning=false;

   @Override
   public void onCreate(Bundle icicle) {
     super.onCreate(icicle);
     setContentView(R.layout.main);
     bar=(ProgressBar)findViewById(R.id.progress);
   }

   public void onStart() {
     super.onStart();
     bar.setProgress(0);

     Thread background=new Thread(new Runnable() {
       public void run() {
         try {
           for (int i=0;i<20 && isRunning;i++) {
             Thread.sleep(1000);
             handler.sendMessage(handler.obtainMessage());
           }
         }
         catch (Throwable t) {
           // just end the background thread
         }
       }
     });

     isRunning=true;
     background.start();
   }

   public void onStop() {
     super.onStop();
     isRunning=false;
   }
}
```

As part of constructing the Activity, we create an instance of Handler, with our implementation of handleMessage(). Basically, for any message received, we update the ProgressBar by 5 points, then exit the message handler.

In onStart(), we set up a background thread. In a real system, this thread would do something meaningful. Here, we just sleep one second, post a Message to the Handler, and repeat for a total of 20 passes. This, combined with the 5-point increase in the ProgressBar position, will march the bar clear across the screen, as the default maximum value for ProgressBar is 100.

You can adjust that maximum via setMax(), such as setting the maximum to be the number of database rows you are processing, and updating once per row.

Note that we then *leave* onStart(). This is crucial. The onStart() method is invoked on the activity UI thread, so it can update widgets and anything else that affects the UI, such as the title bar. However, that means we need to get out of onStart(), both to let the Handler get its work done, and also so Android does not think our activity is stuck.

The resulting activity is simply a horizontal progress bar (see Figure 15-1).

Figure 15-1. *The HandlerDemo sample application*

Runnables

If you would rather not fuss with Message objects, you can also pass Runnable objects to the Handler, which will run those Runnable objects on the activity UI thread. Handler offers a set of post...() methods for passing Runnable objects in for eventual processing.

Running in Place

Just as Handler supports post() and postDelayed() to add Runnable objects to the event queue, you can use those same methods on View. This slightly simplifies your code, in that you can then skip the Handler object. However, you lose a bit of flexibility, and the Handler has been around longer in the Android toolkit and may be more tested.

Where, Oh Where Has My UI Thread Gone?

Sometimes, you may not know if you are currently executing on the UI thread of your application. For example, if you package some of your code in a JAR for others to reuse, you might not know whether your code is being executed on the UI thread or from a background thread.

To help combat this problem, `Activity` offers `runOnUiThread()`. This works similar to the `post()` methods on `Handler` and `View`, in that it queues up a `Runnable` to run on the UI thread, if you are not on the UI thread right now. If you already are on the UI thread, it invokes the `Runnable` immediately. This gives you the best of both worlds: no delay if you are on the UI thread, yet safety in case you are not.

Now, the Caveats

Background threads, while eminently possible using the Android `Handler` system, are not all happiness and warm puppies. Background threads not only add complexity, but they have real-world costs in terms of available memory, CPU, and battery life.

To that end, there are a wide range of scenarios you need to account for with your background thread, including

- The possibility that users will interact with your activity's UI while the background thread is chugging along. If the work that the background thread is doing is altered or invalidated by the user input, you will need to communicate this to the background thread. Android includes many classes in the `java.util.concurrent` package that will help you communicate safely with your background thread.

- The possibility that the activity will be killed off while background work is going on. For example, after starting your activity, the user might have a call come in, followed by a text message, then a need to look up a contact—all of which might be sufficient to kick your activity out of memory. Chapter 16 will cover the various events Android will take your activity through; hook the proper ones and be sure to shut down your background thread cleanly when you have the chance.

- The possibility that your user will get irritated if you chew up a lot of CPU time and battery life without giving any payback. Tactically, this means using `ProgressBar` or other means of letting the user know that something is happening. Strategically, this means you still need to be efficient at what you do—background threads are no panacea for sluggish or pointless code.

- The possibility that you will encounter an error during background processing. For example, if you are gathering information off the Internet, the device might lose connectivity. Alerting the user of the problem via a `Notification` and shutting down the background thread may be your best option.

CHAPTER 16

■ ■ ■

Handling Activity Lifecycle Events

While this may sound like a broken record please remember that Android devices, by and large, are phones. As such, some activities are more important that others—taking a call is probably more important to users than is playing Sudoku. And, since it is a phone, it probably has less RAM than does your current desktop or notebook.

As a result, your activity may find itself being killed off because other activities are going on and the system needs your activity's memory. Think of it as the Android equivalent of the "circle of life"—your activity dies so others may live, and so on. You cannot assume that your activity will run until you think it is complete, or even until the user thinks it is complete.

This is one example—perhaps the most important example—of how an activity's lifecycle will affect your own application logic. This chapter covers the various states and callbacks that make up an activity's lifecycle and how you can hook into them appropriately.

Schroedinger's Activity

An activity, generally speaking, is in one of four states at any point in time:

- **Active**: The activity was started by the user, is running, and is in the foreground. This is what you're used to thinking of in terms of your activity's operation.

- **Paused**: The activity was started by the user, is running, and is visible, but a notification or something is overlaying part of the screen. During this time, the user can see your activity but may not be able to interact with it. For example, if a call comes in, the user will get the opportunity to take the call or ignore it.

- **Stopped**: The activity was started by the user, is running, but it is hidden by other activities that have been launched or switched to. Your application will not be able to present anything meaningful to the user directly, only by way of a `Notification`.

- **Dead**: Either the activity was never started (e.g., just after a phone reset) or the activity was terminated, perhaps due to lack of available memory.

Life, Death, and Your Activity

Android will call into your activity as the activity transitions between the four states previously listed, using the methods shown in this section. Some transitions may result in multiple calls to your activity, and sometimes Android will kill your application without calling it. This whole area is rather murky and probably subject to change, so pay close attention to the official Android documentation as well as this section when deciding which events to pay attention to and which you can safely ignore.

Note that for all of these, you should chain upward and invoke the superclass' edition of the method, or Android may raise an exception.

onCreate() and onDestroy()

We have been implementing onCreate() in all of our Activity subclasses in every example. This will get called in three situations:

- When the activity is first started (e.g., since a system restart), onCreate() will be invoked with a null parameter.

- If the activity had been running, then sometime later was killed off, onCreate() will be invoked with the Bundle from onSaveInstanceState() as a parameter.

- If the activity had been running and you have set up your activity to have different resources based on different device states (e.g., landscape versus portrait), your activity will be re-created and onCreate() will be called.

Here is where you initialize your user interface and set up anything that needs to be done once, regardless of how the activity gets used.

On the other end of the lifecycle, onDestroy() may be called when the activity is shutting down, either because the activity called finish() (which "finishes" the activity) or because Android needs RAM and is closing the activity prematurely. Note that onDestroy() may not get called if the need for RAM is urgent (e.g., incoming phone call) and that the activity will just get shut down regardless. Hence, onDestroy() is mostly for cleanly releasing resources you obtained in onCreate() (if any).

onStart(), onRestart(), and onStop()

An activity can come to the foreground either because it is first being launched, or because it is being brought back to the foreground after having been hidden (e.g., by another activity or by an incoming phone call).

The onStart() method is called in either of those cases. The onRestart() method is called in the case where the activity had been stopped and is now restarting.

Conversely, onStop() is called when the activity is about to be stopped.

onPause() and onResume()

The onResume() method is called just before your activity comes to the foreground, either after being initially launched, being restarted from a stopped state, or after a pop-up dialog (e.g., incoming call) is cleared. This is a great place to refresh the UI based on things that may have occurred since the user was last looking at your activity. For example, if you are polling a service for changes to some information (e.g., new entries for a feed), onResume() is a fine time to both refresh the current view and, if applicable, kick off a background thread to update the view (e.g., via a Handler).

Conversely, anything that steals your user away from your activity—mostly, the activation of another activity—will result in your onPause() being called. Here, you should undo anything you did in onResume(), such as stopping background threads, releasing any exclusive-access resources you may have acquired (e.g., camera), and the like.

Once onPause() is called, Android reserves the right to kill off your activity's process at any point. Hence, you should not be relying upon receiving any further events.

The Grace of State

Mostly, the aforementioned methods are for dealing with things at the application-general level (e.g., wiring together the last pieces of your UI in onCreate(), closing down background threads in onPause()).

However, a large part of the goal of Android is to have a patina of seamlessness. Activities may come and go as dictated by memory requirements, but users are, ideally, unaware that this is going on. If, for example, they were using a calculator, and come back to that calculator after an absence, they should see whatever number(s) they were working on originally—unless they themselves took some action to close down the calculator.

To make all this work, activities need to be able to save their application-instance state, and to do so quickly and cheaply. Since activities could get killed off at any time, activities may need to save their state more frequently than one might expect. Then, when the activity restarts, the activity should get its former state back, so it can restore the activity to the way it appeared previously.

Saving instance state is handled by onSaveInstanceState(). This supplies a Bundle into which activities can pour whatever data they need (e.g., the number showing on the calculator's display). This method implementation needs to be speedy, so do not try to be too fancy—just put your data in the Bundle and exit the method.

That instance state is provided to you again in:

- onCreate()

- onRestoreInstanceState()

It is your choice when you wish to re-apply the state data to your activity—either callback is a reasonable option.

PART 3

Data Stores, Network Services, and APIs

CHAPTER 17

■ ■ ■

Using Preferences

Android has many different ways for you to store data for long-term use by your activity. The simplest to use is the preferences system.

Android allows activities and applications to keep preferences, in the form of key/value pairs (akin to a Map), that will hang around between invocations of an activity. As the name suggests, the primary purpose is for you to store user-specified configuration details, such as the last feed the user looked at in your feed reader, or what sort order to use by default on a list, or whatever. Of course, you can store in the preferences whatever you like, so long as it is keyed by a String and has a primitive value (boolean, String, etc.).

Preferences can either be for a single activity or shared among all activities in an application. Eventually preferences might be shareable across applications, but that is not supported as of the time of this writing.

Getting What You Want

To get access to the preferences, you have three APIs to choose from:

- getPreferences() from within your Activity, to access activity-specific preferences

- getSharedPreferences() from within your Activity (or other application Context), to access application-level preferences

- getDefaultSharedPreferences(), on PreferencesManager, to get the shared preferences that work in concert with Android's overall preference framework

The first two take a security-mode parameter—for now, pass in 0. The getSharedPreferences() method also takes a name of a set of preferences—getPreferences() effectively calls getSharedPreferences() with the activity's class name as the preference set name. The getDefaultSharedPreferences() method takes the Context for the preferences (e.g., your Activity).

All of those methods return an instance of SharedPreferences, which offers a series of getters to access named preferences, returning a suitably typed result (e.g., getBoolean() to return a Boolean preference). The getters also take a default value, which is returned if there is no preference set under the specified key.

Stating Your Preference

Given the appropriate SharedPreferences object, you can use edit() to get an "editor" for the preferences. This object has a group of setters that mirror the getters on the parent SharedPreferences object. It also has the following:

- remove() to get rid of a single named preference
- clear() to get rid of all preferences
- commit() to persist your changes made via the editor

The last one is important—if you modify preferences via the editor and fail to commit() the changes, those changes will evaporate once the editor goes out of scope.

Conversely, since the preferences object supports live changes, if one part of your application (say, an activity) modifies shared preferences, another part of your application (say, a service) will have access to the changed value immediately.

And Now, a Word from Our Framework

Beginning with the 0.9 SDK, Android has a framework for managing preferences. This framework does not change anything mentioned previously. Instead, the framework is more for presenting consistent preference-setting options for users so different applications do not have to reinvent the wheel.

The linchpin to the preferences framework is yet another XML data structure. You can describe your application's preferences in an XML file stored in your project's res/xml/ directory. Given that, Android can present a pleasant UI for manipulating those preferences, which are then stored in the SharedPreferences you get back from getDefaultSharedPreferences().

The following is the preference XML for the Prefs/Simple preferences sample project available in the Source Code section at http://apress.com:

```
<PreferenceScreen
  xmlns:android="http://schemas.android.com/apk/res/android">
  <CheckBoxPreference
    android:key="@string/checkbox"
    android:title="Checkbox Preference"
    android:summary="Check it on, check it off" />
  <RingtonePreference
    android:key="@string/ringtone"
    android:title="Ringtone Preference"
    android:showDefault="true"
    android:showSilent="true"
    android:summary="Pick a tone, any tone" />
</PreferenceScreen>
```

The root of the preference XML is a PreferenceScreen element. (I will explain why it is named that later in this chapter; for now, take it on faith that it is a sensible name.) One of the things you can have inside a PreferenceScreen element, not surprisingly, is preference definitions—subclasses of Preference, such as CheckBoxPreference or RingtonePreference, as shown in the preceding code. As one might expect, these allow you to check a checkbox and choose a ringtone, respectively. In the case of RingtonePreference, you have the option of allowing users to choose the system-default ringtone or to choose "silence" as a ringtone.

Letting Users Have Their Say

Given that you have set up the preference XML, you can use a nearly built-in activity for allowing your users to set their preferences. The activity is "nearly built-in" because you merely need to subclass it and point it to your preference XML, plus hook the activity into the rest of your application.

So, for example, here is the EditPreferences activity of the Prefs/Simple project available on the Apress Web site:

```
package com.commonsware.android.prefs;

import android.app.Activity;
import android.os.Bundle;
import android.preference.PreferenceActivity;


public class EditPreferences extends PreferenceActivity {
  @Override
  public void onCreate(Bundle savedInstanceState) {
    super.onCreate(savedInstanceState);

    addPreferencesFromResource(R.xml.preferences);
  }
}
```

As you can see, there is not much *to* see. All you need to do is call addPreferencesFromResource() and specify the XML resource containing your preferences. You will also need to add this as an activity to your AndroidManifest.xml file:

```
<?xml version="1.0" encoding="utf-8"?>
<manifest xmlns:android="http://schemas.android.com/apk/res/android"
    package="com.commonsware.android.prefs">
    <application android:label="@string/app_name">
        <activity
            android:name=".SimplePrefsDemo"
            android:label="@string/app_name">
            <intent-filter>
                <action android:name="android.intent.action.MAIN" />
                <category android:name="android.intent.category.LAUNCHER" />
            </intent-filter>
        </activity>
```

```
        <activity
            android:name=".EditPreferences"
            android:label="@string/app_name">
        </activity>
    </application>
</manifest>
```

And you will need to arrange to invoke the activity, such as from a menu option, here pulled from `SimplePrefsDemo` at `http://apress.com`:

```
@Override
public boolean onCreateOptionsMenu(Menu menu) {
  menu.add(Menu.NONE, EDIT_ID, Menu.NONE, "Edit Prefs")
      .setIcon(R.drawable.misc)
      .setAlphabeticShortcut('e');
  menu.add(Menu.NONE, CLOSE_ID, Menu.NONE, "Close")
      .setIcon(R.drawable.eject)
      .setAlphabeticShortcut('c');

  return(super.onCreateOptionsMenu(menu));
}

@Override
public boolean onOptionsItemSelected(MenuItem item) {
  switch (item.getItemId()) {
    case EDIT_ID:
      startActivity(new Intent(this, EditPreferences.class));
      return(true);

    case CLOSE_ID:
      finish();
      return(true);
  }

  return(super.onOptionsItemSelected(item));
}
```

However, that is all that is needed, and it really is not that much code outside of the preferences XML. What you get for your effort is an Android-supplied preference UI, as shown in Figure 17-1.

Figure 17-1. *The Simple project's preferences UI*

The checkbox can be directly checked or unchecked. To change the ringtone preference, just click on the entry in the preference list to bring up a selection dialog like the one in Figure 17-2.

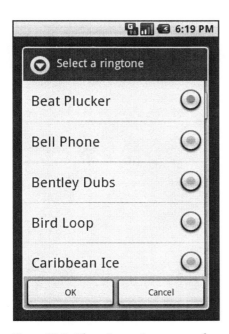

Figure 17-2. *Choosing a ringtone preference*

Note that there is no explicit Save or Commit button or menu—changes are persisted as soon as they are made.

The SimplePrefsDemo activity, beyond having the aforementioned menu, also displays the current preferences via a TableLayout:

```
<?xml version="1.0" encoding="utf-8"?>
<TableLayout
  xmlns:android="http://schemas.android.com/apk/res/android"
  android:layout_width="fill_parent"
  android:layout_height="fill_parent"
>
  <TableRow>
    <TextView
        android:text="Checkbox:"
        android:paddingRight="5px"
    />
    <TextView android:id="@+id/checkbox"
    />
  </TableRow>
  <TableRow>
    <TextView
        android:text="Ringtone:"
        android:paddingRight="5px"
    />
    <TextView android:id="@+id/ringtone"
    />
  </TableRow>
</TableLayout>
```

The fields for the table are found in onCreate():

```
@Override
public void onCreate(Bundle savedInstanceState) {
  super.onCreate(savedInstanceState);
  setContentView(R.layout.main);

  checkbox=(TextView)findViewById(R.id.checkbox);
  ringtone=(TextView)findViewById(R.id.ringtone);
}
```

The fields are updated on each onResume():

```
@Override
public void onResume() {
  super.onResume();

  SharedPreferences prefs=PreferenceManager
                         .getDefaultSharedPreferences(this);

  checkbox.setText(new Boolean(prefs
                              .getBoolean("checkbox", false))
                  .toString());
  ringtone.setText(prefs.getString("ringtone", "<unset>"));
}
```

This means the fields will be updated when the activity is opened and after the preferences activity is left (e.g., via the back button); see Figure 17-3.

Figure 17-3. *The Simple project's list of saved preferences*

Adding a Wee Bit o' Structure

If you have a lot of preferences for users to set, having them all in one big list may become trouble-some. Android's preference framework gives you a few ways to impose a bit of structure on your bag of preferences, including categories and screens.

Categories are added via a `PreferenceCategory` element in your preference XML and are used to group together related preferences. Rather than have your preferences all as children of the root `PreferenceScreen`, you can put a few `PreferenceCategory` elements in the `PreferenceScreen`, and then put your preferences in their appropriate categories. Visually, this adds a divider with the category title between groups of preferences.

If you have lots and lots of preferences—more than is convenient for users to scroll through— you can also put them on separate "screens" by introducing the `PreferenceScreen` element.

Yes, *that* `PreferenceScreen` element.

Any children of `PreferenceScreen` go on their own screen. If you nest `PreferenceScreens`, the parent screen displays the screen as a placeholder entry—tapping that entry brings up the child screen. For example, from the `Prefs/Structured` sample project on the Apress Web site, here is a preference XML file that contains both `PreferenceCategory` and nested `PreferenceScreen` elements:

```
<PreferenceScreen
  xmlns:android="http://schemas.android.com/apk/res/android">
  <PreferenceCategory android:title="Simple Preferences">
    <CheckBoxPreference
      android:key="@string/checkbox"
      android:title="Checkbox Preference"
      android:summary="Check it on, check it off"
    />
    <RingtonePreference
      android:key="@string/ringtone"
      android:title="Ringtone Preference"
      android:showDefault="true"
      android:showSilent="true"
      android:summary="Pick a tone, any tone"
    />
  </PreferenceCategory>
  <PreferenceCategory android:title="Detail Screens">
    <PreferenceScreen
      android:key="detail"
      android:title="Detail Screen"
      android:summary="Additional preferences held in another page">
      <CheckBoxPreference
        android:key="@string/checkbox2"
        android:title="Another Checkbox"
        android:summary="On. Off. It really doesn't matter."
      />
    </PreferenceScreen>
  </PreferenceCategory>
</PreferenceScreen>
```

The result, when you use this preference XML with your `PreferenceActivity` implementation, is a categorized list of elements like those in Figure 17-4.

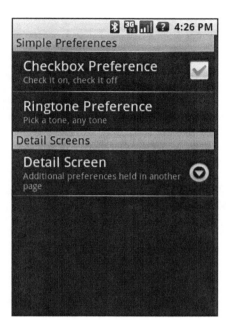

Figure 17-4. *The Structured project's preference UI, showing categories and a screen placeholder*

And if you tap on the Detail Screen entry, you are taken to the child preference screen (Figure 17-5).

Figure 17-5. *The child preference screen of the Structured project's preference UI*

The Kind of Pop-Ups You Like

Of course, not all preferences are checkboxes and ringtones.

For others, like entry fields and lists, Android uses pop-up dialogs. Users do not enter their preference directly in the preference UI activity, but rather tap on a preference, fill in a value, and click OK to commit the change.

Structurally, in the preference XML, fields and lists are not significantly different from other preference types, as seen in this preference XML from the Prefs/Dialogs sample project available at http://apress.com:

```
<PreferenceScreen
  xmlns:android="http://schemas.android.com/apk/res/android">
  <PreferenceCategory android:title="Simple Preferences">
    <CheckBoxPreference
      android:key="@string/checkbox"
      android:title="Checkbox Preference"
      android:summary="Check it on, check it off"
    />
    <RingtonePreference
      android:key="@string/ringtone"
      android:title="Ringtone Preference"
      android:showDefault="true"
      android:showSilent="true"
      android:summary="Pick a tone, any tone"
    />
  </PreferenceCategory>
  <PreferenceCategory android:title="Detail Screens">
    <PreferenceScreen
      android:key="detail"
      android:title="Detail Screen"
      android:summary="Additional preferences held in another page">
      <CheckBoxPreference
        android:key="@string/checkbox2"
        android:title="Another Checkbox"
        android:summary="On. Off. It really doesn't matter."
      />
    </PreferenceScreen>
  </PreferenceCategory>
  <PreferenceCategory android:title="Simple Preferences">
    <EditTextPreference
      android:key="@string/text"
      android:title="Text Entry Dialog"
      android:summary="Click to pop up a field for entry"
      android:dialogTitle="Enter something useful"
    />
```

```
    <ListPreference
      android:key="@string/list"
      android:title="Selection Dialog"
      android:summary="Click to pop up a list to choose from"
      android:entries="@array/cities"
      android:entryValues="@array/airport_codes"
      android:dialogTitle="Choose a Pennsylvania city" />
  </PreferenceCategory>
</PreferenceScreen>
```

With the field (`EditTextPreference`), in addition to the title and summary you put on the preference itself, you can also supply the title to use for the dialog.

With the list (`ListPreference`), you supply both a dialog title and two string-array resources: one for the display names, one for the values. These need to be in the same order— the index of the chosen display name determines which value is stored as the preference in the `SharedPreferences`. For example, here are the arrays for use by the `ListPreference` shown previously:

```
<?xml version="1.0" encoding="utf-8"?>
<resources>
  <string-array name="cities">
    <item>Philadelphia</item>
    <item>Pittsburgh</item>
    <item>Allentown/Bethlehem</item>
    <item>Erie</item>
    <item>Reading</item>
    <item>Scranton</item>
    <item>Lancaster</item>
    <item>Altoona</item>
    <item>Harrisburg</item>
  </string-array>
  <string-array name="airport_codes">
    <item>PHL</item>
    <item>PIT</item>
    <item>ABE</item>
    <item>ERI</item>
    <item>RDG</item>
    <item>AVP</item>
    <item>LNS</item>
    <item>AOO</item>
    <item>MDT</item>
  </string-array>
</resources>
```

When you bring up the preference UI, you start with another category with another pair of preference entries (see Figure 17-6).

Figure 17-6. *The preference screen of the Dialogs project's preference UI*

Tapping the Text Entry Dialog preference brings up . . . a text-entry dialog—in this case, with the prior preference entry pre–filled in (Figure 17-7).

Figure 17-7. *Editing a text preference*

Tapping the Selection Dialog preference brings up . . . a selection dialog, showing the display names (Figure 17-8).

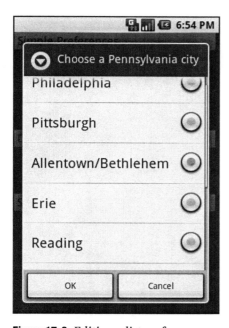

Figure 17-8. *Editing a list preference*

CHAPTER 18

■ ■ ■

Accessing Files

While Android offers structured storage, via preferences and databases, sometimes a simple file will suffice. Android offers two models for accessing files: one for files pre-packaged with your application, and one for files created on-device by your application.

You and the Horse You Rode in On

Let's suppose you have some static data you want to ship with the application, such as a list of words for a spell-checker. The easiest way to deploy that is to put the file in the res/raw directory, so it gets put in the Android application APK file as part of the packaging process as a raw resource.

To access this file, you need a Resources object. From an activity, that is as simple as calling getResources(). A Resources object offers openRawResource() to get an InputStream on the file you specify. Rather than a path, openRawResource() expects an integer identifier for the file as packaged. This works just like accessing widgets via findViewById()—if you put a file named words.xml in res/raw, the identifier is accessible in Java as R.raw.words.

Since you can get only an InputStream, you have no means of modifying this file. Hence, it is really useful only for static reference data. Moreover, since it is unchanging until the user installs an updated version of your application package, either the reference data has to be valid for the foreseeable future, or you need to provide some means of updating the data. The simplest way to handle that is to use the reference data to bootstrap some other modifiable form of storage (e.g., a database), but this makes for two copies of the data in storage. An alternative is to keep the reference data as is but keep modifications in a file or database, and merge them together when you need a complete picture of the information. For example, if your application ships a file of URLs, you could have a second file that tracks URLs added by the user or reference URLs that were deleted by the user.

In the Files/Static sample project available in the Source Code section of http://apress.com, you will find a reworking of the listbox example from Chapter 8, this time using a static XML file instead of a hard-wired array in Java. The layout is the same:

```
<?xml version="1.0" encoding="utf-8"?>
<LinearLayout xmlns:android="http://schemas.android.com/apk/res/android"
  android:orientation="vertical"
  android:layout_width="fill_parent"
  android:layout_height="fill_parent" >
```

```
  <TextView
    android:id="@+id/selection"
    android:layout_width="fill_parent"
    android:layout_height="wrap_content"
  />
  <ListView
    android:id="@android:id/list"
    android:layout_width="fill_parent"
    android:layout_height="fill_parent"
    android:drawSelectorOnTop="false"
  />
</LinearLayout>
```

In addition to that XML file, you need an XML file with the words to show in the list:

```
<words>
  <word value="lorem" />
  <word value="ipsum" />
  <word value="dolor" />
  <word value="sit" />
  <word value="amet" />
  <word value="consectetuer" />
  <word value="adipiscing" />
  <word value="elit" />
  <word value="morbi" />
  <word value="vel" />
  <word value="ligula" />
  <word value="vitae" />
  <word value="arcu" />
  <word value="aliquet" />
  <word value="mollis" />
  <word value="etiam" />
  <word value="vel" />
  <word value="erat" />
  <word value="placerat" />
  <word value="ante" />
  <word value="porttitor" />
  <word value="sodales" />
  <word value="pellentesque" />
  <word value="augue" />
  <word value="purus" />
</words>
```

While this XML structure is not exactly a model of space efficiency, it will suffice for a demo.

The Java code now must read in that XML file, parse out the words, and put them some-place for the list to pick up:

```
public class StaticFileDemo extends ListActivity {
  TextView selection;
  ArrayList<String> items=new ArrayList<String>();

  @Override
  public void onCreate(Bundle icicle) {
    super.onCreate(icicle);
    setContentView(R.layout.main);
    selection=(TextView)findViewById(R.id.selection);

    try {
      InputStream in=getResources().openRawResource(R.raw.words);
      DocumentBuilder builder=DocumentBuilderFactory
                                  .newInstance()
                                  .newDocumentBuilder();
      Document doc=builder.parse(in, null);
      NodeList words=doc.getElementsByTagName("word");

      for (int i=0;i<words.getLength();i++) {
        items.add(((Element)words.item(i)).getAttribute("value"));
      }

      in.close();
    }
    catch (Throwable t) {
      Toast
        .makeText(this, "Exception: "+t.toString(), 2000)
        .show();
    }

    setListAdapter(new ArrayAdapter<String>(this,
                             android.R.layout.simple_list_item_1,
                             items));
  }

  public void onListItemClick(ListView parent, View v, int position,
               long id) {
    selection.setText(items.get(position).toString());
  }
}
```

The differences between the Chapter 8 example and this one mostly lie within onCreate().
We get an InputStream for the XML file (getResources().openRawResource(R.raw.words)), then
use the built-in XML parsing logic to parse the file into a DOM Document, pick out the word
elements, then pour the value attributes into an ArrayList for use by the ArrayAdapter.

The resulting activity looks the same as before (Figure 18-1), since the list of words is the
same, just relocated.

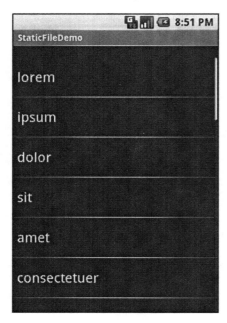

Figure 18-1. *The StaticFileDemo sample application*

Of course, there are even easier ways to have XML files available to you as pre-packaged files, such as by using an XML resource. That is covered in the next chapter. However, while this example uses XML, the file could just as easily have been a simple one-word-per-line list, or in some other format not handled natively by the Android resource system.

Readin' 'n' Writin'

Reading and writing your own, application-specific data files is nearly identical to what you might do in a desktop Java application. The key is to use openFileInput() and openFileOutput() on your Activity or other Context to get an InputStream and OutputStream, respectively. From that point forward, the process is not much different from using regular Java I/O logic:

- Wrap those streams as needed, such as using an InputStreamReader or OutputStreamWriter for text-based I/O.
- Read or write the data.
- Use close() to release the stream when done.

If two applications both try reading a notes.txt file via openFileInput(), they will each access their own edition of the file. If you need to have one file accessible from many places, you probably want to create a content provider, as will be described in Chapter 28.

Note that openFileInput() and openFileOutput() do not accept file paths (e.g., path/to/file.txt), just simple filenames.

The following code shows the layout for the world's most trivial text editor, pulled from the Files/ReadWrite sample application available on the Apress Web site:

```xml
<?xml version="1.0" encoding="utf-8"?>
<LinearLayout xmlns:android="http://schemas.android.com/apk/res/android"
  android:layout_width="fill_parent"
  android:layout_height="fill_parent"
  android:orientation="vertical">
  <Button android:id="@+id/close"
    android:layout_width="wrap_content"
    android:layout_height="wrap_content"
    android:text="Close" />
  <EditText
    android:id="@+id/editor"
    android:layout_width="fill_parent"
    android:layout_height="fill_parent"
    android:singleLine="false"
    />
</LinearLayout>
```

All we have here is a large text-editing widget with a Close button above it. The Java is only slightly more complicated:

```java
package com.commonsware.android.files;

import android.app.Activity;
import android.os.Bundle;
import android.view.View;
import android.widget.Button;
import android.widget.EditText;
import android.widget.Toast;
import java.io.BufferedReader;
import java.io.File;
import java.io.InputStream;
import java.io.InputStreamReader;
import java.io.OutputStream;
import java.io.OutputStreamWriter;

public class ReadWriteFileDemo extends Activity {
  private final static String NOTES="notes.txt";
  private EditText editor;

  @Override
  public void onCreate(Bundle icicle) {
    super.onCreate(icicle);
    setContentView(R.layout.main);
    editor=(EditText)findViewById(R.id.editor);
```

```
      Button btn=(Button)findViewById(R.id.close);

      btn.setOnClickListener(new Button.OnClickListener() {
        public void onClick(View v) {
          finish();
        }
      });
    }

    public void onResume() {
      super.onResume();

      try {
        InputStream in=openFileInput(NOTES);

        if (in!=null) {
          InputStreamReader tmp=new InputStreamReader(in);
          BufferedReader reader=new BufferedReader(tmp);
          String str;
          StringBuffer buf=new StringBuffer();

          while ((str = reader.readLine()) != null) {
            buf.append(str+"\n");
          }

          in.close();
          editor.setText(buf.toString());
        }
      }
      catch (java.io.FileNotFoundException e) {
        // that's OK, we probably haven't created it yet
      }
      catch (Throwable t) {
        Toast
          .makeText(this, "Exception: "+t.toString(), 2000)
          .show();
      }
    }

    public void onPause() {
      super.onPause();

      try {
        OutputStreamWriter out=
            new OutputStreamWriter(openFileOutput(NOTES, 0));
```

```
      out.write(editor.getText().toString());
      out.close();
    }
    catch (Throwable t) {
      Toast
        .makeText(this, "Exception: "+t.toString(), 2000)
        .show();
    }
  }
}
```

First we wire up the button to close out our activity when it's clicked, by using setOnClickListener() to invoke finish() on the activity.

Next we hook into onResume() so we get control when our editor is coming to life, from a fresh launch or after having been frozen. We use openFileInput() to read in notes.txt and pour the contents into the text editor. If the file is not found, we assume this is the first time the activity was run (or that the file was deleted by other means), and we just leave the editor empty.

Finally we hook into onPause() so we get control as our activity gets hidden by another activity or is closed, such as via our Close button. Here we use openFileOutput() to open notes.txt, into which we pour the contents of the text editor.

The net result is that we have a persistent notepad: whatever is typed in will remain until deleted, surviving our activity being closed, the phone being turned off, and similar situations.

■ ■ ■

CHAPTER 19

Working with Resources

Resources are static bits of information held outside the Java source code. You have seen one type of resource—the layout—frequently in the examples in this book. There are many other types of resource, such as images and strings, that you can take advantage of in your Android applications.

The Resource Lineup

Resources are stored as files under the `res/` directory in your Android project layout. With the exception of raw resources (`res/raw/`), all the other types of resources are parsed for you, either by the Android packaging system or by the Android system on the device or emulator. For example, when you lay out an activity's UI via a layout resource (`res/layout/`), you do not have to parse the layout XML yourself—Android handles that for you.

In addition to layout resources (first seen in Chapter 5) and raw resources (introduced in Chapter 18), there are several other types of resources available to you, including:

- Animations (`res/anim/`), designed for short clips as part of a user interface, such as an animation suggesting the turning of a page when a button is clicked

- Images (`res/drawable`), for putting static icons or other pictures in an user interface

- Strings, colors, arrays, and dimensions (`res/values/`), to both give these sorts of constants symbolic names and to keep them separate from the rest of the code (e.g., for internationalization and localization)

- XML (`res/xml/`), for static XML files containing your own data and structure

String Theory

Keeping your labels and other bits of text outside the main source code of your application is generally considered to be a very good idea. In particular, it helps with internationalization (I18N) and localization (L10N), covered in the section "Different Strokes for Different Folks" later on in this chapter. Even if you are not going to translate your strings to other languages, it is easier to make corrections if all the strings are in one spot instead of scattered throughout your source code.

Android supports regular externalized strings, along with "string formats", where the string has placeholders for dynamically-inserted information. On top of that, Android supports simple text formatting, called "styled text", so you can make your words be bold or italic intermingled with normal text.

Plain Strings

Generally speaking, all you need to have for plain strings is an XML file in the res/values directory (typically named res/values/strings.xml), with a resources root element, and one child string element for each string you wish to encode as a resource. The string element takes a name attribute, which is the unique name for this string, and a single text element containing the text of the string:

```
<resources>
  <string name="quick">The quick brown fox...</string>
  <string name="laughs">He who laughs last...</string>
</resources>
```

The only tricky part is if the string value contains a quote (") or an apostrophe ('). In those cases, you will want to escape those values, by preceding them with a backslash (e.g., These are the times that try men\'s souls). Or, if it is just an apostrophe, you could enclose the value in quotes (e.g., "These are the times that try men's souls.").

You can then reference this string from a layout file (as @string/..., where the ellipsis is the unique name—e.g., @string/laughs). Or you can get the string from your Java code by calling getString() with the resource ID of the string resource, that being the unique name prefixed with R.string. (e.g., getString(R.string.quick)).

String Formats

As with other implementations of the Java language, Android's Dalvik VM supports string formats. Here, the string contains placeholders representing data to be replaced at runtime by variable information (e.g., My name is %1$s). Plain strings stored as resources can be used as string formats:

```
String strFormat=getString(R.string.my_name);
String strResult=String.format(strFormat, "Tim");
((TextView)findViewById(R.layout.some_label))
  .setText(strResult);
```

Styled Text

If you want really rich text, you should have raw resources containing HTML, then pour those into a WebKit widget. However, for light HTML formatting, using <b>, <i>, and <u>, you can just use a string resource:

```
<resources>
  <string name="b">This has <b>bold</b> in it.</string>
  <string name="i">Whereas this has <i>italics</i>!</string>
</resources>
```

You can access these the same as with plain strings, with the exception that the result of the getString() call is really an object supporting the android.text.Spanned interface:

```
((TextView)findViewById(R.layout.another_label))
        .setText(getString(R.string.laughs));
```

Styled Formats

Where styled text gets tricky is with styled string formats, as String.format() works on String objects, not Spanned objects with formatting instructions. If you really want to have styled string formats, here is the workaround:

1. Entity-escape the angle brackets in the string resource (e.g., this is <b>%1$s</b>).

2. Retrieve the string resource as normal, though it will not be styled at this point (e.g., getString(R.string.funky_format)).

3. Generate the format results, being sure to escape any string values you substitute in, in case they contain angle brackets or ampersands.

   ```
   String.format(getString(R.string.funky_format),
               TextUtils.htmlEncode(strName));
   ```

4. Convert the entity-escaped HTML into a Spanned object via Html.fromHtml().

   ```
   someTextView.setText(Html
                   .fromHtml(resultFromStringFormat));
   ```

To see this in action, let's look at the Resources/Strings demo, which can be found in the Source Code area of http://apress.com. Here is the layout file:

```xml
<?xml version="1.0" encoding="utf-8"?>
<LinearLayout xmlns:android="http://schemas.android.com/apk/res/android"
  android:orientation="vertical"
  android:layout_width="fill_parent"
  android:layout_height="fill_parent"
  >
  <LinearLayout xmlns:android="http://schemas.android.com/apk/res/android"
    android:orientation="horizontal"
    android:layout_width="fill_parent"
    android:layout_height="wrap_content"
    >
  <Button android:id="@+id/format"
    android:layout_width="wrap_content"
    android:layout_height="wrap_content"
    android:text="@string/btn_name"
    />
  <EditText android:id="@+id/name"
    android:layout_width="fill_parent"
    android:layout_height="wrap_content"
    />
```

```
    </LinearLayout>
    <TextView android:id="@+id/result"
      android:layout_width="fill_parent"
      android:layout_height="wrap_content"
      />
</LinearLayout>
```

As you can see, it is just a button, a field, and a label. The intent is for somebody to enter their name in the field, then click the button to cause the label to be updated with a formatted message containing their name.

The Button in the layout file references a string resource (@string/btn_name), so we need a string resource file (res/values/strings.xml):

```
<?xml version="1.0" encoding="utf-8"?>
<resources>
  <string name="app_name">StringsDemo</string>
  <string name="btn_name">Name:</string>
  <string name="funky_format">My name is &lt;b&gt;%1$s&lt;/b&gt;</string>
</resources>
```

The app_name resource is automatically created by the activityCreator script. The btn_name string is the caption of the Button, while our styled string format is in funky_format.

Finally, to hook all this together, we need a pinch of Java:

```
package com.commonsware.android.resources;

import android.app.Activity;
import android.os.Bundle;
import android.text.TextUtils;
import android.text.Html;
import android.view.View;
import android.widget.Button;
import android.widget.EditText;
import android.widget.TextView;

public class StringsDemo extends Activity {
  EditText name;
  TextView result;

  @Override
  public void onCreate(Bundle icicle) {
    super.onCreate(icicle);
    setContentView(R.layout.main);

    name=(EditText)findViewById(R.id.name);
    result=(TextView)findViewById(R.id.result);

    Button btn=(Button)findViewById(R.id.format);
```

```
    btn.setOnClickListener(new Button.OnClickListener() {
      public void onClick(View v) {
        applyFormat();
      }
    });
  }

  private void applyFormat() {
    String format=getString(R.string.funky_format);
    String simpleResult=String.format(format,
                   TextUtils.htmlEncode(name.getText().toString()));
    result.setText(Html.fromHtml(simpleResult));
  }
}
```

The string resource manipulation can be found in applyFormat(), which is called when the button is clicked. First, we get our format via getString()—something we could have done at onCreate() time for efficiency. Next, we format the value in the field using this format, getting a String back, since the string resource is in entity-encoded HTML. Note the use of TextUtils. htmlEncode() to entity-encode the entered name, in case somebody decides to use an ampersand or something. Finally, we convert the simple HTML into a styled text object via Html.fromHtml() and update our label.

When the activity is first launched, we have an empty label (see Figure 19-1).

Figure 19-1. *The StringsDemo sample application, as initially launched*

However, if we fill in a name and click the button, we get the result seen in Figure 19-2.

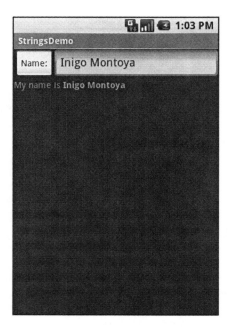

Figure 19-2. *The same application, after filling in some heroic figure's name*

Get the Picture?

Android supports images in the PNG, JPEG, and GIF formats. GIF is officially discouraged, however; PNG is the overall preferred format. Images can be used anywhere that requires a Drawable, such as the image and background of an ImageView.

Using images is simply a matter of putting your image files in res/drawable/ and then referencing them as a resource. Within layout files, images are referenced as @drawable/... where the ellipsis is the base name of the file (e.g., for res/drawable/foo.png, the resource name is @drawable/foo). In Java, where you need an image resource ID, use R.drawable. plus the base name (e.g., R.drawable.foo).

If you need a Uri to an image resource, you can use one of two different string formats for the path:

- `android.resource://com.example.app/...`, where `com.example.app` is the name of the Java package used by your application in `AndroidManifest.xml` and `...` is the numeric resource ID for the resource in question (e.g., the value of `R.drawable.foo`)

- `android.resource://com.example.app/raw/...`, where `com.example.app` is the name of the Java package used by your application in `AndroidManifest.xml` and `...` is the textual name of the raw resource (e.g., `foo` for `res/drawable/foo.png`)

Note that Android ships with some image resources built in. Those are addressed in Java with an `android.R.drawable` prefix to distinguish them from application-specific resources (e.g., `android.R.drawable.picture_frame`).

Let's update the previous example to use an icon for the button instead of the string resource. This can be found as `Resources/Images`. First, we slightly adjust the layout file, using an `ImageButton` and referencing a drawable named `@drawable/icon`:

```xml
<?xml version="1.0" encoding="utf-8"?>
<LinearLayout xmlns:android="http://schemas.android.com/apk/res/android"
  android:orientation="vertical"
  android:layout_width="fill_parent"
  android:layout_height="fill_parent"
  >
  <LinearLayout xmlns:android="http://schemas.android.com/apk/res/android"
    android:orientation="horizontal"
    android:layout_width="fill_parent"
    android:layout_height="wrap_content"
    >
    <ImageButton android:id="@+id/format"
      android:layout_width="wrap_content"
      android:layout_height="wrap_content"
      android:src="@drawable/icon"
      />
    <EditText android:id="@+id/name"
      android:layout_width="fill_parent"
      android:layout_height="wrap_content"
      />
  </LinearLayout>
  <TextView android:id="@+id/result"
    android:layout_width="fill_parent"
    android:layout_height="wrap_content"
    />
</LinearLayout>
```

Next, we need to put an image file in res/drawable with a base name of icon. In this case, we use a 32×32 PNG file from the Nuvola[1] icon set. Finally, we twiddle the Java source, replacing our Button with an ImageButton:

```
package com.commonsware.android.resources;

import android.app.Activity;
import android.os.Bundle;
import android.text.TextUtils;
import android.text.Html;
import android.view.View;
import android.widget.Button;
import android.widget.ImageButton;
import android.widget.EditText;
import android.widget.TextView;

public class ImagesDemo extends Activity {
  EditText name;
  TextView result;

  @Override
  public void onCreate(Bundle icicle) {
    super.onCreate(icicle);
    setContentView(R.layout.main);

    name=(EditText)findViewById(R.id.name);
    result=(TextView)findViewById(R.id.result);

    ImageButton btn=(ImageButton)findViewById(R.id.format);

    btn.setOnClickListener(new Button.OnClickListener() {
      public void onClick(View v) {
        applyFormat();
      }
    });
  }

  private void applyFormat() {
    String format=getString(R.string.funky_format);
    String simpleResult=String.format(format,
                  TextUtils.htmlEncode(name.getText().toString()));
    result.setText(Html.fromHtml(simpleResult));
  }
}
```

---

1. http://en.wikipedia.org/wiki/Nuvola

Now, our button has the desired icon (see Figure 19-3).

Figure 19-3. *The ImagesDemo sample application*

XML: The Resource Way

In Chapter 18, we showed how you can package XML files as raw resources and get access to them for parsing and usage. There is another way of packaging static XML with your application: the XML resource.

Simply put the XML file in res/xml/, and you can access it by getXml() on a Resources object, supplying it a resource ID of R.xml. plus the base name of your XML file. So, in an activity, with an XML file of words.xml, you could call getResources().getXml(R.xml.words).

This returns an instance of the currently-undocumented XmlPullParser, found in the org.xmlpull.v1 Java namespace. Documentation for this library can be found at the parser's site[2] as of this writing.

An XML pull parser is event-driven: you keep calling next() on the parser to get the next event, which could be START_TAG, END_TAG, END_DOCUMENT, etc. On a START_TAG event, you can access the tag's name and attributes; a single TEXT event represents the concatenation of all text nodes that are direct children of this element. By looping, testing, and invoking per-element logic, you parse the file.

To see this in action, let's rewrite the Java code for the Files/Static sample project to use an XML resource. This new project, Resources/XML, requires that you place the words.xml file from Static not in res/raw/, but in res/xml/. The layout stays the same, so all that needs replacing is the Java source:

---

2. http://www.xmlpull.org/v1/doc/api/org/xmlpull/v1/package-summary.html

```java
package com.commonsware.android.resources;

import android.app.Activity;
import android.os.Bundle;
import android.app.ListActivity;
import android.view.View;
import android.widget.AdapterView;
import android.widget.ArrayAdapter;
import android.widget.ListView;
import android.widget.TextView;
import android.widget.Toast;
import java.io.InputStream;
import java.util.ArrayList;
import org.xmlpull.v1.XmlPullParser;
import org.xmlpull.v1.XmlPullParserException;

public class XMLResourceDemo extends ListActivity {
  TextView selection;
  ArrayList<String> items=new ArrayList<String>();

  @Override
  public void onCreate(Bundle icicle) {
    super.onCreate(icicle);
    setContentView(R.layout.main);
    selection=(TextView)findViewById(R.id.selection);

    try {
      XmlPullParser xpp=getResources().getXml(R.xml.words);

      while (xpp.getEventType()!=XmlPullParser.END_DOCUMENT) {
        if (xpp.getEventType()==XmlPullParser.START_TAG) {
          if (xpp.getName().equals("word")) {
            items.add(xpp.getAttributeValue(0));
          }
        }

        xpp.next();
      }
    }
    catch (Throwable t) {
      Toast
        .makeText(this, "Request failed: "+t.toString(), 4000)
        .show();
    }
```

```
    setListAdapter(new ArrayAdapter<String>(this,
                        android.R.layout.simple_list_item_1,
                        items));
  }

  public void onListItemClick(ListView parent, View v, int position,
                   long id) {
    selection.setText(items.get(position).toString());
  }
}
```

Now, inside our try...catch block, we get our XmlPullParser and loop until the end of the document. If the current event is START_TAG and the name of the element is word (xpp.getName(). equals("word")), then we get the one-and-only attribute and pop that into our list of items for the selection widget. Since we're in complete control over the XML file, it is safe enough to assume there is exactly one attribute. But, if you were not as comfortable that the XML is properly defined, you might consider checking the attribute count (getAttributeCount()) and the name of the attribute (getAttributeName()) before blindly assuming the 0-index attribute is what you think it is.

As you can see in Figure 19-4, the result looks the same as before, albeit with a different name in the title bar.

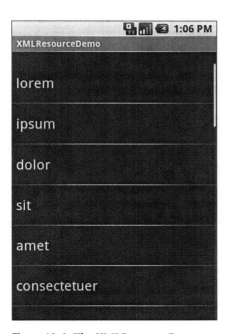

Figure 19-4. *The XMLResourceDemo sample application*

Miscellaneous Values

In the res/values/ directory, you can place one (or more) XML files describing simple resources: dimensions, colors, and arrays. We have already seen uses of dimensions and colors in previous examples, where they were passed as simple strings (e.g., "10px") as parameters to calls. You can, of course, set these up as Java static final objects and use their symbolic names . . . but this only works inside Java source, not in layout XML files. By putting these values in resource XML files, you can reference them from both Java and layouts, plus have them centrally located for easy editing.

Resource XML files have a root element of resources; everything else is a child of that root.

Dimensions

Dimensions are used in several places in Android to describe distances, such as a widget's padding. While this book usually uses pixels (e.g., 10px for ten pixels), there are several different units of measurement available to you:

- in and mm for inches and millimeters, respectively, based on the actual size of the screen

- pt for points, which in publishing terms is 1/72nd of an inch (again, based on the actual physical size of the screen)

- dp and sp for device-independent pixels and scale-independent pixels—one pixel equals one dp for a 160dpi resolution screen, with the ratio scaling based on the actual screen pixel density (scale-independent pixels also take into account the user's preferred font size)

To encode a dimension as a resource, add a dimen element, with a name attribute for your unique name for this resource, and a single child text element representing the value:

```
<resources>
  <dimen name="thin">10px</dimen>
  <dimen name="fat">1in</dimen>
</resources>
```

In a layout, you can reference dimensions as @dimen/..., where the ellipsis is a placeholder for your unique name for the resource (e.g., thin and fat from the previous sample). In Java, you reference dimension resources by the unique name prefixed with R.dimen. (e.g., Resources.getDimen(R.dimen.thin)).

Colors

Colors in Android are hexadecimal RGB values, also optionally specifying an alpha channel. You have your choice of single-character hex values or double-character hex values, leaving you with four styles:

- #RGB

- #ARGB

- #RRGGBB

- #AARRGGBB

These work similarly to their counterparts in Cascading Style Sheets (CSS).

You can, of course, put these RGB values as string literals in Java source or layout resources. If you wish to turn them into resources, though, all you need to do is add color elements to the resources file, with a name attribute for your unique name for this color, and a single text element containing the RGB value itself:

```
<resources>
  <color name="yellow_orange">#FFD555</color>
  <color name="forest_green">#005500</color>
  <color name="burnt_umber">#8A3324</color>
</resources>
```

In a layout, you can reference colors as @color/..., replacing the ellipsis with your unique name for the color (e.g., burnt_umber). In Java, you reference color resources by the unique name prefixed with R.color. (e.g., Resources.getColor(R.color.forest_green)).

Arrays

Array resources are designed to hold lists of simple strings, such as a list of honorifics (Mr., Mrs., Ms., Dr., etc.).

In the resource file, you need one string-array element per array, with a name attribute for the unique name you are giving the array. Then, add one or more child item elements, each of which have a single text element with the value for that entry in the array:

```
<?xml version="1.0" encoding="utf-8"?>
<resources>
  <string-array name="cities">
    <item>Philadelphia</item>
    <item>Pittsburgh</item>
    <item>Allentown/Bethlehem</item>
    <item>Erie</item>
    <item>Reading</item>
    <item>Scranton</item>
    <item>Lancaster</item>
    <item>Altoona</item>
    <item>Harrisburg</item>
  </string-array>
  <string-array name="airport_codes">
    <item>PHL</item>
    <item>PIT</item>
    <item>ABE</item>
    <item>ERI</item>
    <item>RDG</item>
    <item>AVP</item>
    <item>LNS</item>
    <item>AOO</item>
    <item>MDT</item>
  </string-array>
</resources>
```

From your Java code, you can then use `Resources.getStringArray()` to get a `String[]` of the items in the list. The parameter to `getStringArray()` is your unique name for the array, prefixed with `R.array`. (e.g., `Resources.getStringArray(R.array.honorifics)`).

Different Strokes for Different Folks

One set of resources may not fit all situations where your application may be used. One obvious area comes with string resources and dealing with internationalization (I18N) and localization (L10N). Putting strings all in one language works fine—probably at least for the developer—but only covers one language.

That is not the only scenario where resources might need to differ, though. Here are others:

- **Screen orientation:** is the screen in a portrait orientation? Landscape? Is the screen square and, therefore, does not really have an orientation?

- **Screen size:** how many pixels does the screen have, so you can size your resources accordingly (e.g., large versus small icons)?

- **Touchscreen:** does the device have a touchscreen? If so, is the touchscreen set up to be used with a stylus or a finger?

- **Keyboard:** what keyboard does the user have (QWERTY, numeric, neither), either now or as an option?

- **Other input:** does the device have some other form of input, like a directional pad or click-wheel?

The way Android currently handles this is by having multiple resource directories, with the criteria for each embedded in their names.

Suppose, for example, you want to support strings in both English and Spanish. Normally, for a single-language setup, you would put your strings in a file named `res/values/strings.xml`. To support both English and Spanish, you would create two folders, `res/values-en` and `res/values-es`, where the value after the hyphen is the ISO 639-1[3] two-letter code for the language you want. Your English-language strings would go in `res/values-en/strings.xml` and the Spanish ones in `res/values-es/strings.xml`. Android will choose the proper file based on the user's device settings.

Seems easy, right?

Where things start to get complicated is when you need to use multiple disparate criteria for your resources. For example, let us suppose you want to develop both for the T-Mobile G1 and two currently-fictitious devices. One device (the Fictional One) has a VGA screen normally in a landscape orientation (640×480), an always-open QWERTY keyboard, a directional pad, but no touch-screen. The other device (the Fictional Two) has a G1-sized screen (320×480), a numeric keyboard but no QWERTY, a directional pad, and no touch-screen.

You may want to have somewhat different layouts for these devices, to take advantage of different screen real estate and different input options:

---

3. `http://en.wikipedia.org/wiki/ISO_639-1`

- You want different layouts for each combination of resolution and orientation

- You want different layouts for touch-screen devices versus ones without touch-screens

- You want different layouts for QWERTY versus non-QWERTY devices

Once you get into these sorts of situations, though, all sorts of rules come into play, such as:

- The configuration options (e.g., -en) have a particular order of precedence, and they must appear in the directory name in that order. The Android documentation[4] outlines the specific order in which these options can appear. For the purposes of this example, screen orientation must precede touchscreen type, which must precede screen size.

- There can only be one value of each configuration option category per directory.

- Options are case sensitive.

So, for the scenario described previously, in theory, we would need the following directories:

- `res/layout-port-notouch-qwerty-640x480`

- `res/layout-port-notouch-qwerty-480x320`

- `res/layout-port-notouch-12key-640x480`

- `res/layout-port-notouch-12key-480x320`

- `res/layout-port-notouch-nokeys-640x480`

- `res/layout-port-notouch-nokeys-480x320`

- `res/layout-port-stylus-qwerty-640x480`

- `res/layout-port-stylus-qwerty-480x320`

- `res/layout-port-stylus-12key-640x480`

- `res/layout-port-stylus-12key-480x320`

- `res/layout-port-stylus-nokeys-640x480`

- `res/layout-port-stylus-nokeys-480x320`

- `res/layout-port-finger-qwerty-640x480`

- `res/layout-port-finger-qwerty-480x320`

- `res/layout-port-finger-12key-640x480`

- `res/layout-port-finger-12key-480x320`

- `res/layout-port-finger-nokeys-640x480`

---

4. `http://code.google.com/android/devel/resources-i18n.html#AlternateResources`

- `res/layout-port-finger-nokeys-480x320`

- `res/layout-land-notouch-qwerty-640x480`

- `res/layout-land-notouch-qwerty-480x320`

- `res/layout-land-notouch-12key-640x480`

- `res/layout-land-notouch-12key-480x320`

- `res/layout-land-notouch-nokeys-640x480`

- `res/layout-land-notouch-nokeys-480x320`

- `res/layout-land-stylus-qwerty-640x480`

- `res/layout-land-stylus-qwerty-480x320`

- `res/layout-land-stylus-12key-640x480`

- `res/layout-land-stylus-12key-480x320`

- `res/layout-land-stylus-nokeys-640x480`

- `res/layout-land-stylus-nokeys-480x320`

- `res/layout-land-finger-qwerty-640x480`

- `res/layout-land-finger-qwerty-480x320`

- `res/layout-land-finger-12key-640x480`

- `res/layout-land-finger-12key-480x320`

- `res/layout-land-finger-nokeys-640x480`

- `res/layout-land-finger-nokeys-480x320`

Don't panic! We will shorten this list in just a moment!

Note that for many of these, the actual layout files will be identical. For example, we only care about touch-screen layouts being different than the other two layouts, but since we cannot combine those two, we would theoretically have to have separate directories with identical contents for `finger` and `stylus`.

Also note that there is nothing preventing you from also having a directory with the unadorned base name (`res/layout`). In fact, this is probably a good idea, in case future editions of the Android runtime introduce other configuration options you did not consider— having a default layout might make the difference between your application working or failing on that new device.

Now, we can "cheat" a bit, by decoding the rules Android uses for determining which, among a set of candidates, is the "right" resource directory to use:

1. First up, Android tosses out ones that are specifically invalid. So, for example, if the screen size of the device is 320×240, the 640x480 directories would be dropped as candidates, since they specifically call for some other size.

2. Next, Android counts the number of matches for each folder, and only pays attention to those with the most matches.

3. Finally, Android goes in the order of precedence of the options—in other words, it goes from left to right in the directory name.

So we could skate by with only the following configurations:

- `res/layout-port-notouch-qwerty-640x480`

- `res/layout-port-notouch-qwerty`

- `res/layout-port-notouch-640x480`

- `res/layout-port-notouch`

- `res/layout-port-qwerty-640x480`

- `res/layout-port-qwerty`

- `res/layout-port-640x480`

- `res/layout-port`

- `res/layout-land-notouch-qwerty-640x480`

- `res/layout-land-notouch-qwerty`

- `res/layout-land-notouch-640x480`

- `res/layout-land-notouch`

- `res/layout-land-qwerty-640x480`

- `res/layout-land-qwerty`

- `res/layout-land-640x480`

- `res/layout-land`

Here, we take advantage of the fact that specific matches take precedence over "unspecified" values. So, a device with a QWERTY keyboard will choose a resource with qwerty in the directory over a resource that does not specify its keyboard type. Combine that with the "most matches wins" rule, we see that res/layout-port will only match devices with 480×320 screens, no QWERTY keyboard, and a touch-screen in portrait orientation.

We could refine this even further, to only cover the specific devices we are targeting (the T-Mobile G1, the Fictional One, and the Fictional Two), plus take advantage of res/layout being the overall default:

- res/layout-port-notouch-640x480

- res/layout-port-notouch

- res/layout-land-notouch-640x480

- res/layout-land-notouch

- res/layout-land

- res/layout

Here, 640x480 differentiates the Fictional One from the other two devices, while notouch differentiates the Fictional Two from the T-Mobile G1.

CHAPTER 20

■ ■ ■

Managing and Accessing Local Databases

SQLite[1] is a very popular embedded database, as it combines a clean SQL interface with a very small memory footprint and decent speed. Moreover, it is public domain, so everyone can use it. Lots of firms (Adobe, Apple, Google, Sun, Symbian) and open-source projects (Mozilla, PHP, Python) all ship products with SQLite.

For Android, SQLite is "baked into" the Android runtime, so every Android application can create SQLite databases. Since SQLite uses a SQL interface, it is fairly straightforward to use for people with experience in other SQL-based databases. However, its native API is not JDBC, and JDBC might be too much overhead for a memory-limited device like a phone, anyway. Hence, Android programmers have a different API to learn—the good news is that it is not very difficult.

This chapter will cover the basics of SQLite use in the context of working on Android. It by no means is a thorough coverage of SQLite as a whole. If you want to learn more about SQLite and how to use it in environments other than Android, a fine book is *The Definitive Guide to SQLite*[2] by Mike Owens (Apress, 2006).

Activities will typically access a database via a content provider or service. Therefore, this chapter does not have a full example. You will find a full example of a content provider that accesses a database in Chapter 28.

A Quick SQLite Primer

SQLite, as the name suggests, uses a dialect of SQL for queries (SELECT), data manipulation (INSERT, et al), and data definition (CREATE TABLE, et al). SQLite has a few places where it deviates from the SQL-92 standard, no different than most SQL databases. The good news is that SQLite is so space-efficient that the Android runtime can include all of SQLite, not some arbitrary subset to trim it down to size.

The biggest difference from other SQL databases you will encounter is probably the data typing. While you can specify the data types for columns in a CREATE TABLE statement, and while SQLite will use those as a hint, that is as far as it goes. You can put whatever data you want

---

1. http://www.sqlite.org
2. http://www.amazon.com/Definitive-Guide-SQLite/dp/1590596730

in whatever column you want. Put a string in an INTEGER column? Sure! No problem! Vice versa? Works too! SQLite refers to this as "manifest typing," as described in the documentation:[3]

> *In manifest typing, the datatype is a property of the value itself, not of the column in which the value is stored. SQLite thus allows the user to store any value of any datatype into any column regardless of the declared type of that column.*

In addition, there is a handful of standard SQL features not supported in SQLite, notably FOREIGN KEY constraints, nested transactions, RIGHT OUTER JOIN and FULL OUTER JOIN, and some flavors of ALTER TABLE.

Beyond that, though, you get a full SQL system, complete with triggers, transactions, and the like. Stock SQL statements, like SELECT, work pretty much as you might expect.

If you are used to working with a major database, like Oracle, you may look upon SQLite as being a "toy" database. Please bear in mind that Oracle and SQLite are meant to solve different problems, and that you will not likely be seeing a full copy of Oracle on a phone any time soon.

Start at the Beginning

No databases are automatically supplied to you by Android. If you want to use SQLite, you have to create your own database, then populate it with your own tables, indexes, and data.

To create and open a database, your best option is to craft a subclass of SQLiteOpenHelper. This class wraps up the logic to create and upgrade a database, per your specifications, as needed by your application. Your subclass of SQLiteOpenHelper will need three methods:

- The constructor, chaining upward to the SQLiteOpenHelper constructor. This takes the Context (e.g., an Activity), the name of the database, an optional cursor factory (typically, just pass null), and an integer representing the version of the database schema you are using.

- onCreate(), which passes you a SQLiteDatabase object that you need to populate with tables and initial data, as appropriate.

- onUpgrade(), which passes you a SQLiteDatabase object and the old and new version numbers, so you can figure out how best to convert the database from the old schema to the new one. The simplest, albeit least friendly, approach is to simply drop the old tables and create new ones. This is covered in greater detail in Chapter 28.

The rest of this chapter will discuss how you actually create tables, insert data, drop tables, etc., and will show sample code from a SQLiteOpenHelper subclass.

To use your SQLiteOpenHelper subclass, create an instance and ask it to getReadableDatabase() or getWriteableDatabase(), depending upon whether or not you will be changing its contents:

```
db=(new DatabaseHelper(getContext())).getWritableDatabase();

return (db == null) ? false : true;
```

---

3. http://www.sqlite.org/different.html

This will return a `SQLiteDatabase` instance, which you can then use to query the database or modify its data.

When you are done with the database (e.g., your activity is being closed), simply call `close()` on the `SQLiteDatabase` to release your connection.

Setting the Table

For creating your tables and indexes, you will need to call `execSQL()` on your `SQLiteDatabase`, providing the DDL statement you wish to apply against the database. Barring a database error, this method returns nothing.

So, for example, you can use the following code:

```
db.execSQL("CREATE TABLE constants (_id INTEGER PRIMARY KEY AUTOINCREMENT,➥
  title TEXT, value REAL);");
```

This will create a table, named `constants`, with a primary key column named `_id` that is an auto-incremented integer (i.e., SQLite will assign the value for you when you insert rows), plus two data columns: `title` (text) and `value` (a float, or "real" in SQLite terms). SQLite will automatically create an index for you on your primary-key column—you could add other indices here via some `CREATE INDEX` statements, if you so chose.

Most likely, you will create tables and indexes when you first create the database, or possibly when the database needs upgrading to accommodate a new release of your application. If you do not change your table schemas, you might never drop your tables or indexes, but if you do, just use `execSQL()` to invoke `DROP INDEX` and `DROP TABLE` statements as needed.

Makin' Data

Given that you have a database and one or more tables, you probably want to put some data in them and such. You have two major approaches for doing this.

You can always use `execSQL()`, just like you did for creating the tables. The `execSQL()` method works for any SQL that does not return results, so it can handle `INSERT`, `UPDATE`, `DELETE`, etc. just fine. So, for example you could use this code:

```
db.execSQL("INSERT INTO widgets (name, inventory)"+
        "VALUES ('Sprocket', 5)");
```

Your alternative is to use the `insert()`, `update()`, and `delete()` methods on the `SQLiteDatabase` object. These are "builder" sorts of methods, in that they break down the SQL statements into discrete chunks, then take those chunks as parameters.

These methods make use of `ContentValues` objects, which implement a `Map`-esque interface, albeit one that has additional methods for working with SQLite types. For example, in addition to `get()` to retrieve a value by its key, you have `getAsInteger()`, `getAsString()`, and so forth.

The `insert()` method takes the name of the table, the name of one column as the *null column hack*, and a `ContentValues` with the initial values you want put into this row. The null column hack is for the case where the `ContentValues` instance is empty—the column named as the null column hack will be explicitly assigned the value `NULL` in the SQL `INSERT` statement generated by `insert()`.

```
ContentValues cv=new ContentValues();

cv.put(Constants.TITLE, "Gravity, Death Star I");
cv.put(Constants.VALUE, SensorManager.GRAVITY_DEATH_STAR_I);
db.insert("constants", getNullColumnHack(), cv);
```

The update() method takes the name of the table, a ContentValues representing the columns and replacement values to use, an optional WHERE clause, and an optional list of parameters to fill into the WHERE clause, to replace any embedded question marks (?). Since update() replaces only columns with fixed values, versus ones computed based on other information, you may need to use execSQL() to accomplish some ends.

The WHERE clause and parameter list work akin to the positional SQL parameters you may be used to from other SQL APIs. Consider this example:

```
// replacements is a ContentValues instance
String[] parms=new String[] {"snicklefritz"};
db.update("widgets", replacements, "name=?", parms);
```

The delete() method works akin to update(), taking the name of the table, the optional WHERE clause, and the corresponding parameters to fill into the WHERE clause.

What Goes Around Comes Around

As with INSERT, UPDATE, and DELETE, you have two main options for retrieving data from a SQLite database using SELECT:

- You can use rawQuery() to invoke a SELECT statement directly.

- You can use query() to build up a query from its component parts.

Confounding matters is the SQLiteQueryBuilder class and the issue of cursors and cursor factories. Let's take all of this one piece at a time.

Raw Queries

The simplest solution, at least in terms of the API, is rawQuery(). Simply call it with your SQL SELECT statement. The SELECT statement can include positional parameters; the array of these forms your second parameter to rawQuery(). So, we wind up with this:

```
Cursor c=db.rawQuery("SELECT name FROM sqlite_master WHERE type='table' AND ➡
  name='constants'", null);
```

In this example, we actually query a SQLite system table (sqlite_master) to see if our constants table already exists. The return value is a Cursor, which contains methods for iterating over results (see the "Using Cursors" section).

If your queries are pretty much baked into your application, this is a very straightforward way to use them. However, it gets complicated if parts of the query are dynamic, beyond what positional parameters can really handle. For example, if the set of columns you need to retrieve is not known at compile time, puttering around concatenating column names into a comma-delimited list can be annoying—which is where query() comes in.

Regular Queries

The query() method takes the discrete pieces of a SELECT statement and builds the query from them. The pieces, in the order they appear as parameters to query(), are as follows:

1. The name of the table to query against

2. The list of columns to retrieve

3. The WHERE clause, optionally including positional parameters

4. The list of values to substitute in for those positional parameters

5. The GROUP BY clause, if any

6. The ORDER BY clause, if any

7. The HAVING clause, if any

These can be null when they are not needed (except the table name, of course):

```
String[] columns={"ID", "inventory"};
String[] parms={"snicklefritz"};
Cursor result=db.query("widgets", columns, "name=?",
                        parms, null, null, null);
```

Building with Builders

Yet another option is to use SQLiteQueryBuilder, which offers much richer query-building options, particularly for nasty queries involving things like the union of multiple sub-query results. More importantly, the SQLiteQueryBuilder interface dovetails nicely with the ContentProvider interface for executing queries. Hence, a common pattern for your content provider's query() implementation is to create a SQLiteQueryBuilder, fill in some defaults, then allow it to build up (and optionally execute) the full query combining the defaults with what is provided to the content provider on the query request.

For example, here is a snippet of code from a content provider using SQLiteQueryBuilder:

```
@Override
public Cursor query(Uri url, String[] projection, String selection,
                    String[] selectionArgs, String sort) {
  SQLiteQueryBuilder qb=new SQLiteQueryBuilder();

  qb.setTables(getTableName());

  if (isCollectionUri(url)) {
    qb.setProjectionMap(getDefaultProjection());
  }
  else {
    qb.appendWhere(getIdColumnName()+"="+url.getPathSegments().get(1));
  }
```

```
    String orderBy;

    if (TextUtils.isEmpty(sort)) {
      orderBy=getDefaultSortOrder();
    } else {
      orderBy=sort;
    }

    Cursor c=qb.query(db, projection, selection, selectionArgs,
                      null, null, orderBy);
    c.setNotificationUri(getContext().getContentResolver(), url);
    return c;
}
```

Content providers are explained in greater detail in Part 5 of this book, so some of this you will have to take on faith until then. Here, we see the following:

1. A SQLiteQueryBuilder is constructed.

2. It is told the table to use for the query (setTables(getTableName())).

3. It is either told the default set of columns to return (setProjectionMap()), or is given a piece of a WHERE clause to identify a particular row in the table by an identifier extracted from the Uri supplied to the query() call (appendWhere()).

4. Finally, it is told to execute the query, blending the preset values with those supplied on the call to query() (qb.query(db, projection, selection, selectionArgs, null, null, orderBy)).

Instead of having the SQLiteQueryBuilder execute the query directly, we could have called buildQuery() to have it generate and return the SQL SELECT statement we needed, which we could then execute ourselves.

Using Cursors

No matter how you execute the query, you get a Cursor back. This is the Android/SQLite edition of the database cursor, a concept used in many database systems. With the cursor, you can do the following:

- Find out how many rows are in the result set via getCount()

- Iterate over the rows via moveToFirst(),moveToNext(), and isAfterLast()

- Find out the names of the columns via getColumnNames(), convert those into column numbers via getColumnIndex(), and get values for the current row for a given column via methods like getString(),getInt(), etc.

- Re-execute the query that created the cursor, via requery()

- Release the cursor's resources via close()

For example, here we iterate over the `widgets` table entries from the previous snippets:

```
Cursor result=
  db.rawQuery("SELECT ID, name, inventory FROM widgets");

result.moveToFirst();

while (!result.isAfterLast()) {
 int id=result.getInt(0);
 String name=result.getString(1);
 int inventory=result.getInt(2);

 // do something useful with these

 result.moveToNext();
}

result.close();
```

Making Your Own Cursors

There may be circumstances in which you want to use your own `Cursor` subclass rather than the stock implementation provided by Android. In those cases, you can use `queryWithFactory()` and `rawQueryWithFactory()`, which take a `SQLiteDatabase.CursorFactory` instance as a parameter. The factory, as one might expect, is responsible for creating new cursors via its `newCursor()` implementation.

Finding and implementing a valid use for this facility is left as an exercise for the reader. Suffice it to say that you should not need to create your own cursor classes much, if at all, in ordinary Android development.

Data, Data, Everywhere

If you are used to developing for other databases, you are also probably used to having tools to inspect and manipulate the contents of the database, beyond merely the database's API. With Android's emulator, you have two main options for this.

First, the emulator is supposed to bundle in the `sqlite3` console program and makes it available from the `adb shell` command. Once you are in the emulator's shell, just execute `sqlite3`, providing it the path to your database file. Your database file can be found at the following location:

```
/data/data/your.app.package/databases/your-db-name
```

Here `your.app.package` is the Java package for your application (e.g., `com.commonsware.android`) and `your-db-name` is the name of your database, as supplied to `createDatabase()`.

Note, however, that the Android 0.9 SDK appears to be missing the `sqlite3` command, though it has returned in Android 1.0.

The sqlite3 program works, and if you are used to poking around your tables using a console interface, you are welcome to use it. If you prefer something a little bit friendlier, you can always copy the SQLite database off the device onto your development machine, then use a SQLite-aware client program to putter around. Note, though, that you are working off a copy of the database; if you want your changes to go back to the device, you will need to transfer the database back over to the device.

To get the database off the device, you can use the adb pull command (or the equivalent in your IDE), which takes the path to the on-device database and the local destination as parameters. To store a modified database on the device, use adb push, which takes the local path to the database and the on-device destination as parameters.

One of the most accessible SQLite clients is the SQLite Manager[4] extension for Firefox (Figure 20-1), as it works across all platforms.

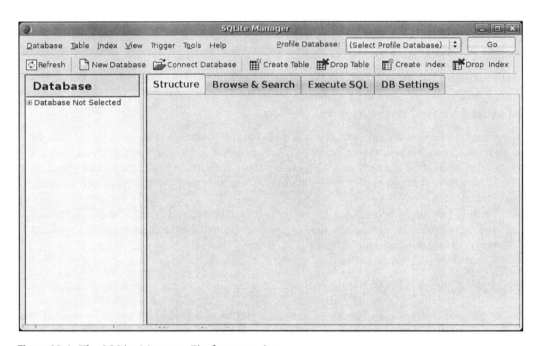

Figure 20-1. *The SQLite Manager Firefox extension*

You can find other client tools[5] on the SQLite Web site.[6]

---

4. https://addons.mozilla.org/en-US/firefox/addon/5817
5. http://www.sqlite.org/cvstrac/wiki?p=SqliteTools
6. http://www.sqlite.org

CHAPTER 21

■ ■ ■

Leveraging Java Libraries

Java has as many, if not more, third-party libraries than any other modern programming language. Here, "third-party libraries" refers to the innumerable JARs that you can include in a server or desktop Java application—the things that the Java SDKs themselves do not provide.

In the case of Android, the Dalvik Virtual Machine (Dalvik VM) at its heart is not precisely Java, and what it provides in its SDK is not precisely the same as any traditional Java SDK. That being said, many Java third-party libraries still provide capabilities that Android lacks natively and therefore the ones you can get working with Android's flavor of Java may be of use to you in your project.

This chapter explains what it will take for you to leverage such libraries, and the limitations on Android's support for arbitrary third-party code.

The Outer Limits

Not all available Java code, of course, will work well with Android. There are a number of factors to consider, including the following:

- *Expected Platform APIs*: Does the code assume a newer JVM than the one Android is based on? Or does the code assume the existence of Java APIs that ship with J2SE but not with Android, such as Swing?

- *Size*: Existing Java code designed for use on desktops or servers need not worry too much about on-disk size, or even in-RAM size. Android, of course, is short on both. Using third-party Java code, particularly when pre-packaged as JARs, may balloon the size of your application.

- *Performance*: Does the Java code effectively assume a much more powerful CPU than what you may find on many Android devices? Just because a desktop computer can run it without issue doesn't mean your average mobile phone will handle it well.

- *Interface*: Does the Java code assume a console interface? Or is it a pure API that you can wrap your own interface around?

One trick for addressing some of these concerns is to use open-source Java code, and actually work with the code to make it more Android-friendly. For example, if you're only using 10% of the third-party library, maybe it's worthwhile to recompile the subset of the project to be only what you need, or at least to remove the unnecessary classes from the JAR. The former approach is safer in that you get compiler help to make sure you're not discarding some essential piece of code, though it may be more tedious to do.

Ants and JARs

You have two choices for integrating third-party code into your project: use source code or use pre-packaged JARs.

If you choose to use the third-party source code, all you need to do is copy it into your own source tree (under `src/` in your project) so it can sit alongside your existing code, then let the compiler perform its magic.

If you choose to use an existing JAR, perhaps one for which you do not have the source code, you will need to teach your build chain how to use the JAR. If you are using an IDE, that's a matter of telling it to reference the JAR. If, on the other hand, you are not using an IDE and are relying upon the `build.xml` Ant script, put the JAR in the `libs/` directory created for you by `activityCreator`, and the Ant build process will pick it up.

For example, in a previous draft of this book, we had a MailBuzz project. MailBuzz, as the name suggests, dealt with email. It leveraged the JavaMail APIs and needed two JavaMail JARs: `mail-1.4.jar` and `activation-1.1.jar`. With both of those in the `libs/` directory, the `classpath` told `javac` to link against those JARs, so any JavaMail references in the MailBuzz code could be correctly resolved. Then, those JARs were listed, along with the MailBuzz compiled classes, in the task that invokes the `dex` tool to convert the Java code into Dalvik VM instructions. Without this step, even though your code may compile, it won't find the JavaMail classes at runtime and will fail with an exception.

As it turned out, though, the Dalvik VM and compiler supplied with the Android 0.9 and newer SDKs no longer supported some Java language features used by JavaMail. And, while the JavaMail source code is available, it is under an open-source license (Common Development and Distribution License; CDDL) that . . . has issues.

Following the Script

Unlike other mobile-device operating systems, Android has no restrictions on what you can run on it, so long as you can do it in Java using the Dalvik VM. This includes incorporating your own scripting language into your application, something that is expressly prohibited on some other devices.

One possible Java scripting language is BeanShell.[1] BeanShell gives you Java-compatible syntax with implicit typing and no compilation required.

So, to add BeanShell scripting, you need to put the BeanShell interpreter's JAR file in your `libs/` directory. The 2.0b4 JAR available for download from the BeanShell site, unfortunately, does not work out of the box with the Android 0.9 and newer SDKs, perhaps due to the compiler that was used to build it. Instead, you should probably check out the source code from Subversion[2] and execute `ant jarcore` to build it, then copy the resulting JAR (in BeanShell's `dist/` directory) to your own project's `libs/`. Or just use the BeanShell JAR that accompanies the source code for this book, in the `Java/AndShell` project available in the Source Code area at `http://apress.com`.

---

1. `http://beanshell.org`
2. `http://beanshell.org/developer.html`

From there, using BeanShell on Android is no different from using BeanShell in any other Java environment:

1. Create an instance of the BeanShell Interpreter class.

2. Set any globals for the script's use via Interpreter#set().

3. Call Interpreter#eval() to run the script and, optionally, get the result of the last statement.

For example, here is the XML layout for the world's smallest BeanShell IDE:

```xml
<?xml version="1.0" encoding="utf-8"?>
<LinearLayout xmlns:android="http://schemas.android.com/apk/res/android"
    android:orientation="vertical"
    android:layout_width="fill_parent"
    android:layout_height="fill_parent"
    >
<Button
    android:id="@+id/eval"
    android:layout_width="fill_parent"
    android:layout_height="wrap_content"
    android:text="Go!"
    />
<EditText
    android:id="@+id/script"
    android:layout_width="fill_parent"
    android:layout_height="fill_parent"
    android:singleLine="false"
    android:gravity="top"
    />
</LinearLayout>
```

Couple that with the following activity implementation:

```java
package com.commonsware.android.andshell;

import android.app.Activity;
import android.app.AlertDialog;
import android.os.Bundle;
import android.view.View;
import android.widget.Button;
import android.widget.EditText;
import android.widget.Toast;
import bsh.Interpreter;

public class MainActivity extends Activity {
  private Interpreter i=new Interpreter();
```

```java
@Override
public void onCreate(Bundle icicle) {
  super.onCreate(icicle);
  setContentView(R.layout.main);

  Button btn=(Button)findViewById(R.id.eval);
  final EditText script=(EditText)findViewById(R.id.script);

  btn.setOnClickListener(new View.OnClickListener() {
    public void onClick(View view) {
      String src=script.getText().toString();

      try {
        i.set("context", MainActivity.this);
        i.eval(src);
      }
      catch (bsh.EvalError e) {
        AlertDialog.Builder builder=
                  new AlertDialog.Builder(MainActivity.this);

        builder
          .setTitle("Exception!")
          .setMessage(e.toString())
          .setPositiveButton("OK", null)
          .show();
      }
    }
  });
}
}
```

Compile and run it (including incorporating the BeanShell JAR as mentioned earlier), and install it on the emulator. Fire it up, and you get a trivial IDE with a large text area for your script and a big Go! button (see Figure 21-1) to execute it.

```java
import android.widget.Toast;

Toast.makeText(context, "Hello, world!", 5000).show();
```

Note the use of context to refer to the activity when making the Toast. That is the global set by the activity to reference back to itself. You could call this global variable anything you want, so long as the set() call and the script code use the same name.

When you click the Go! button, you get the result shown in Figure 21-2.

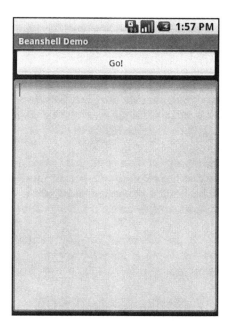

Figure 21-1. *The AndShell BeanShell IDE*

Figure 21-2. *The AndShell BeanShell IDE, executing some code*

And now, some caveats.

First, not all scripting languages will work. For example, those that implement their own form of just-in-time (JIT) compilation, generating Java bytecodes on the fly, would probably have to be augmented to generate Dalvik VM bytecodes instead of those for stock Java implementations. Simpler languages that execute from parsed scripts, calling Java reflection APIs to call back into compiled classes, will likely work better. Even there, though, not every feature of the language may work if the feature relies upon some facility in a traditional Java API that does not exist in Dalvik—for example, there could be stuff hidden inside BeanShell or the add-on JARs that does not work on today's Android.

Second, scripting languages without JIT will inevitably be slower than compiled Dalvik applications. Slower may mean users experience sluggishness. Slower definitely means more battery life is consumed for the same amount of work. So, building a whole Android application in BeanShell, simply because you feel it is easier to program in may cause your users to be unhappy.

Third, scripting languages that expose the whole Java API, like BeanShell, can pretty much do anything the underlying Android security model allows. So, if your application has the READ_CONTACTS permission, expect any BeanShell scripts your application runs to have the same permission.

Last, but certainly not least, is that language interpreter JARs tend to be . . . portly. The BeanShell JAR used in this example is 200KB. That is not ridiculous, considering what it does, but it will make applications that use BeanShell that much bigger to download, take up that much more space on the device, etc.

. . . And Not a Drop to Drink

Not all Java code will work on Android and Dalvik. Specifically consider the following:

- If the Java code assumes it runs on Java SE, Java ME, or Java EE, it may be missing some APIs that those platforms provide that Android does not. For example, some charting libraries assume the existence of Swing or Abstract Window Toolkit (AWT) drawing primitives, which are generally unavailable on Android.

- The Java code might have a dependency on other Java code that, in turn, might have problems running on Android. For example, you might want to use a JAR that relies upon an earlier (or newer) version of the Apache HTTPComponents than the one that is bundled with Android.

- The Java code may use language capabilities beyond what the Dalvik engine is capable of using.

In all these cases, if you have only a compiled JAR to work with, you may not encounter problems at compile time, but rather when running the application. Hence, where possible it is best to use open-source code with Android so you can build the third-party code alongside your own and find out about difficulties sooner.

CHAPTER 22

■■■

Communicating via the Internet

The expectation is that most, if not all, Android devices will have built-in Internet access. That could be WiFi, cellular data services (EDGE, 3G, etc.), or possibly something else entirely. Regardless, most people—or at least those with a data plan or WiFi access—will be able to get to the Internet from their Android phone.

Not surprisingly, the Android platform gives developers a wide range of ways to make use of this Internet access. Some offer high-level access, such as the integrated WebKit browser component we saw in Chapter 13. If you want, you can drop all the way down to using raw sockets. Or, in between, you can leverage APIs—both on-device and from 3rd-party JARs—that give you access to specific protocols: HTTP, XMPP, SMTP, and so on.

The emphasis of this book is on the higher-level forms of access: the WebKit component and Internet-access APIs, as busy coders should be trying to reuse existing components versus rolling one's own on-the-wire protocol wherever possible.

REST and Relaxation

Android does not have built-in SOAP or XML-RPC client APIs. However, it does have the Apache HttpComponents library baked in. You can either layer a SOAP/XML-RPC layer atop this library, or use it "straight" for accessing REST-style Web services. For the purposes of this book, "REST-style Web services" is defined as simple HTTP requests for ordinary URLs over the full range of HTTP verbs, with formatted payloads (XML, JSON, etc.) as responses.

More expansive tutorials, FAQs, and HOWTOs can be found at the HttpComponents Web site.[1] Here, we'll cover the basics, while checking the weather.

HTTP Operations via Apache HttpComponents

The HTTPClient component of HttpComponents handles all HTTP requests on your behalf. The first step to using HttpClient is, not surprisingly, to create an `HttpClient` object. Since `HttpClient` is an interface, you will need to actually instantiate some implementation of that interface, such as `DefaultHttpClient`.

---

1. `http://hc.apache.org/`

Those requests are bundled up into HttpRequest instances, with different HttpRequest implementations for each different HTTP verb (e.g., HttpGet for HTTP GET requests). You create an HttpRequest implementation instance, fill in the URL to retrieve and other configuration data (e.g., form values if you are doing an HTTP POST via HttpPost), then pass the method to the client to actually make the HTTP request via execute().

What happens at this point can be as simple or as complicated as you want. You can get an HttpResponse object back, with response code (e.g., 200 for OK), HTTP headers, and the like. Or, you can use a flavor of execute() that takes a ResponseHandler<String> as a parameter—the net result there being that execute() returns just the String representation of the request body. In practice, this is not a recommended approach, because you really should be checking your HTTP response codes for errors. However, for trivial applications, like book examples, the ResponseHandler<String> approach works just fine.

For example, let's take a look at the Internet/Weather sample project. This implements an activity that retrieves weather data for your current location from the National Weather Service (Note: this probably only works in the US). That data is converted into an HTML page, which is poured into a WebKit widget for display. Rebuilding this demo using a ListView is left as an exercise for the reader. Also, since this sample is relatively long, we will only show relevant pieces of the Java code here in this chapter, though you can always download the full source from the CommonsWare Web site.[2]

To make this a bit more interesting, we use the Android location services to figure out where we are . . . sort of. The full details of how that works is described in Chapter 33.

In the onResume() method, we toggle on location updates, so we will be informed where we are now and when we move a significant distance (10km). When a location is available—either at the start or based on movement—we retrieve the National Weather Service data via our updateForecast() method:

```
private void updateForecast(Location loc) {
  String url=String.format(format, loc.getLatitude(), loc.getLongitude());
  HttpGet getMethod=new HttpGet(url);

  try {
    ResponseHandler<String> responseHandler = new BasicResponseHandler();
    String responseBody=client.execute(getMethod, responseHandler);

    buildForecasts(responseBody);

    String page=generatePage();

    browser.loadDataWithBaseURL(null, page, "text/html",
                                "UTF-8", null);
  }
```

---

2. http://commonsware.com/Android/

```
  catch (Throwable t) {
    Toast
      .makeText(this, "Request failed: "+t.toString(), 4000)
      .show();
  }
}
```

The updateForecast() method takes a Location as a parameter, obtained from the location update process. For now, all you need to know is that Location sports getLatitude() and getLongitude() methods that return the latitude and longitude of the device's position, respectively.

We hold the URL to the National Weather Service XML in a string resource, and pour in the latitude and longitude at runtime. Given our HttpClient object created in onCreate(), we populate an HttpGet with that customized URL, then execute that method. Given the resulting XML from the REST service, we build the forecast HTML page (see "Parsing Responses") and pour that into the WebKit widget. If the HttpClient blows up with an exception, we provide that error as a Toast.

Parsing Responses

The response you get will be formatted using some system—HTML, XML, JSON, whatever. It is up to you, of course, to pick out what information you need and do something useful with it. In the case of the WeatherDemo, we need to extract the forecast time, temperature, and icon (indicating sky conditions and precipitation) and generate an HTML page from it.

Android includes:

- Three XML parsers: the traditional W3C DOM (org.w3c.dom), a SAX parser (org.xml.sax), and the XML pull parser discussed in Chapter 19

- A JSON parser (org.json)

You are also welcome to use third-party Java code, where possible, to handle other formats, such as a dedicated RSS/Atom parser for a feed reader. The use of third-party Java code is discussed in Chapter 21.

For WeatherDemo, we use the W3C DOM parser in our buildForecasts() method:

```
void buildForecasts(String raw) throws Exception {
  DocumentBuilder builder=DocumentBuilderFactory
                             .newInstance()
                             .newDocumentBuilder();
  Document doc=builder.parse(new InputSource(new StringReader(raw)));
  NodeList times=doc.getElementsByTagName("start-valid-time");
```

```java
for (int i=0;i<times.getLength();i++) {
  Element time=(Element)times.item(i);
  Forecast forecast=new Forecast();

  forecasts.add(forecast);
  forecast.setTime(time.getFirstChild().getNodeValue());
}

NodeList temps=doc.getElementsByTagName("value");

for (int i=0;i<temps.getLength();i++) {
  Element temp=(Element)temps.item(i);
  Forecast forecast=forecasts.get(i);

  forecast.setTemp(new Integer(temp.getFirstChild().getNodeValue()));
}

NodeList icons=doc.getElementsByTagName("icon-link");

for (int i=0;i<icons.getLength();i++) {
  Element icon=(Element)icons.item(i);
  Forecast forecast=forecasts.get(i);

  forecast.setIcon(icon.getFirstChild().getNodeValue());
}
}
```

The National Weather Service XML format is . . . curiously structured, relying heavily on sequential position in lists versus the more object-oriented style you find in formats like RSS or Atom. That being said, we can take a few liberties and simplify the parsing somewhat, taking advantage of the fact that the elements we want (start-valid-time for the forecast time, value for the temperature, and icon-link for the icon URL) are all unique within the document.

The HTML comes in as an InputStream and is fed into the DOM parser. From there, we scan for the start-valid-time elements and populate a set of Forecast models using those start times. Then, we find the temperature value elements and icon-link URLs and fill those into the Forecast objects.

In turn, the generatePage() method creates a rudimentary HTML table with the forecasts:

```java
String generatePage() {
  StringBuffer bufResult=new StringBuffer("<html><body><table>");

  bufResult.append("<tr><th width=\"50%\">Time</th>"+
                   "<th>Temperature</th><th>Forecast</th></tr>");

  for (Forecast forecast : forecasts) {
    bufResult.append("<tr><td align=\"center\">");
    bufResult.append(forecast.getTime());
    bufResult.append("</td><td align=\"center\">");
```

```
    bufResult.append(forecast.getTemp());
    bufResult.append("</td><td><img src=\"");
    bufResult.append(forecast.getIcon());
    bufResult.append("\"></td></tr>");
  }

  bufResult.append("</table></body></html>");

  return(bufResult.toString());
}
```

The result can be seen in Figure 22-1.

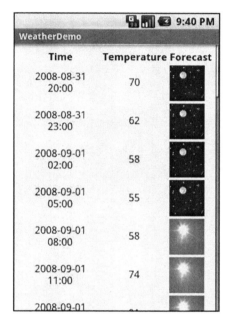

Figure 22-1. *The WeatherDemo sample application*

Stuff to Consider

If you need to use SSL, bear in mind that the default HttpClient setup does not include SSL support. Mostly, this is because you need to decide how to handle SSL certificate presentation—do you blindly accept all certificates, even self-signed or expired ones? Or do you want to ask the user if they really want to use some strange certificates?

Similarly, HttpClient, by default, is designed for single-threaded use. If you will be using HttpClient from a service or some other place where multiple threads might be an issue, you can readily set up HttpClient to support multiple threads.

For these sorts of topics, you are best served by checking out the HttpComponents Web site for documentation and support.

PART 4

Intents

CHAPTER 23

■ ■ ■

Creating Intent Filters

Up to now, the focus of this book has been on activities opened directly by the user from the device's launcher. This, of course, is the most obvious case for getting your activity up and visible to the user. In many cases it is the primary way the user will start using your application.

However, the Android system is based upon lots of loosely-coupled components. What you might accomplish in a desktop GUI via dialog boxes, child windows, and the like are mostly supposed to be independent activities. While one activity will be "special", in that it shows up in the launcher, the other activities all need to be reached . . . somehow.

The "how" is via intents.

An intent is basically a message that you pass to Android saying, "Yo! I want to do . . . er . . . something! Yeah!" How specific the "something" is depends on the situation—sometimes you know exactly what you want to do (e.g., open up one of your other activities), and sometimes you don't.

In the abstract, Android is all about intents and receivers of those intents. So, now that we are well-versed in creating activities, let's dive into intents, so we can create more complex applications while simultaneously being "good Android citizens."

What's Your Intent?

When Sir Tim Berners-Lee cooked up the Hypertext Transfer Protocol—HTTP—he set up a system of verbs plus addresses in the form of URLs. The address indicated a resource, such as a Web page, graphic, or server-side program. The verb indicated what should be done: GET to retrieve it, POST to send form data to it for processing, etc.

Intents are similar, in that they represent an action plus context. There are more actions and more components to the context with Android intents than there are with HTTP verbs and resources, but the concept is still the same.

Just as a Web browser knows how to process a verb + URL pair, Android knows how to find activities or other application logic that will handle a given intent.

Pieces of Intents

The two most important pieces of an intent are the action and what Android refers to as the "data". These are almost exactly analogous to HTTP verbs and URLs—the action is the verb, and the "data" is a Uri, such as `content://contacts/people/1` representing a contact in the contacts database. Actions are constants, such as `ACTION_VIEW` (to bring up a viewer for the resource), `ACTION_EDIT` (to edit the resource), or `ACTION_PICK` (to choose an available item given a Uri representing a collection, such as `content://contacts/people`).

If you were to create an intent combining ACTION_VIEW with a content Uri of content://
contacts/people/1, and pass that intent to Android, Android would know to find and open an
activity capable of viewing that resource.

There are other criteria you can place inside an intent (represented as an Intent object),
besides the action and "data" Uri, such as:

- A category. Your "main" activity will be in the LAUNCHER category, indicating it should
  show up on the launcher menu. Other activities will probably be in the DEFAULT or
  ALTERNATIVE categories.

- A MIME type, indicating the type of resource you want to operate on, if you don't know
  a collection Uri.

- A component, which is to say, the class of the activity that is supposed to receive this
  intent. Using components this way obviates the need for the other properties of the intent.
  However, it does make the intent more fragile, as it assumes specific implementations.

- "Extras", which is a Bundle of other information you want to pass along to the receiver
  with the intent, that the receiver might want to take advantage of. What pieces of information a given receiver can use is up to the receiver and (hopefully) is well-documented.

You will find rosters of the standard actions and categories in the Android SDK documentation for the Intent class.

Intent Routing

As previously noted, if you specify the target component in your intent, Android has no doubt
where the intent is supposed to be routed to—it will launch the named activity. This might be
OK if the target intent is in your application. It definitely is not recommended for sending
intents to other applications. Component names, by and large, are considered private to the
application and are subject to change. Content Uri templates and MIME types are the preferred
ways of identifying services you wish third-party code to supply.

If you do not specify the target component, then Android has to figure out what activities
(or other intent receivers) are eligible to receive the intent. Note the use of the plural "activities", as a broadly-written intent might well resolve to several activities. That is the . . . ummm
. . . intent (pardon the pun), as you will see later in this chapter. This routing approach is referred to
as implicit routing.

Basically, there are three rules, all of which must be true for a given activity to be eligible
for a given intent:

1. The activity must support the specified action.

2. The activity must support the stated MIME type (if supplied).

3. The activity must support all of the categories named in the intent.

The upshot is that you want to make your intents specific enough to find the right
receiver(s), and no more specific than that.

This will become clearer as we work through some examples later in this chapter.

Stating Your Intent(ions)

All Android components that wish to be notified via intents must declare intent filters, so Android knows which intents should go to that component. To do this, you need to add `intent-filter` elements to your `AndroidManifest.xml` file.

All of the example projects have intent filters defined, courtesy of the Android application-building script (`activityCreator` or the IDE equivalent). They look something like this:

```
<manifest xmlns:android="http://schemas.android.com/apk/res/android"
    package="com.commonsware.android.skeleton">
    <application>
        <activity android:name=".Now" android:label="Now">
            <intent-filter>
                <action android:name="android.intent.action.MAIN" />
                <category android:name="android.intent.category.LAUNCHER" />
            </intent-filter>
        </activity>
    </application>
</manifest>
```

Note the `intent-filter` element under the `activity` element. Here, we declare that this activity:

- is the main activity for this application

- is in the LAUNCHER category, meaning it gets an icon in the Android main menu

Because this activity is the main one for the application, Android knows this is the component it should launch when somebody chooses the application from the main menu.

You are welcome to have more than one action or more than one category in your intent filters. That indicates that the associated component (e.g., activity) handles multiple different sorts of intents.

More than likely, you will also want to have your secondary (non-MAIN) activities specify the MIME type of data they work on. Then, if an intent is targeted for that MIME type—either directly, or indirectly by the Uri referencing something of that type—Android will know that the component handles such data.

For example, you could have an activity declared like this:

```
<activity android:name=".TourViewActivity">
  <intent-filter>
    <action android:name="android.intent.action.VIEW" />
    <category android:name="android.intent.category.DEFAULT" />
    <data android:mimeType="vnd.android.cursor.item/vnd.commonsware.tour" />
  </intent-filter>
</activity>
```

This activity will get launched by an intent requesting to view a Uri representing a vnd. android.cursor.item/vnd.commonsware.tour piece of content. That intent could come from another activity in the same application (e.g., the MAIN activity for this application) or from another activity in another Android application that happens to know a Uri that this activity handles.

Narrow Receivers

In the examples shown previously, the intent filters were set up on activities. Sometimes, tying intents to activities is not exactly what we want:

- Some system events might cause us to want to trigger something in a service rather than an activity.

- Some events might need to launch different activities in different circumstances, where the criteria are not solely based on the intent itself, but some other state (e.g., if we get intent X and the database has a Y, then launch activity M; if the database does not have a Y, then launch activity N).

For these cases, Android offers the intent receiver, defined as a class implementing the BroadcastReceiver interface. Intent receivers are disposable objects designed to receive intents— particularly broadcast intents—and take action, typically involving launching other intents to trigger logic in an activity, service, or other component.

The BroadcastReceiver interface has only one method: onReceive(). Intent receivers implement that method, where they do whatever it is they wish to do upon an incoming intent. To declare an intent receiver, add a receiver element to your AndroidManifest.xml file:

```
<receiver android:name=".MyIntentReceiverClassName" />
```

An intent receiver is only alive for as long as it takes to process onReceive()—as soon as that method returns, the receiver instance is subject to garbage collection and will not be reused. This means intent receivers are somewhat limited in what they can do, mostly to avoid anything that involves any sort of callback. For example, they cannot bind to a service, and they cannot open a dialog box.

The exception is if the BroadcastReceiver is implemented on some longer-lived component, such as an activity or service—in that case, the intent receiver lives as long as its "host" does (e.g., until the activity is frozen). However, in this case, you cannot declare the intent receiver via AndroidManifest.xml. Instead, you need to call registerReceiver() on your Activity's onResume() callback to declare interest in an intent, then call unregisterReceiver() from your Activity's onPause() when you no longer need those intents.

The Pause Caveat

There is one hiccup with using Intent objects to pass arbitrary messages around: it only works when the receiver is active. To quote from the documentation for BroadcastReceiver:

> *If registering a receiver in your Activity.onResume() implementation, you should unregister it in Activity.onPause(). (You won't receive intents when paused, and this will cut down on unnecessary system overhead). Do not unregister in Activity.onSaveInstanceState(), because this won't be called if the user moves back in the history stack.*

Hence, you can only really use the Intent framework as an arbitrary message bus if:

- Your receiver does not care if it misses messages because it was not active.

- You provide some means of getting the receiver "caught up" on messages it missed while it was inactive.

In Chapters 30 and 31 on creating and using services, you will see an example of the former condition, where the receiver (service client) will use Intent-based messages when they are available but does not need them if the client is not active.

CHAPTER 24

■ ■ ■

Launching Activities and Sub-Activities

The theory behind the Android UI architecture is that developers should decompose their application into distinct activities, each implemented as an `Activity`, each reachable via `Intents`, with one "main" activity being the one launched by the Android launcher. For example, a calendar application could have activities for viewing the calendar, viewing a single event, editing an event (including adding a new one), and so forth.

This, of course, implies that one of your activities has the means to start up another activity. For example, if somebody clicks on an event from the view-calendar activity, you might want to show the view-event activity for that event. This means that, somehow, you need to be able to cause the view-event activity to launch and show a specific event (the one the user clicked upon).

This can be further broken down into two scenarios:

- You know what activity you want to launch, probably because it is another activity in your own application.

- You have a content `Uri` to . . . something, and you want your users to be able to do . . . something with it, but you do not know up front what the options are.

This chapter covers the first scenario; the next chapter handles the second.

Peers and Subs

One key question you need to answer when you decide to launch an activity is, does your activity need to know when the launched activity ends?

For example, suppose you want to spawn an activity to collect authentication information for some Web service you are connecting to—maybe you need to authenticate with OpenID[1] in order to use an OAuth[2] service. In this case, your main activity will need to know when the authentication is complete so it can start to use the Web service.

In this case the launched activity is clearly subordinate to the launching activity. Therefore you probably want to launch the child as a sub-activity, which means your activity will be notified when the child activity is complete.

---

1. http://openid.net/
2. http://oauth.net/

On the other hand, imagine an email application in Android. When the user elects to view an attachment, neither you nor the user necessarily expects the main activity to know when the user is done viewing that attachment.

In this scenario, the launched activity is more a peer of your activity, so you probably want to launch the "child" just as a regular activity. Your activity will not be informed when the "child" is done, but, then again, your activity really doesn't need to know.

Start 'Em Up

The two requirements for starting an activity are an Intent and your choice of how to start it up.

Make an Intent

As discussed in Chapter 1, Intents encapsulate a request, made to Android, for some activity or other Intent receiver to do something.

If the activity you intend to launch is one of your own, you may find it simplest to create an explicit Intent, naming the component you wish to launch. For example, from within your activity, you could create an Intent like this:

```
new Intent(this, HelpActivity.class);
```

This would stipulate that you wanted to launch the HelpActivity. This activity would need to be named in your AndroidManifest.xml file, though not necessarily with any Intent filter, since you are trying to request it directly.

Or you could put together an Intent for some Uri, requesting a particular action:

```
Uri uri=Uri.parse("geo:"+lat.toString()+","+lon.toString());
Intent i=new Intent(Intent.ACTION_VIEW, uri);
```

Here, given that we have the latitude and longitude of some position (lat and lon, respectively) of type Double, we construct a geo scheme Uri and create an Intent requesting to view this Uri (ACTION_VIEW).

Make the Call

Once you have your Intent, you need to pass it to Android and get the child activity to launch. You have four choices:

- The simplest option is to call startActivity() with the Intent—this will cause Android to find the best-match activity and pass the Intent to it for handling. Your activity will not be informed when the "child" activity is complete.

- You can call startActivityForResult(), passing it the Intent and a number (unique to the calling activity). Android will find the best-match activity and pass the Intent over to it. However, your activity will be notified when the child activity is complete via the onActivityResult() callback (see the text following this list).

- You can call sendBroadcast(). In this case, Android will pass the Intent to all registered BroadcastReceivers that could possibly want this Intent, not just the best match.

- You can call sendOrderedBroadcast(). Here Android will pass the Intent to all candidate BroadcastReceivers one at a time—if any one "consumes" the Intent, the rest of the candidates are not notified.

Most of the time, you will wind up using startActivity() or startActivityForResult()—broadcast Intents are more typically raised by the Android system itself.

With startActivityForResult(), as noted, you can implement the onActivityResult() callback to be notified when the child activity has completed its work. The callback receives the unique number supplied to startActivityForResult(), so you can determine which child activity is the one that has completed. You also get the following:

- A result code from the child activity calling setResult(). Typically this is RESULT_OK or RESULT_CANCELLED, though you can create your own return codes (pick a number starting with RESULT_FIRST_USER).

- An optional String containing some result data, possibly a URL to some internal or external resource—for example, an ACTION_PICK Intent typically returns the selected bit of content via this data string.

- An optional Bundle containing additional information beyond the result code and data string.

To demonstrate launching a peer activity, take a peek at the Activities/Launch sample application in the Source Code section at http://apress.com. The XML layout is fairly straightforward: two fields for the latitude and longitude, plus a button:

```xml
<?xml version="1.0" encoding="utf-8"?>
<LinearLayout xmlns:android="http://schemas.android.com/apk/res/android"
  android:orientation="vertical"
  android:layout_width="fill_parent"
  android:layout_height="fill_parent"
  >
  <TableLayout
    android:layout_width="fill_parent"
    android:layout_height="wrap_content"
    android:stretchColumns="1,2"
  >
    <TableRow>
      <TextView
        android:layout_width="wrap_content"
        android:layout_height="wrap_content"
        android:paddingLeft="2dip"
        android:paddingRight="4dip"
        android:text="Location:"
      />
```

```
      <EditText android:id="@+id/lat"
        android:layout_width="fill_parent"
        android:layout_height="wrap_content"
        android:cursorVisible="true"
        android:editable="true"
        android:singleLine="true"
        android:layout_weight="1"
      />
      <EditText android:id="@+id/lon"
        android:layout_width="fill_parent"
        android:layout_height="wrap_content"
        android:cursorVisible="true"
        android:editable="true"
        android:singleLine="true"
        android:layout_weight="1"
      />
    </TableRow>
  </TableLayout>
  <Button android:id="@+id/map"
    android:layout_width="fill_parent"
    android:layout_height="wrap_content"
    android:text="Show Me!"
  />
</LinearLayout>
```

The button's OnClickListener simply takes the latitude and longitude, pours them into a geo scheme Uri, then starts the activity.

```
package com.commonsware.android.activities;

import android.app.Activity;
import android.content.Intent;
import android.net.Uri;
import android.os.Bundle;
import android.view.View;
import android.widget.Button;
import android.widget.EditText;

public class LaunchDemo extends Activity {
  private EditText lat;
  private EditText lon;

  @Override
  public void onCreate(Bundle icicle) {
    super.onCreate(icicle);
    setContentView(R.layout.main);
```

```
Button btn=(Button)findViewById(R.id.map);
lat=(EditText)findViewById(R.id.lat);
lon=(EditText)findViewById(R.id.lon);

btn.setOnClickListener(new View.OnClickListener() {
  public void onClick(View view) {
    String _lat=lat.getText().toString();
    String _lon=lon.getText().toString();
    Uri uri=Uri.parse("geo:"+_lat+","+_lon);

    startActivity(new Intent(Intent.ACTION_VIEW, uri));
  }
});
}
}
```

The activity is not much to look at (Figure 24-1).

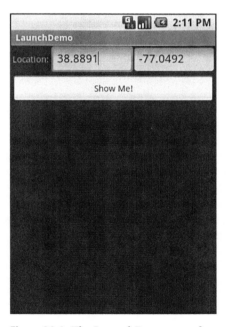

Figure 24-1. *The LaunchDemo sample application, with a location filled in*

If you fill in a location (e.g., 38.8891 latitude and -77.0492 longitude) and click the button, the resulting map is more interesting (Figure 24-2). Note that this is the built-in Android map activity—we did not create our own activity to display this map.

In a Chapter 34, you will see how you can create maps in your own activities, in case you need greater control over how the map is displayed.

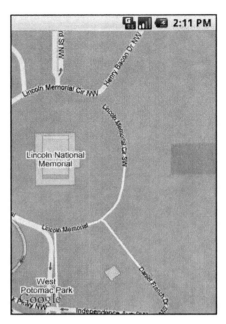

Figure 24-2. *The map launched by LaunchDemo, showing the Lincoln Memorial in Washington DC*

Tabbed Browsing, Sort Of

One of the main features of the modern desktop Web browser is tabbed browsing, where a single browser window can show several pages split across a series of tabs. On a mobile device this may not make a lot of sense, given that you lose screen real estate for the tabs themselves.

In this book, however, we do not let little things like sensibility stop us, so let me demonstrate a tabbed browser, using TabActivity and Intents.

As you may recall from Chapter 10, a tab can have either a View or an Activity as its content. If you want to use an Activity as the content of a tab, you provide an Intent that will launch the desired Activity; Android's tab-management framework will then pour the Activity's user interface into the tab.

Your natural instinct might be to use an http: Uri the way we used a geo: Uri in the previous example:

```
Intent i=new Intent(Intent.ACTION_VIEW);
i.setData(Uri.parse("http://commonsware.com"));
```

That way, you could use the built-in Browser application and get all of the features that it offers.

Alas, this does not work. You cannot host other applications' activities in your tabs—only your own activities, for security reasons.

So, we dust off our WebView demos from Chapter 13 and use those instead, repackaged as Activities/IntentTab.

Here is the source to the main activity, the one hosting the TabView:

```
public class IntentTabDemo extends TabActivity {
  @Override
  public void onCreate(Bundle savedInstanceState) {
    super.onCreate(savedInstanceState);

    TabHost host=getTabHost();

    host.addTab(host.newTabSpec("one")
            .setIndicator("CW")
            .setContent(new Intent(this, CWBrowser.class)));
    host.addTab(host.newTabSpec("two")
            .setIndicator("Android")
            .setContent(new Intent(this, AndroidBrowser.class)));
  }
}
```

As you can see, we are using TabActivity as the base class, and so we do not need our own layout XML—TabActivity supplies it for us. All we do is get access to the TabHost and add two tabs, each specifying an Intent that directly refers to another class. In this case, our two tabs will host a CWBrowser and an AndroidBrowser, respectively.

Those activities are simple modifications to the earlier browser demos:

```
public class CWBrowser extends Activity {
  WebView browser;

  @Override
  public void onCreate(Bundle icicle) {
    super.onCreate(icicle);

    browser=new WebView(this);
    setContentView(browser);
    browser.loadUrl("http://commonsware.com");
  }
}
public class AndroidBrowser extends Activity {
  WebView browser;

  @Override
  public void onCreate(Bundle icicle) {
    super.onCreate(icicle);

    browser=new WebView(this);
    setContentView(browser);
    browser.loadUrl("http://code.google.com/android");
  }
}
```

They simply load a different URL into the browser: the CommonsWare home page in one (Figure 24-3), the Android home page in the other (Figure 24-4). The resulting UI shows what tabbed browsing could look like on Android.

Figure 24-3. *The IntentTabDemo sample application, showing the first tab*

Figure 24-4. *The IntentTabDemo sample application, showing the second tab*

Using distinct subclasses for each targeted page is rather wasteful. Instead we could have packaged the URL to open as an "extra" in an Intent and used that Intent to spawn a general-purpose BrowserTab activity, which would read the URL out of the Intent "extra," and use that. The proof of this is left as an exercise for the reader.

CHAPTER 25

■ ■ ■

Finding Available Actions via Introspection

Sometimes you know just what you want to do, such as display one of your other activities. Sometimes, you have a pretty good idea of what you want to do, such as view the content represented by a Uri, or have the user pick a piece of content of some MIME type. Sometimes you're lost. All you have is a content Uri, and you don't really know what you can do with it.

For example, suppose you were creating a common tagging sub-system for Android, where users could tag pieces of content—contacts, Web URLs, geographic locations, etc. Your sub-system would hold onto the Uri of the content plus the associated tags, so other sub-systems could, say, ask for all pieces of content referencing some tag.

That's all well and good. However, you probably need some sort of maintenance activity, where users could view all their tags and the pieces of content so tagged. This might even serve as a quasi-bookmark service for items on their phone. The problem is, the user is going to expect to be able to do useful things with the content they find in your sub-system, such as dial a contact or show a map for a location.

The problem is, you have absolutely no idea what is possible with any given content Uri. You probably can view any of them, but can you edit them? Can you dial them? Since new applications with new types of content could be added by any user at any time, you can't even assume you know all possible combinations just by looking at the stock applications shipped on all Android devices.

Fortunately, the Android developers thought of this.

Android offers various means by which you can present to your users a set of likely activities to spawn for a given content Uri—even if you have no idea what that content Uri really represents. This chapter explores some of these Uri action introspection tools.

Pick 'Em

Sometimes you know your content Uri represents a collection of some type, such as content://contacts/people representing the list of contacts in the stock Android contacts list. In this case, you can let the user pick a contact that your activity can then use (e.g., tag it, dial it).

To do this, you need to create an Intent for the ACTION_PICK on the target Uri, then start a sub-activity (via startActivityForResult()) to allow the user to pick a piece of content of the specified type. If your onActivityResult() callback for this request gets a RESULT_OK result code, your data string can be parsed into a Uri representing the chosen piece of content.

For example, take a look at Introspection/Pick in the sample applications in the Source Code section of http://apress.com. This activity gives you a field for a collection Uri (with content://contacts/people pre-filled in for your convenience), plus a really big Gimme! button:

```xml
<?xml version="1.0" encoding="utf-8"?>
<LinearLayout xmlns:android="http://schemas.android.com/apk/res/android"
  android:orientation="vertical"
  android:layout_width="fill_parent"
  android:layout_height="fill_parent"
  >
  <EditText android:id="@+id/type"
    android:layout_width="fill_parent"
    android:layout_height="wrap_content"
    android:cursorVisible="true"
    android:editable="true"
    android:singleLine="true"
    android:text="content://contacts/people"
  />
  <Button
    android:id="@+id/pick"
    android:layout_width="fill_parent"
    android:layout_height="fill_parent"
    android:text="Gimme!"
    android:layout_weight="1"
  />
</LinearLayout>
```

Upon being clicked, the button creates the ACTION_PICK on the user-supplied collection Uri and starts the sub-activity. When that sub-activity completes with RESULT_OK, the ACTION_VIEW is invoked on the resulting content Uri.

```java
public class PickDemo extends Activity {
  static final int PICK_REQUEST=1337;
  private EditText type;

  @Override
  public void onCreate(Bundle icicle) {
    super.onCreate(icicle);
    setContentView(R.layout.main);
    type=(EditText)findViewById(R.id.type);

    Button btn=(Button)findViewById(R.id.pick);
```

```
  btn.setOnClickListener(new View.OnClickListener() {
    public void onClick(View view) {
      Intent i=new Intent(Intent.ACTION_PICK,
                Uri.parse(type.getText().toString()));

      startActivityForResult(i, PICK_REQUEST);
    }
  });
}

@Override
protected void onActivityResult(int requestCode, int resultCode,
                                Intent data) {
  if (requestCode==PICK_REQUEST) {
    if (resultCode==RESULT_OK) {
        startActivity(new Intent(Intent.ACTION_VIEW,
                                 data.getData()));
    }
  }
 }
}
```

The result: the user chooses a collection (Figure 25-1), picks a piece of content (Figure 25-2), and views it (Figure 25-3).

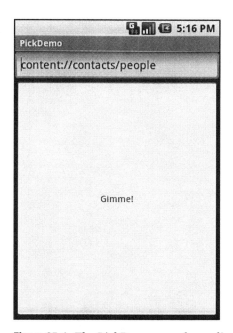

Figure 25-1. *The PickDemo sample application, as initially launched*

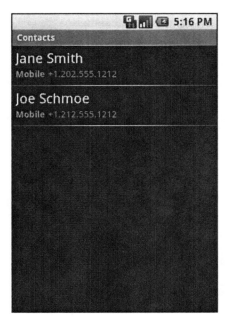

Figure 25-2. *The same application, after the user has clicked the Gimme! button, showing the list of available people*

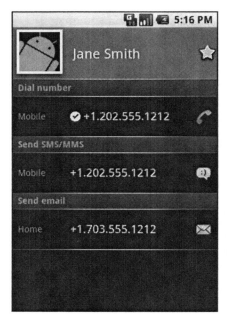

Figure 25-3. *A view of a contact, launched by PickDemo after the user has chosen one of the people from the pick list*

Would You Like to See the Menu?

Another way to give the user ways to take actions on a piece of content, without you knowing what actions are possible, is to inject a set of menu choices into the options menu via addIntentOptions(). This method, available on Menu, takes an Intent and other parameters and fills in a set of menu choices on the Menu instance, each representing one possible action. Choosing one of those menu choices spawns the associated activity.

The canonical example of using addIntentOptions() illustrates another flavor of having a piece of content and not knowing the actions that can be taken. In the previous example, showing ActivityAdapter, the content was from some other Android application, and we know nothing about it. It is also possible, though, that we know full well what the content is—it's ours. However, Android applications are perfectly capable of adding new actions to existing content types, so even though you wrote your application and know what you expect to be done with your content, there may be other options you are unaware of that are available to users.

For example, imagine the tagging sub-system mentioned in the introduction to this chapter. It would be very annoying to users if every time they wanted to tag a piece of content, they had to go to a separate tagging tool then turn around and pick the content they just had been working on (if that is even technically possible) before associating tags with it. Instead they would probably prefer a menu choice in the content's own "home" activity where they can indicate they want to tag it, which leads them to the set-a-tag activity and tells that activity what content should get tagged.

To accomplish this, the tagging sub-system should set up an Intent filter, supporting any piece of content with its own action (e.g., ACTION_TAG) and a category of CATEGORY_ALTERNATIVE, which is the convention for one application adding actions to another application's content.

If you want to write activities that are aware of possible add-ons like tagging, you should use addIntentOptions() to add those add-ons' actions to your options menu, such as the following:

```
Intent intent = new Intent(null, myContentUri);

intent.addCategory(Intent.ALTERNATIVE_CATEGORY);
menu.addIntentOptions(Menu.ALTERNATIVE, 0,
                   new ComponentName(this,
                                     MyActivity.class),
                   null, intent, 0, null);
```

Here, myContentUri is the content Uri of whatever is being viewed by the user in this activity, MyActivity is the name of the activity class, and menu is the menu being modified.

In this case, the Intent we are using to pick actions from requires that appropriate Intent receivers support the CATEGORY_ALTERNATIVE. Then we add the options to the menu with addIntentOptions() and the following parameters:

- The sort position for this set of menu choices, typically set to 0 (which appear in the order added to the menu) or ALTERNATIVE (which appear after other menu choices).

- A unique number for this set of menu choices, or 0 if you do not need a number.

- A ComponentName instance representing the activity that is populating its menu—this is used to filter out the activity's own actions so the activity can handle its own actions as it sees fit.

- An array of Intent instances that are the "specific" matches—any actions matching those Intents are shown in the menu before any other possible actions.

- The Intent for which you want the available actions.

- A set of flags. The only one of likely relevance is represented as MATCH_DEFAULT_ONLY, which means matching actions must also implement the DEFAULT_CATEGORY category. If you do not need this, use a value of 0 for the flags.

- An array of Menu.Items, which will hold the menu items matching the array of Intent instances supplied as the "specifics," or null if you do not need those items (or are not using "specifics").

Asking Around

Both the ActivityAdapter family and addIntentOptions() use queryIntentActivityOptions() for the "heavy lifting" of finding possible actions. The queryIntentActivityOptions() method is implemented on PackageManager, which is available to your activity via getPackageManager().

The queryIntentActivityOptions() method takes some of the same parameters as does addIntentOptions(), notably the caller ComponentName, the "specifics" array of Intent instances, the overall Intent representing the actions you are seeking, and the set of flags. It returns a List of Intent instances matching the stated criteria, with the "specifics" ones first.

If you would like to offer alternative actions to users, but by means other than addIntentOptions(), you could call queryIntentActivityOptions(), get the Intent instances, then use them to populate some other user interface (e.g., a toolbar).

CHAPTER 26

■ ■ ■

Handling Rotation

Some Android handsets, like the T-Mobile G1, offer a slide-out keyboard that triggers rotating the screen from portrait to landscape. Other handsets might use accelerometers to determine screen rotation, like the iPhone does. As a result, it is reasonable to assume that switching from portrait to landscape and back again may be something your users will look to do.

Android has a number of ways for you to handle screen rotation, so your application can properly handle either orientation. All these facilities do is help you detect and manage the rotation process—you are still required to make sure you have layouts that look decent on each orientation.

A Philosophy of Destruction

By default, when there is a change in the phone configuration that might affect resource selection, Android will destroy and re-create any running or paused activities the next time they are to be viewed. While this could happen for a variety of different configuration changes (e.g., change of language selection), it will most likely trip you up mostly for rotations, since a change in orientation can cause you to load a different set of resources (e.g., layouts).

The key here is that this is the default behavior. It may even be the behavior that is best for one or more of your activities. You do have some control over the matter, though, and can tailor how your activities respond to orientation changes or similar configuration switches.

It's All The Same, Just Different

Since, by default, Android destroys and re-creates your activity on a rotation, you may only need to hook into the same onSaveInstanceState() that you would if your activity were destroyed for any other reason (e.g., low memory). Implement that method in your activity and fill in the supplied Bundle with enough information to get you back to your current state. Then, in onCreate() (or onRestoreInstanceState(), if you prefer), pick the data out of the Bundle and use it to bring your activity back to the way it was.

To demonstrate this, let's take a look at the Rotation/RotationOne project. It, and the other sample projects used in this chapter, which are also found in the source code section of the Apress web site, use a pair of main.xml layouts, one in res/layout/ and one in res/layout-land/ for use in landscape mode. Here is the portrait layout:

```xml
<?xml version="1.0" encoding="utf-8"?>
<LinearLayout xmlns:android="http://schemas.android.com/apk/res/android"
  android:orientation="vertical"
  android:layout_width="fill_parent"
  android:layout_height="fill_parent"
  >
  <Button android:id="@+id/pick"
    android:layout_width="fill_parent"
    android:layout_height="fill_parent"
    android:layout_weight="1"
    android:text="Pick"
    android:enabled="true"
  />
  <Button android:id="@+id/view"
    android:layout_width="fill_parent"
    android:layout_height="fill_parent"
    android:layout_weight="1"
    android:text="View"
    android:enabled="false"
  />
</LinearLayout>
```

while here is the similar landscape layout:

```xml
<?xml version="1.0" encoding="utf-8"?>
<LinearLayout xmlns:android="http://schemas.android.com/apk/res/android"
  android:orientation="horizontal"
  android:layout_width="fill_parent"
  android:layout_height="fill_parent"
  >
  <Button android:id="@+id/pick"
    android:layout_width="fill_parent"
    android:layout_height="fill_parent"
    android:layout_weight="1"
    android:text="Pick"
    android:enabled="true"
  />
  <Button android:id="@+id/view"
    android:layout_width="fill_parent"
    android:layout_height="fill_parent"
    android:layout_weight="1"
    android:text="View"
    android:enabled="false"
  />
</LinearLayout>
```

Basically, it is a pair of buttons, each taking up half the screen. In portrait mode, the buttons are stacked; in landscape mode, they are side-by-side.

If you were to simply create a project, put in those two layouts, and compile it, the application would appear to work just fine—a rotation (<Ctrl>-<F12> in the emulator) will cause the layout to change. And while buttons lack state, if you were using other widgets (e.g., EditText), you would even find that Android hangs onto some of the widget state for you (e.g., the text entered in the EditText).

What Android cannot automatically help you with is anything held outside the widgets.

This application is derived from the Pick demo used in Chapter 24. There, clicking one button would let you pick a contact, then view the contact. Here, we split those into separate buttons, with the "View" button only enabled when we actually have a contact.

Let's see how we handle this, using onSaveInstanceState():

```
public class RotationOneDemo extends Activity {
  static final int PICK_REQUEST=1337;
  Button viewButton=null;
  Uri contact=null;

  @Override
  public void onCreate(Bundle savedInstanceState) {
    super.onCreate(savedInstanceState);
    setContentView(R.layout.main);

    Button btn=(Button)findViewById(R.id.pick);

    btn.setOnClickListener(new View.OnClickListener() {
      public void onClick(View view) {
        Intent i=new Intent(Intent.ACTION_PICK,
                  Uri.parse("content://contacts/people"));

        startActivityForResult(i, PICK_REQUEST);
      }
    });

    viewButton=(Button)findViewById(R.id.view);

    viewButton.setOnClickListener(new View.OnClickListener() {
      public void onClick(View view) {
        startActivity(new Intent(Intent.ACTION_VIEW, contact));
      }
    });

    restoreMe(savedInstanceState);

    viewButton.setEnabled(contact!=null);
  }
```

```java
  @Override
  protected void onActivityResult(int requestCode, int resultCode,
                                    Intent data) {
    if (requestCode==PICK_REQUEST) {
      if (resultCode==RESULT_OK) {
        contact=data.getData();
        viewButton.setEnabled(true);
      }
    }
  }

  @Override
  protected void onSaveInstanceState(Bundle outState) {
    super.onSaveInstanceState(outState);

    if (contact!=null) {
      outState.putString("contact", contact.toString());
    }
  }

  private void restoreMe(Bundle state) {
    contact=null;

    if (state!=null) {
      String contactUri=state.getString("contact");

      if (contactUri!=null) {
        contact=Uri.parse(contactUri);
      }
    }
  }
}
```

By and large, it looks like a normal activity . . . because it is. Initially, the "model"—a Uri named contact—is null. It is set as the result of spawning the ACTION_PICK sub-activity. Its string representation is saved in onSaveInstanceState() and restored in restoreMe() (called from onCreate()). If the contact is not null, the "View" button is enabled and can be used to view the chosen contact.

Visually, it looks like Figures 26-1 and 26-2.

The benefit to this implementation is that it handles a number of system events beyond mere rotation, such as being closed by Android due to low memory.

For fun, comment out the restoreMe() call in onCreate() and try running the application. You will see that the application "forgets" a contact selected in one orientation when you rotate the emulator or device.

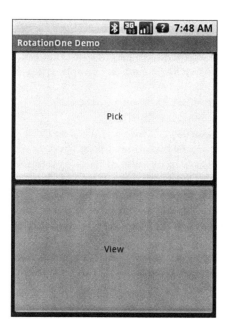

Figure 26-1. *The RotationOne application, in portrait mode*

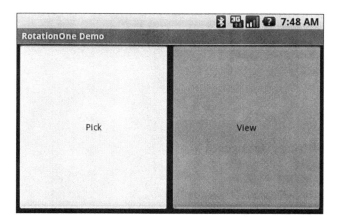

Figure 26-2. *The RotationOne application, in landscape mode*

Now With More Savings!

The problem with onSaveInstanceState() is that you are limited to a Bundle. That's because this callback is also used in cases where your whole process might be terminated (e.g., low memory), so the data to be saved has to be something that can be serialized and has no dependencies upon your running process.

For some activities, that limitation is not a problem. For others, though, it is more annoying. Take an online chat, for example. You have no means of storing a socket in a Bundle, so by default, you will have to drop your connection to the chat server and re-establish it. That not only may be a performance hit, but it might also affect the chat itself, such as you appearing in the chat logs as disconnecting and reconnecting.

One way to get past this is to use onRetainNonConfigurationInstance() instead of onSaveInstanceState() for "light" changes like a rotation. Your activity's onRetainNonConfigurationInstance() callback can return an Object, which you can retrieve later via getLastNonConfigurationInstance(). The Object can be just about anything you want —typically, it will be some kind of "context" object holding activity state, such as running threads, open sockets, and the like. Your activity's onCreate() can call getLastNonConfigurationInstance()—if you get a non-null response, you now have your sockets and threads and whatnot. The biggest limitation is that you do not want to put in the saved context anything that might reference a resource that will get swapped out, such as a Drawable loaded from a resource.

Let's take a look at the Rotation/RotationTwo sample project, which uses this approach to handling rotations. The layouts, and hence the visual appearance, is the same as with Rotation/RotationOne. Where things differ slightly is in the Java code:

```java
public class RotationTwoDemo extends Activity {
  static final int PICK_REQUEST=1337;
  Button viewButton=null;
  Uri contact=null;

  @Override
  public void onCreate(Bundle savedInstanceState) {
    super.onCreate(savedInstanceState);
    setContentView(R.layout.main);

    Button btn=(Button)findViewById(R.id.pick);

    btn.setOnClickListener(new View.OnClickListener() {
      public void onClick(View view) {
        Intent i=new Intent(Intent.ACTION_PICK,
                   Uri.parse("content://contacts/people"));

        startActivityForResult(i, PICK_REQUEST);
      }
    });

    viewButton=(Button)findViewById(R.id.view);

    viewButton.setOnClickListener(new View.OnClickListener() {
      public void onClick(View view) {
        startActivity(new Intent(Intent.ACTION_VIEW, contact));
      }
    });
```

```
    restoreMe();

    viewButton.setEnabled(contact!=null);
  }

  @Override
  protected void onActivityResult(int requestCode, int resultCode,
                                  Intent data) {
    if (requestCode==PICK_REQUEST) {
      if (resultCode==RESULT_OK) {
        contact=data.getData();
        viewButton.setEnabled(true);
      }
    }
  }

  @Override
  public Object onRetainNonConfigurationInstance() {
    return(contact);
  }

  private void restoreMe() {
    contact=null;

    if (getLastNonConfigurationInstance()!=null) {
      contact=(Uri)getLastNonConfigurationInstance();
    }
  }
}
```

In this case, we override onRetainNonConfigurationInstance(), returning the actual Uri for our contact, rather than a string representation of it. In turn, restoreMe() calls getLastNonConfigurationInstance(), and if it is not null, we hold onto it as our contact and enable the "View" button.

The advantage here is that we are passing around the Uri rather than a string representation. In this case, that is not a big saving. But our state could be much more complicated, including threads and sockets and other things we cannot pack into a Bundle.

DIY Rotation

Even this, though, may still be too intrusive to your application. Suppose, for example, you are creating a real-time game, such as a first-person shooter. The "hiccup" your users experience as your activity is destroyed and re-created might be enough to get them shot, which they may not appreciate. While this would be less of an issue on the T-Mobile G1, since a rotation requires sliding open the keyboard and therefore is unlikely to be done mid-game, other devices might rotate based solely upon the device's position as determined by accelerometers.

The third possibility for handling rotations, therefore, is to tell Android that you will handle them completely yourself and that you do not want assistance from the framework. To do this:

1. Put an android:configChanges entry in your AndroidManifest.xml file, listing the configuration changes you want to handle yourself versus allowing Android to handle for you.

2. Implement onConfigurationChanged() in your Activity, which will be called when one of the configuration changes you listed in android:configChanges occurs.

Now, for any configuration change you want, you can bypass the whole activity-destruction process and simply get a callback letting you know of the change.

To see this in action, turn to the Rotation/RotationThree sample application. Once again, our layouts are the same, so the application looks the same as the preceding two samples. However, the Java code is significantly different, because we are no longer concerned with saving our state, but rather with updating our UI to deal with the layout.

But first, we need to make a small change to our manifest:

```
<?xml version="1.0" encoding="utf-8"?>
<manifest xmlns:android="http://schemas.android.com/apk/res/android"
    package="com.commonsware.android.rotation.three"
    android:versionCode="1"
    android:versionName="1.0.0">
    <application android:label="@string/app_name">
        <activity android:name=".RotationThreeDemo"
                android:label="@string/app_name"
                android:configChanges="keyboardHidden|orientation">
            <intent-filter>
                <action android:name="android.intent.action.MAIN" />
                <category android:name="android.intent.category.LAUNCHER" />
            </intent-filter>
        </activity>
    </application>
</manifest>
```

Here, we state that we will handle keyboardHidden and orientation configuration changes ourselves. This covers us for any cause of the "rotation"—whether it is a sliding keyboard or a physical rotation. Note that this is set on the activity, not the application—if you have several activities, you will need to decide for each which of the tactics outlined in this chapter you wish to use.

The Java code for this project follows:

```java
public class RotationThreeDemo extends Activity {
  static final int PICK_REQUEST=1337;
  Button viewButton=null;
  Uri contact=null;

  @Override
  public void onCreate(Bundle savedInstanceState) {
    super.onCreate(savedInstanceState);

    setupViews();
  }

  @Override
  protected void onActivityResult(int requestCode, int resultCode,
                                  Intent data) {
    if (requestCode==PICK_REQUEST) {
      if (resultCode==RESULT_OK) {
        contact=data.getData();
        viewButton.setEnabled(true);
      }
    }
  }

  public void onConfigurationChanged(Configuration newConfig) {
    super.onConfigurationChanged(newConfig);

    setupViews();
  }

  private void setupViews() {
    setContentView(R.layout.main);

    Button btn=(Button)findViewById(R.id.pick);

    btn.setOnClickListener(new View.OnClickListener() {
      public void onClick(View view) {
        Intent i=new Intent(Intent.ACTION_PICK,
                    Uri.parse("content://contacts/people"));
```

```
          startActivityForResult(i, PICK_REQUEST);
        }
      });

    viewButton=(Button)findViewById(R.id.view);

    viewButton.setOnClickListener(new View.OnClickListener() {
      public void onClick(View view) {
        startActivity(new Intent(Intent.ACTION_VIEW, contact));
      }
    });

    viewButton.setEnabled(contact!=null);
  }
}
```

The onCreate() implementation delegates most of its logic to a setupViews() method,
which loads the layout and sets up the buttons. The reason this logic was broken out into its
own method is because it is also called from onConfigurationChanged().

Forcing the Issue

In the previous three sections, we covered ways to deal with rotational events. There is, of course,
a radical alternative: tell Android not to rotate your activity at all. If the activity does not rotate,
you do not have to worry about writing code to deal with rotations.

To block Android from rotating your activity, all you need to do is add android:
screenOrientation = "portrait" (or "landscape", as you prefer) to your AndroidManifest.xml
file, as shown (from the Rotation/RotationFour sample project):

```
<?xml version="1.0" encoding="utf-8"?>
<manifest xmlns:android="http://schemas.android.com/apk/res/android"
    package="com.commonsware.android.rotation.four"
    android:versionCode="1"
    android:versionName="1.0.0">
  <application android:label="@string/app_name">
    <activity android:name=".RotationFourDemo"
            android:screenOrientation="portrait"
            android:label="@string/app_name">
      <intent-filter>
        <action android:name="android.intent.action.MAIN" />
        <category android:name="android.intent.category.LAUNCHER" />
      </intent-filter>
    </activity>
  </application>
</manifest>
```

Since this is applied on a per-activity basis, you will need to decide which of your activities may need this turned on.

At this point, your activity is locked into whatever orientation you specified, regardless of what you do. The following screen shots show the same activity as in the previous three sections, but using the previous manifest and with the emulator set for both portrait and landscape orientation. Note that the UI does not move a bit, but remains in portrait mode as can be seen in Figures 26-3 and 26-4.

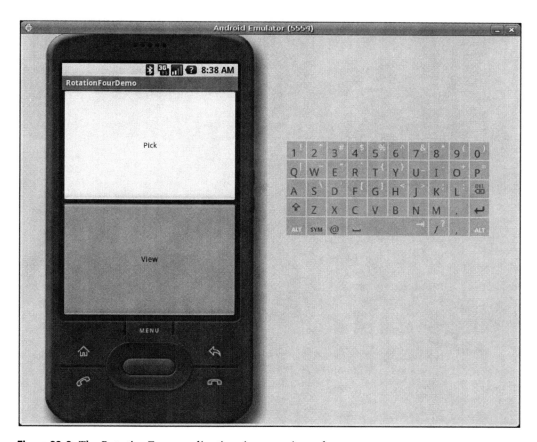

Figure 26-3. *The RotationFour application, in portrait mode*

Figure 26-4. *The RotationFour application, in landscape mode*

Making Sense of it All

All of these scenarios assume that you rotate the screen by opening up the keyboard on the device (or pressing <Ctrl>-<F12> in the emulator). Certainly, this is the norm for Android applications.

However, we haven't covered the iPhone Scenario.

You may have seen one (or several) commercials for the iPhone, showing how the screen rotates just by turning the device. By default, you do not get this behavior with the T-Mobile G1—instead, the screen rotates based on whether the keyboard is open or closed.

However, it is very easy for you to change this behavior, so your screen will rotate based on the position of the phone: just add android:screenOrientation = "sensor" to your AndroidManifest. xml file (as seen in the Rotation/RotationFive sample project):

```
<?xml version="1.0" encoding="utf-8"?>
<manifest xmlns:android="http://schemas.android.com/apk/res/android"
    package="com.commonsware.android.rotation.five"
    android:versionCode="1"
    android:versionName="1.0.0">
```

```
    <application android:label="@string/app_name">
        <activity android:name=".RotationFiveDemo"
                android:screenOrientation="sensor"
                android:label="@string/app_name">
            <intent-filter>
                <action android:name="android.intent.action.MAIN" />
                <category android:name="android.intent.category.LAUNCHER" />
            </intent-filter>
        </activity>
    </application>
</manifest>
```

The "sensor", in this case, tells Android you want the accelerometers to control the screen orientation, so the physical shift in the device orientation controls the screen orientation.

At least on the G1, this appears to only work when going from the traditional upright portrait position to the traditional landscape position—rotating 90 degrees counter-clockwise. Rotating the device 90 degrees clockwise results in no change in the screen.

Also note that this setting disables having the keyboard trigger a rotation event. Leaving the device in the portrait position, if you slide out the keyboard, in a "normal" Android activity, the screen will rotate; in a android:screenOrientation = "sensor" activity, the screen will not rotate.

PART 5

Content Providers and Services

CHAPTER 27

■ ■ ■

Using a Content Provider

Any Uri in Android that begins with the content:// scheme represents a resource served up by a content provider. Content providers offer data encapsulation using Uri instances as handles—you neither know nor care where the data represented by the Uri comes from, so long as it is available to you when needed. The data could be stored in a SQLite database, or in flat files, or retrieved off a device, or be stored on some far-off server accessed over the Internet.

Given a Uri, you can perform basic CRUD (create, read, update, delete) operations using a content provider. Uri instances can represent either collections or individual pieces of content. Given a collection Uri, you can create new pieces of content via insert operations. Given an instance Uri, you can read data represented by the Uri, update that data, or delete the instance outright.

Android lets you use existing content providers or create your own. This chapter covers using content providers; Chapter 28 will explain how you can serve up your own data using the content provider framework.

Pieces of Me

The simplified model of the construction of a content Uri is the scheme, the namespace of data, and, optionally, the instance identifier, all separated by slashes in URL-style notation. The scheme of a content Uri is always content://.

So, a content Uri of content://constants/5 represents the constants instance with an identifier of 5.

The combination of the scheme and the namespace is known as the "base Uri" of a content provider, or a set of data supported by a content provider. In the previous example, content://constants is the base Uri for a content provider that serves up information about "constants" (in this case, physical constants).

The base Uri can be more complicated. For example, the base Uri for contacts is content://contacts/people, as the contacts content provider may serve up other data using other base Uri values.

The base Uri represents a collection of instances. The base Uri combined with an instance identifier (e.g., 5) represents a single instance.

Most of the Android APIs expect these to be Uri objects, though in common discussion, it is simpler to think of them as strings. The Uri.parse() static method creates a Uri out of the string representation.

Getting a Handle

Where do these Uri instances come from?

The most popular starting point, if you know the type of data you want to work with, is to get the base Uri from the content provider itself in code. For example, CONTENT_URI is the base Uri for contacts represented as people—this maps to content://contacts/people. If you just need the collection, this Uri works as is; if you need an instance and know its identifier, you can call addId() on the Uri to inject it, so you have a Uri for the instance.

You might also get Uri instances handed to you from other sources, such as getting Uri handles for contacts via sub-activities responding to ACTION_PICK intents. In this case, the Uri is truly an opaque handle . . . unless you decide to pick it apart using the various getters on the Uri class.

You can also hard-wire literal String objects and convert them into Uri instances via Uri.parse(). For example, in Chapter 25, the sample code used an EditText with content:// contacts/people pre-filled in. This isn't an ideal solution, as the base Uri values could conceivably change over time.

Making Queries

Given a base Uri, you can run a query to return data out of the content provider related to that Uri. This has much of the feel of SQL: you specify the "columns" to return, the constraints to determine which "rows" to return, a sort order, etc. The difference is that this request is being made of a content provider, not directly of some database (e.g., SQLite).

The nexus of this is the managedQuery() method available to your activity. This method takes five parameters:

1. The base Uri of the content provider to query, or the instance Uri of a specific object to query

2. An array of properties of instances from that content provider that you want returned by the query

3. A constraint statement, functioning like a SQL WHERE clause

4. An optional set of parameters to bind into the constraint clause, replacing any ?s that appear there

5. An optional sort statement, functioning like a SQL ORDER BY clause

This method returns a Cursor object, which you can use to retrieve the data returned by the query.

"Properties" is to content providers as columns are to databases. In other words, each instance (row) returned by a query consists of a set of properties (columns), each representing some piece of data.

This will hopefully make more sense given an example.

Our content provider examples come from the ContentProvider/Constants sample application, specifically the ConstantsBrowser class:

```
constantsCursor=managedQuery(Provider.Constants.CONTENT_URI,
                             PROJECTION, null, null, null);
```

In the call to managedQuery(), we provide:

- The Uri passed into the activity by the caller (CONTENT_URI), in this case representing the collection of physical constants managed by the content provider

- A list of properties to retrieve (see the following code)

- Three null values, indicating that we do not need a constraint clause (the Uri represents the instance we need), nor parameters for the constraint, nor a sort order (we should only get one entry back)

```
private static final String[] PROJECTION = new String[] {
    Provider.Constants._ID, Provider.Constants.TITLE,
    Provider.Constants.VALUE};
```

The biggest "magic" here is the list of properties. The lineup of what properties are possible for a given content provider should be provided by the documentation (or source code) for the content provider itself. In this case, we define logical values on the Provider content provider implementation class that represent the various properties (namely, the unique identifier, the display name or title, and the value of the constant).

Adapting to the Circumstances

Now that we have a Cursor via managedQuery(), we have access to the query results and can do whatever we want with them. You might, for example, manually extract data from the Cursor to populate widgets or other objects.

However, if the goal of the query was to return a list from which the user should choose an item, you probably should consider using SimpleCursorAdapter. This class bridges between the Cursor and a selection widget, such as a ListView or Spinner. Pour the Cursor into a SimpleCursorAdapter, hand the adapter off to the widget, and you're set—your widget will show the available options.

For example, here is the onCreate() method from ConstantsBrowser, which gives the user a list of physical constants:

```
@Override
public void onCreate(Bundle savedInstanceState) {
  super.onCreate(savedInstanceState);

  constantsCursor=managedQuery(Provider.Constants.CONTENT_URI,
                               PROJECTION, null, null, null);
```

```
ListAdapter adapter=new SimpleCursorAdapter(this,
                    R.layout.row, constantsCursor,
                    new String[] {Provider.Constants.TITLE,
                                  Provider.Constants.VALUE},
                    new int[] {R.id.title, R.id.value});

setListAdapter(adapter);
registerForContextMenu(getListView());
}
```

After executing the managedQuery() and getting the Cursor, ConstantsBrowser creates a SimpleCursorAdapter with the following parameters:

- The activity (or other Context) creating the adapter; in this case, the ConstantsBrowser itself

- The identifier for a layout to be used for rendering the list entries (R.layout.row)

- The cursor (constantsCursor)

- The properties to pull out of the cursor and use for configuring the list entry View instances (TITLE and VALUE)

- The corresponding identifiers of TextView widgets in the list entry layout that those properties should go into (R.id.title and R.id.value)

After that, we put the adapter into the ListView, and we get the results shown in Figure 27-1.

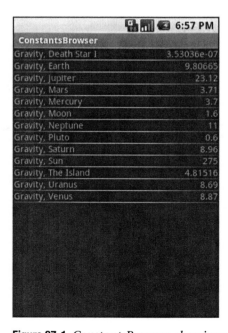

Figure 27-1. *ConstantsBrowser, showing a list of physical constants*

If you need more control over the views than you can reasonably achieve with the stock view construction logic, subclass SimpleCursorAdapter and override getView() to create your own widgets to go into the list, as demonstrated in Chapter 9.

Doing It By Hand

Of course, you can always do it the "hard way"—pulling data out of the Cursor by hand. The Cursor interface is similar in concept to other database access APIs offering cursors as objects, though, as always, the devil is in the details.

Position

Cursor instances have a built-in notion of position, akin to the Java Iterator interface. To get to the various rows, you can use:

- moveToFirst() to move to the first row in the result set or moveToLast() to move to the last row in the result set

- moveToNext() to move to the next row and determine if there is yet another row to process (moveToNext() returns true if it points to another row after moving, false otherwise)

- moveToPrevious() to move to the previous row, as the opposite to moveToNext()

- moveToPosition() to move to a specific index, or move() to move to a relative position plus or minus from your current position

- getPosition() to return your current index

- a whole host of condition methods, including isFirst(), isLast(), isBeforeFirst(), and isAfterLast()

Getting Properties

Once you have the Cursor positioned at a row of interest, you have a variety of methods to retrieve properties from that row, with different methods supporting different types (getString(), getInt(), getFloat(), etc.). Each method takes the zero-based index of the property you want to retrieve.

If you want to see if a given property has a value, you can use isNull() to test it for null-ness.

Give and Take

Of course, content providers would be astonishingly weak if you couldn't add or remove data from them, only update what is there. Fortunately, content providers offer these abilities as well.

To insert data into a content provider, you have two options available on the ContentProvider interface (available through getContentProvider() to your activity):

- Use insert() with a collection Uri and a ContentValues structure describing the initial set of data to put in the row

- Use bulkInsert() with a collection Uri and an array of ContentValues structures to populate several rows at once

The insert() method returns a Uri for you to use for future operations on that new object. The bulkInsert() method returns the number of created rows; you would need to do a query to get back at the data you just inserted.

For example, here is a snippet of code from ConstantsBrowser to insert a new constant into the content provider, given a DialogWrapper that can provide access to the title and value of the constant:

```
private void processAdd(DialogWrapper wrapper) {
  ContentValues values=new ContentValues(2);

  values.put(Provider.Constants.TITLE, wrapper.getTitle());
  values.put(Provider.Constants.VALUE, wrapper.getValue());

  getContentResolver().insert(Provider.Constants.CONTENT_URI,
                              values);
  constantsCursor.requery();
}
```

Since we already have an outstanding Cursor for the content provider's contents, we call requery() on that to update the Cursor's contents. This, in turn, will update any SimpleCursorAdapter you may have wrapping the Cursor—and that will update any selection widgets (e.g., ListView) you have using the adapter.

To delete one or more rows from the content provider, use the delete() method on ContentResolver. This works akin to a SQL DELETE statement and takes three parameters:

1. A Uri representing the collection (or instance) you wish to update

2. A constraint statement, functioning like a SQL WHERE clause, to determine which rows should be updated

3. An optional set of parameters to bind into the constraint clause, replacing any ?s that appear there

Beware of the BLOB!

Binary large objects—BLOBs—are supported in many databases, including SQLite. However, the Android model is more aimed at supporting such hunks of data via their own separate content Uri values. A content provider, therefore, does not provide direct access to binary data, like photos, via a Cursor. Rather, a property in the content provider will give you the content Uri for that particular BLOB. You can use getInputStream() and getOutputStream() on your ContentProvider to read and write the binary data.

Quite possibly, the rationale is to minimize unnecessary data copying. For example, the primary use of a photo in Android is to display it to the user. The ImageView widget can do just that, via a content Uri to a JPEG. By storing the photo in a manner that has its own Uri, you do not need to copy data out of the content provider into some temporary holding area just to be able to display it—just use the Uri. The expectation, presumably, is that few Android applications will do much more than upload binary data and use widgets or built-in activities to display that data.

CHAPTER 28

■■■

Building a Content Provider

Building a content provider is probably the most complicated and tedious task in all of Android development. There are many requirements of a content provider, in terms of methods to implement and public data members to supply. And, until you try using it, you have no great way of telling if you did any of it correctly (versus, say, building an activity and getting validation errors from the resource compiler).

That being said, building a content provider is of huge importance if your application wishes to make data available to other applications. If your application is keeping its data solely to itself, you may be able to avoid creating a content provider, just accessing the data directly from your activities. But if you want your data to possibly be used by others—for example, if you are building a feed reader and you want other programs to be able to access the feeds you are downloading and caching—then a content provider is right for you.

First, Some Dissection

As was discussed in the previous chapter, the content Uri is the linchpin behind accessing data inside a content provider. When using a content provider, all you really need to know is the provider's base Uri; from there you can run queries as needed or construct a Uri to a specific instance if you know the instance identifier.

When building a content provider, though, you need to know a bit more about the innards of the content Uri.

A content Uri has two to four pieces, depending on the situation:

- It always has a scheme (content://), indicating it is a content Uri instead of a Uri to a Web resource (http://).

- It always has an authority, which is the first path segment after the scheme. The authority is a unique string identifying the content provider that handles the content associated with this Uri.

- It may have a data type path, which is the list of path segments after the authority and before the instance identifier (if any). The data type path can be empty if the content provider handles only one type of content. It can be a single path segment (foo) or a chain of path segments (foo/bar/goo) as needed to handle whatever data-access scenarios the content provider requires.

- It may have an instance identifier, which is an integer identifying a specific piece of content. A content Uri without an instance identifier refers to the collection of content represented by the authority (and, where provided, the data path).

For example, a content Uri could be as simple as content://sekrits, which would refer to the collection of content held by whatever content provider was tied to the sekrits authority (e.g., SecretsProvider). Or, it could be as complex as content://sekrits/card/pin/17, which would refer to a piece of content (identified as 17) managed by the sekrits content provider that is of the data type card/pin.

Next, Some Typing

Next you need to come up with some MIME types corresponding with the content from your content provider.

Android uses both the content Uri and the MIME type as ways to identify content on the device. A collection content Uri—or, more accurately, the combination authority and data type path—should map to a pair of MIME types. One MIME type will represent the collection; the other will represent an instance. These map to the Uri patterns discussed in the previous section for no-identifier and identifier cases, respectively. As you saw in Chapters 24 and 25, you can fill a MIME type into an Intent to route the Intent to the proper activity (e.g., ACTION_PICK on a collection MIME type to call up a selection activity to pick an instance out of that collection).

The collection MIME type should be of the form vnd.X.cursor.dir/Y, where X is the name of your firm, organization, or project, and Y is a dot-delimited type name. So, for example, you might use vnd.tlagency.cursor.dir/sekrits.card.pin as the MIME type for your collection of secrets.

The instance MIME type should be of the form vnd.X.cursor.item/Y, usually for the same values of X and Y as you used for the collection MIME type (though that is not strictly required).

Step #1: Create a Provider Class

Just as an activity and intent receiver are both Java classes, so is a content provider. So, the big step in creating a content provider is crafting its Java class, with a base class of ContentProvider.

In your subclass of ContentProvider, you are responsible for implementing six methods that, when combined, perform the services that a content provider is supposed to offer to activities wishing to create, read, update, or delete content.

onCreate()

As with an activity, the main entry point to a content provider is onCreate(). Here you can do whatever initialization you want. In particular, here is where you should lazy-initialize your data store. For example, if you plan on storing your data in such-and-so directory on an SD card, with an XML file serving as a "table of contents," you should check if that directory and XML file are there and, if not, create them so the rest of your content provider knows they are out there and available for use.

Similarly, if you have rewritten your content provider sufficiently to cause the data store to shift structure, you should check to see what structure you have now and adjust it if what you have is out-of-date. You don't write your own "installer" program and so have no great way of determining if, when onCreate() is called, this is the first time ever for the content provider, the first time for a new release of a content provider that was upgraded in place, or just a normal startup.

If your content provider uses SQLite for storage, you can detect if your tables exist by querying on the sqlite_master table. This is useful for lazy-creating a table your content provider will need.

For example, here is the onCreate() method for Provider, from the ContentProvider/ Constants sample application available in the Source Code section of http://apress.com:

```
@Override
public boolean onCreate() {
  db=(new DatabaseHelper(getContext())).getWritableDatabase();

  return (db == null) ? false : true;
}
```

While that doesn't seem all that special, the "magic" is in the private DatabaseHelper object, described in the chapter on database access.

query()

As one might expect, the query() method is where your content provider gets details on a query some activity wants to perform. It is up to you to actually process said query.

The query method gets the following as parameters:

- A Uri representing the collection or instance being queried

- A String[] representing the list of properties that should be returned

- A String representing what amounts to a SQL WHERE clause, constraining which instances should be considered for the query results

- A String[] representing values to "pour into" the WHERE clause, replacing any ? found there

- A String representing what amounts to a SQL ORDER BY clause

You are responsible for interpreting these parameters however they make sense and returning a Cursor that can be used to iterate over and access the data.

As you can imagine, these parameters are aimed toward people using a SQLite database for storage. You are welcome to ignore some of these parameters (e.g., you can elect not to try to roll your own SQL WHERE-clause parser), but you need to document that fact so activities attempt to query you only by instance Uri and not using parameters you elect not to handle.

For SQLite-backed storage providers, however, the query() method implementation should be largely boilerplate. Use a SQLiteQueryBuilder to convert the various parameters into a single SQL statement, then use query() on the builder to actually invoke the query and give you a Cursor back. The Cursor is what your query() method then returns.

For example, here is query() from Provider:

```
@Override
public Cursor query(Uri url, String[] projection, String selection,
                    String[] selectionArgs, String sort) {
  SQLiteQueryBuilder qb=new SQLiteQueryBuilder();

  qb.setTables(getTableName());
```

```
    if (isCollectionUri(url)) {
      qb.setProjectionMap(getDefaultProjection());
    }
    else {
      qb.appendWhere(getIdColumnName()+"="+url.getPathSegments().get(1));
    }

    String orderBy;

    if (TextUtils.isEmpty(sort)) {
      orderBy=getDefaultSortOrder();
    } else {
      orderBy=sort;
    }

    Cursor c=qb.query(db, projection, selection, selectionArgs,
                      null, null, orderBy);
    c.setNotificationUri(getContext().getContentResolver(), url);
    return c;
}
```

We create a SQLiteQueryBuilder and pour the query details into the builder. Note that the query could be based on either a collection or an instance Uri—in the latter case, we need to add the instance ID to the query. When done, we use the query() method on the builder to get a Cursor for the results.

insert()

Your insert() method will receive a Uri representing the collection and a ContentValues structure with the initial data for the new instance. You are responsible for creating the new instance, filling in the supplied data, and returning a Uri to the new instance.

If this is a SQLite-backed content provider, once again, the implementation is mostly boilerplate: validate that all required values were supplied by the activity, merge your own notion of default values with the supplied data, and call insert() on the database to actually create the instance.

For example, here is insert() from Provider:

```
@Override
public Uri insert(Uri url, ContentValues initialValues) {
  long rowID;
  ContentValues values;

  if (initialValues!=null) {
    values=new ContentValues(initialValues);
  } else {
    values=new ContentValues();
  }
```

```
  if (!isCollectionUri(url)) {
    throw new IllegalArgumentException("Unknown URL " + url);
  }

  for (String colName : getRequiredColumns()) {
    if (values.containsKey(colName) == false) {
      throw new IllegalArgumentException("Missing column: "+colName);
    }
  }

  populateDefaultValues(values);

  rowID=db.insert(getTableName(), getNullColumnHack(), values);
  if (rowID > 0) {
    Uri uri=ContentUris.withAppendedId(getContentUri(), rowID);
    getContext().getContentResolver().notifyChange(uri, null);
    return uri;
  }

  throw new SQLException("Failed to insert row into " + url);
}
```

The pattern is the same as before: use the provider particulars plus the data to be inserted to actually do the insertion. Please note the following:

- You can insert only into a collection Uri, so we validate that by calling isCollectionUri().

- The provider knows what columns are required (getRequiredColumns()), so we iterate over those and confirm our supplied values cover the requirements.

- The provider is responsible for filling in any default values (populateDefaultValues()) for columns not supplied in the insert() call and not automatically handled by the SQLite table definition.

update()

Your update() method gets the Uri of the instance or collection to change, a ContentValues structure with the new values to apply, a String for a SQL WHERE clause, and a String[] with parameters to use to replace ? found in the WHERE clause. Your responsibility is to identify the instance(s) to be modified (based on the Uri and WHERE clause), then replace those instances' current property values with the ones supplied.

This will be annoying unless you're using SQLite for storage. Then you can pretty much pass all the parameters you received to the update() call to the database, though the update() call will vary slightly depending on whether you are updating one instance or several.

For example, here is update() from Provider:

```
@Override
public int update(Uri url, ContentValues values, String where, String[] whereArgs) {
  int count;

  if (isCollectionUri(url)) {
    count=db.update(getTableName(), values, where, whereArgs);
  }
  else {
    String segment=url.getPathSegments().get(1);
    count=db
        .update(getTableName(), values, getIdColumnName()+"="
            + segment
            + (!TextUtils.isEmpty(where) ? " AND (" + where
                + ')' : ""), whereArgs);
  }

  getContext().getContentResolver().notifyChange(url, null);
  return count;
}
```

In this case, updates can either be to a specific instance or applied across the entire collection, so we check the Uri (isCollectionUri()) and, if it is an update for the collection, just perform the update. If we are updating a single instance, we need to add a constraint to the WHERE clause to only update for the requested row.

delete()

Like update(), delete() receives a Uri representing the instance or collection to work with and a WHERE clause and parameters. If the activity is deleting a single instance, the Uri should represent that instance and the WHERE clause may be null. But the activity might be requesting to delete an open-ended set of instances, using the WHERE clause to constrain which ones to delete.

As with update(), though, this is simple if you are using SQLite for database storage (sense a theme?). You can let it handle the idiosyncrasies of parsing and applying the WHERE clause—all you have to do is call delete() on the database.

For example, here is delete() from Provider:

```
@Override
public int delete(Uri url, String where, String[] whereArgs) {
  int count;
  long rowId=0;

  if (isCollectionUri(url)) {
    count=db.delete(getTableName(), where, whereArgs);
  }
```

```
  else {
    String segment=url.getPathSegments().get(1);
    rowId=Long.parseLong(segment);
    count=db
        .delete(getTableName(), getIdColumnName()+"="
            + segment
            + (!TextUtils.isEmpty(where) ? " AND (" + where
                + ')' : ""), whereArgs);
  }

  getContext().getContentResolver().notifyChange(url, null);
  return count;
}
```

This is almost a clone of the update() implementation described earlier in this chapter—either delete a subset of the entire collection or delete a single instance (if it also satisfies the supplied WHERE clause).

getType()

The last method you need to implement is getType(). This takes a Uri and returns the MIME type associated with that Uri. The Uri could be a collection or an instance Uri; you need to determine which was provided and return the corresponding MIME type.

For example, here is getType() from Provider:

```
@Override
public String getType(Uri url) {
  if (isCollectionUri(url)) {
    return(getCollectionType());
  }

  return(getSingleType());
}
```

As you can see, most of the logic delegates to private getCollectionType() and getSingleType() methods:

```
private String getCollectionType() {
  return("vnd.android.cursor.dir/vnd.commonsware.constant");
}

private String getSingleType() {
  return("vnd.android.cursor.item/vnd.commonsware.constant");
}
```

Step #2: Supply a Uri

You also need to add a public static member . . . somewhere, containing the Uri for each collection your content provider supports. Typically this is a public static final Uri put on the content-provider class itself:

```
public static final Uri CONTENT_URI=
  Uri.parse("content://com.commonsware.android.tourit.Provider/tours");
```

You may wish to use the same namespace for the content Uri that you use for your Java classes, to reduce the chance of collision with others.

Step #3: Declare the Properties

Remember those properties you referenced when you were using a content provider in the previous chapter? Well, you need to have those too for your own content provider.

Specifically, you want a public static class implementing BaseColumns that contains your property names, such as this example from Provider:

```
public static final class Constants implements BaseColumns {
  public static final Uri CONTENT_URI
      =Uri.parse("content://com.commonsware.android.constants.Provider/constants");
  public static final String DEFAULT_SORT_ORDER="title";
  public static final String TITLE="title";
  public static final String VALUE="value";
}
```

If you are using SQLite as a data store, the values for the property name constants should be the corresponding column name in the table, so you can just pass the projection (array of properties) to SQLite on a query(), or pass the ContentValues on an insert() or update().

Note that nothing in here stipulates the types of the properties. They could be strings, integers, or whatever. The biggest limitation is what a Cursor can provide access to via its property getters. The fact that there is nothing in code that enforces type safety means you should document the property types well so people attempting to use your content provider know what they can expect.

Step #4: Update the Manifest

The glue tying the content-provider implementation to the rest of your application resides in your AndroidManifest.xml file. Simply add a <provider> element as a child of the <application> element:

```
<provider
  android:name=".Provider"
  android:authorities="com.commonsware.android.tourit.Provider" />
```

The android:name property is the name of the content-provider class, with a leading dot to indicate it is in the stock namespace for this application's classes (just like you use with activities).

The android:authorities property should be a semicolon-delimited list of the authority values supported by the content provider. Recall, from earlier in this chapter, that each content Uri is made up of a scheme, an authority, a data type path, and an instance identifier. Each authority from each CONTENT_URI value should be included in the android:authorities list.

Now when Android encounters a content Uri, it can sift through the providers registered through manifests to find a matching authority. That tells Android which application and class implements the content provider, and from there Android can bridge between the calling activity and the content provider being called.

Notify-on-Change Support

An optional feature your content provider offers its clients is notify-on-change support. This means that your content provider will let clients know if the data for a given content Uri changes.

For example, suppose you have created a content provider that retrieves RSS and Atom feeds from the Internet based on the user's feed subscriptions (via OPML, perhaps). The content provider offers read-only access to the contents of the feeds, with an eye toward several applications on the phone using those feeds versus everyone implementing their own feed-poll-fetch-and-cache system. You have also implemented a service that will get updates to those feeds asynchronously, updating the underlying data store. Your content provider could alert applications using the feeds that such-and-so feed was updated, so applications using that specific feed could refresh and get the latest data.

On the content-provider side, to do this call notifyChange() on your ContentResolver instance (available in your content provider via getContext().getContentResolver()). This takes two parameters: the Uri of the piece of content that changed, and the ContentObserver that initiated the change. In many cases, the latter will be null; a non-null value simply means the observer that initiated the change will not be notified of its own changes.

On the content-consumer side, an activity can call registerContentObserver() on its ContentResolver (via getContentResolver()). This ties a ContentObserver instance to a supplied Uri—the observer will be notified whenever notifyChange() is called for that specific Uri. When the consumer is done with the Uri, unregisterContentObserver() releases the connection.

CHAPTER 29

■ ■ ■

Requesting and Requiring Permissions

In the late 1990s a wave of viruses spread through the Internet, delivered via email, using contact information culled from Microsoft Outlook. A virus would simply email copies of itself to each of the Outlook contacts that had an email address. This was possible because, at the time, Outlook did not take any steps to protect data from programs using the Outlook API, since that API was designed for ordinary developers, not virus authors.

Nowadays, many applications that hold onto contact data secure that data by requiring that a user explicitly grant rights for other programs to access the contact information. Those rights could be granted on a case-by-case basis or once at install time.

Android is no different, in that it requires permissions for applications to read or write contact data. Android's permission system is useful well beyond contact data, and for content providers and services beyond those supplied by the Android framework.

You, as an Android developer, will frequently need to ensure your applications have the appropriate permissions to do what you want to do with other applications' data. You may also elect to require permissions for other applications to use your data or services, if you make those available to other Android components. This chapter covers how to accomplish both these ends.

Mother, May I?

Requesting the use of other applications' data or services requires the uses-permission element to be added to your AndroidManifest.xml file. Your manifest may have zero or more uses-permission elements, all as direct children of the root manifest element.

The uses-permission element takes a single attribute, android:name, which is the name of the permission your application requires:

```
<uses-permission
  android:name="android.permission.ACCESS LOCATION" />
```

The stock system permissions all begin with `android.permission` and are listed in the Android SDK documentation for `Manifest.permission`. Third-party applications may have their own permissions, which hopefully they have documented for you. Here are some of the more important built-in permissions:

- `INTERNET`, if your application wishes to access the Internet through any means, from raw Java sockets through the `WebView` widget

- `READ CALENDAR`, `READ CONTACTS`, and the like for reading data out of the built-in content providers

- `WRITE CALENDAR`, `WRITE CONTACTS`, and the like for modifying data in the built-in content providers

Permissions are confirmed at the time the application is installed—the user will be prompted to confirm it is OK for your application to do what the permission calls for. This prompt is not available in the current emulator, however.

If you do not have the desired permission and you try to do something that needs it, you may get a `SecurityException` informing you of the missing permission, but this is not a guarantee—failures may come in other forms, depending on if something else is catching and trying to handle that exception.

Halt! Who Goes There?

The other side of the coin, of course, is to secure your own application. If your application is merely activities and intent receivers, security may be just an *outbound* thing, where you request the right to use resources of other applications. If, on the other hand, you put content providers or services in your application, you will want to implement *inbound* security to control which applications can do what with the data.

Note that the issue here is less about whether other applications might "mess up" your data, and more about privacy of the user's information or use of services that might incur expense. That is where the stock permissions for built-in Android applications are focused—can you read or modify contacts, can you send SMS messages, etc. If your application does not store information that might be considered private, security is less of an issue. If, on the other hand, your application stores private data, such as medical information, security is much more important.

The first step to securing your own application using permissions is to declare said permissions, once again in the `AndroidManifest.xml` file. In this case, instead of `uses-permission`, you add `permission` elements. Once again, you can have zero or more `permission` elements, all as direct children of the root `manifest` element.

Declaring a permission is slightly more complicated than using a permission. There are three pieces of information you need to supply:

1. The symbolic name of the permission. To keep your permissions from colliding with those from other applications, you should use your application's Java namespace as a prefix.

2. A label for the permission: something short that is understandable by users.

3. A description for the permission: something a wee bit longer that is understandable by your users.

```
<permission
  android:name="vnd.tlagency.sekrits.SEE SEKRITS"
  android:label="@string/see sekrits label"
  android:description="@string/see sekrits description" />
```

This does not enforce the permission. Rather, it indicates that it is a possible permission; your application must still flag security violations as they occur.

There are two ways for your application to enforce permissions, dictating where and under what circumstances they are required. You can enforce permissions in your code, but the easier option is to indicate in the manifest where permissions are required.

Enforcing Permissions via the Manifest

Activities, services, and intent receivers can all declare an attribute named android:permission, whose value is the name of the permission that is required to access those items:

```
<activity
  android:name=".SekritApp"
  android:label="Top Sekrit"
  android:permission="vnd.tlagency.sekrits.SEE SEKRITS">
  <intent-filter>
    <action android:name="android.intent.action.MAIN" />
    <category
      android:name="android.intent.category.LAUNCHER" />
  </intent-filter>
</activity>
```

Only applications that have requested your indicated permission will be able to access the secured component. In this case, "access" means the following:

- Activities cannot be started without the permission.

- Services cannot be started, stopped, or bound to an activity without the permission.

- Intent receivers ignore messages sent via sendBroadcast() unless the sender has the permission.

Content providers offer two distinct attributes: readPermission and writePermission:

```
<provider
    android:name=".SekritProvider"
    android:authorities="vnd.tla.sekrits.SekritProvider"
    android:readPermission="vnd.tla.sekrits.SEE SEKRITS"
    android:writePermission="vnd.tla.sekrits.MOD SEKRITS" />
```

In this case, readPermission controls access to querying the content provider, while writePermission controls access to insert, update, or delete data in the content provider.

Enforcing Permissions Elsewhere

In your code, you have two additional ways to enforce permissions.

Your services can check permissions on a per-call basis via checkCallingPermission(). This returns PERMISSION GRANTED or PERMISSION DENIED, depending on whether the caller has the permission you specified. For example, if your service implements separate read and write methods, you could get the effect of readPermission and writePermission in code by checking those methods for the permissions you need from Java.

Also, you can include a permission when you call sendBroadcast(). This means that eligible receivers must hold that permission; those without the permission are ineligible to receive it. For example, the Android subsystem presumably includes the RECEIVE SMS permission when it broadcasts that an SMS message has arrived—this will restrict the receivers of that intent to be only those authorized to receive SMS messages.

May I See Your Documents?

There is no automatic discovery of permissions at compile time; all permission failures occur at runtime. Hence, it is important that you document the permissions required for your public APIs, including content providers, services, and activities intended for launching from other activities. Otherwise, the programmers attempting to interface with your application will have to find out the permission rules by trial and error.

Furthermore, you should expect that users of your application will be prompted to confirm any permissions your application says it needs. Hence, you need to document for your users what they should expect, lest they get confused by the question posed by the phone and elect to not install or use your application.

CHAPTER 30

■■■

Creating a Service

As noted previously, Android services are for long-running processes that may need to keep running even when decoupled from any activity. Examples include playing music even if the "player" activity gets garbage-collected, polling the Internet for RSS/Atom feed updates, and maintaining an online chat connection even if the chat client loses focus due to an incoming phone call.

Services are created when manually started (via an API call) or when some activity tries connecting to the service via inter-process communication (IPC). Services will live until no longer needed and if RAM needs to be reclaimed. Running for a long time isn't without its costs, though, so services need to be careful not to use too much CPU or keep radios active much of the time, or else the service causes the device's battery to get used up too quickly.

This chapter covers how you can create your own services; the next chapter covers how you can use such services from your activities or other contexts. Both chapters will analyze the Service/WeatherPlus sample application, with this chapter focusing mostly on the WeatherPlusService implementation. WeatherPlusService extends the weather-fetching logic of the original Internet/Weather sample, by bundling it in a service that monitors changes in location, so the weather is updated as the emulator is "moved".

Service with Class

Creating a service implementation shares many characteristics with building an activity. You inherit from an Android-supplied base class, override some lifecycle methods, and hook the service into the system via the manifest.

The first step in creating a service is to extend the Service class, in our case with our own WeatherPlusService subclass.

Just as activities have onCreate(),onResume(),onPause() and kin, Service implementations can override three different lifecycle methods:

1. onCreate(), which, as with activities, is called when the service process is created

2. onStart(), which is called when a service is manually started by some other process, versus being implicitly started as the result of an IPC request (discussed more in Chapter 31)

3. onDestroy(), which is called as the service is being shut down.

Common startup and shutdown logic should go in `onCreate()` and `onDestroy()`;`onStart()` is mostly if your service needs data passed into it from the starting process and you don't wish to use IPC.

For example, here is the `onCreate()` method for `WeatherPlusService`:

```
@Override
public void onCreate() {
  super.onCreate();

  client=new DefaultHttpClient();
  format=getString(R.string.url);

  myLocationManager=(LocationManager)getSystemService(Context.LOCATION_SERVICE);
  myLocationManager.requestLocationUpdates("gps", 10000,
                                          10000.0f,
                                          onLocationChange);
}
```

First, we chain upward to the superclass, so Android can do any setup work it needs to have done. Then we initialize our `HttpClient` and format string as we did in the Weather demo. We then get the `LocationManager` instance for our application and request to get updates as our location changes, via the `gps` `LocationProvider`, which will be discussed in Chapter 33.

The `onDestroy()` method is much simpler:

```
@Override
public void onDestroy() {
  super.onDestroy();

  myLocationManager.removeUpdates(onLocationChange);
}
```

Here, we just shut down the location-monitoring logic, in addition to chaining upward to the superclass for any Android internal bookkeeping that might be needed.

In addition to those lifecycle methods, though, your service also needs to implement `onBind()`. This method returns an `IBinder`, which is the linchpin behind the IPC mechanism. If you're creating a service class while reading this chapter, just have this method return null for now, and we'll fill in the full implementation in the next section.

When IPC Attacks!

Services will tend to offer inter-process communication (IPC) as a means of interacting with activities or other Android components. Each service declares what methods it is making available over IPC; those methods are then available for other components to call, with Android handling all the messy details involved with making method calls across component or process boundaries.

The core of this, from the standpoint of the developer, is expressed in AIDL: the Android Interface Description Language. If you have used IPC mechanisms like COM, CORBA, or the like, you will recognize the notion of IDL. AIDL describes the public IPC interface, and Android supplies tools to build the client and server side of that interface.

With that in mind, let's take a look at AIDL and IPC.

Write the AIDL

IDLs are frequently written in a "language-neutral" syntax. AIDL, on the other hand, looks a lot like a Java interface. For example, here is the AIDL for the `IWeather`:

```
package com.commonsware.android.service;

// Declare the interface.
interface IWeather {
  String getForecastPage();
}
```

As with a Java interface, you declare a package at the top. As with a Java interface, the methods are wrapped in an interface declaration (`interface IWeather { ... }`). And, as with a Java interface, you list the methods you are making available.

The differences, though, are critical.

First, not every Java type can be used as a parameter. Your choices are:

- Primitive values (`int`, `float`, `double`, `boolean`, etc.)

- `String` and `CharSequence`

- `List` and `Map` (from `java.util`)

- Any other AIDL-defined interfaces

- Any Java classes that implement the `Parcelable` interface, which is Android's flavor of serialization

In the case of the latter two categories, you need to include `import` statements referencing the names of the classes or interfaces that you are using (e.g., `import com.commonsware. android.ISomething`). This is true even if these classes are in your own package—you have to import them anyway.

Next, parameters can be classified as `in`, `out`, or `inout`. Values that are `out` or `inout` can be changed by the service and those changes will be propagated back to the client. Primitives (e.g., `int`) can only be `in`; we included `in` for the AIDL for `enable()` just for illustration purposes.

Also, you cannot throw any exceptions. You will need to catch all exceptions in your code, deal with them, and return failure indications some other way (e.g., error code return values).

Name your AIDL files with the `.aidl` extension and place them in the proper directory based on the package name.

When you build your project, either via an IDE or via Ant, the `aidl` utility from the Android SDK will translate your AIDL into a server stub and a client proxy.

Implement the Interface

Given the AIDL-created server stub, now you need to implement the service, either directly in the stub, or by routing the stub implementation to other methods you have already written.

The mechanics of this are fairly straightforward:

- Create a private instance of the AIDL-generated `.Stub` class (e.g., `IWeather.Stub`)

- Implement methods matching up with each of the methods you placed in the AIDL

- Return this private instance from your `onBind()` method in the `Service` subclass

For example, here is the `IWeather.Stub` instance:

```
private final IWeather.Stub binder=new IWeather.Stub() {
  public String getForecastPage() {
    return(getForecastPageImpl());
  }
};
```

In this case, the stub calls the corresponding method on the service itself. That method, which simply returns the cached most-recent weather forecast for the current location, is shown here:

```
synchronized private String getForecastPageImpl() {
  return(forecast);
}
```

Note that AIDL IPC calls are synchronous, and so the caller is blocked until the IPC method returns. Hence, your services need to be quick about their work.

Manifest Destiny

Finally, you need to add the service to your `AndroidManifest.xml` file, for it to be recognized as an available service for use. That is simply a matter of adding a `service` element as a child of the `application` element, providing `android:name` to reference your service class.

For example, here is the `AndroidManifest.xml` file for WeatherPlus:

```
<?xml version="1.0" encoding="utf-8"?>
<manifest xmlns:android="http://schemas.android.com/apk/res/android"
    package="com.commonsware.android.service">
  <uses-permission android:name="android.permission.INTERNET" />
  <uses-permission android:name="android.permission.ACCESS_COARSE_LOCATION" />
  <uses-permission android:name="android.permission.ACCESS_FINE_LOCATION" />
```

```
  <application android:label="@string/app_name">
    <activity android:name=".WeatherPlus" android:label="@string/app_name">
      <intent-filter>
        <action android:name="android.intent.action.MAIN" />
        <category android:name="android.intent.category.LAUNCHER" />
      </intent-filter>
    </activity>
    <service android:name=".WeatherPlusService" />
  </application>
</manifest>
```

Since the service class is in the same Java namespace as everything else in this application, we can use the shorthand dot-notation (".WeatherPlusService") to reference our class.

If you wish to require some permission of those who wish to start or bind to the service, add an android:permission attribute naming the permission you are mandating—see Chapter 35 for more details.

Lobbing One Over the Fence

Classic IPC is one-way: the client calls functions on the service. It is possible, through the creative use of AIDL, to allow the service to call back into an activity. However, this is a bit fragile, as the service may not know if the activity is still around or if it has been killed off to free up some memory.

An alternative approach, first mentioned in Chapter 23 which discusses Intent filters, is to have the service send a broadcast Intent that can be picked up by the activity . . . assuming the activity is still around and is not paused. We will examine the client side of this exchange in Chapter 31; for now, let us examine how the service can send a broadcast.

The theory behind the WeatherPlusService implementation is that the service gets "tickled" when the device (or emulator) position changes. At that point, the service calls out to the Web service and generates a new forecast Web page for the activity to display. At the same time, though, the service also sends a broadcast, to alert the activity that there is a page update available if it wants it.

Here is the high-level implementation of the aforementioned flow:

```
private void updateForecast(Location loc) {
  String url=String.format(format, loc.getLatitude(),
                           loc.getLongitude());
  HttpGet getMethod=new HttpGet(url);

  try {
    ResponseHandler<String> responseHandler=new BasicResponseHandler();
    String responseBody=client.execute(getMethod, responseHandler);
    String page=generatePage(buildForecasts(responseBody));

    synchronized(this) {
      forecast=page;
    }
```

```
      sendBroadcast(broadcast);
    }
  catch (Throwable t) {
    android.util.Log.e("WeatherPlus",
                    "Exception in updateForecast()", t);
  }
}
```

Much of this is similar to the equivalent piece of the original Weather demo—perform the HTTP request, convert that into a set of Forecast objects, and turn those into a Web page. The first difference is that the Web page is simply cached in the service, since the service cannot directly put the page into the activity's WebView. The second difference is that we call sendBroadcast(), which takes an Intent and sends it out to all interested parties. That Intent is declared up front in the class prologue:

```
private Intent broadcast=new Intent(BROADCAST_ACTION);
```

Here, BROADCAST_ACTION is simply a static String with a value that will distinguish this Intent from all others:

```
public static final String BROADCAST_ACTION=
        "com.commonsware.android.service.ForecastUpdateEvent";
```

Where's the Remote? And the Rest of the Code?

In Android, services can either be local or remote. Local services run in the same process as the launching activity; remote services run in their own process. A detailed discussion of remote services will be added to a future edition of this book.

We will return to this service in Chapter 33, at which point we will flesh out how locations are tracked (and, in this case, mocked up).

CHAPTER 31

■ ■ ■

Invoking a Service

Services can be used by any application component that "hangs around" for a reasonable period of time. This includes activities, content providers, and other services. Notably, it does not include pure intent receivers (i.e., intent receivers that are not part of an activity), since those will get garbage collected immediately after each instance processes one incoming Intent.

To use a service, you need to get an instance of the AIDL interface for the service, then call methods on that interface as if it were a local object. When done, you can release the interface, indicating you no longer need the service.

In this chapter, we will look at the client side of the Service/WeatherPlus sample application. The WeatherPlus activity looks an awful lot like the original Weather application—just a Web page showing a weather forecast as you can see in Figure 31-1.

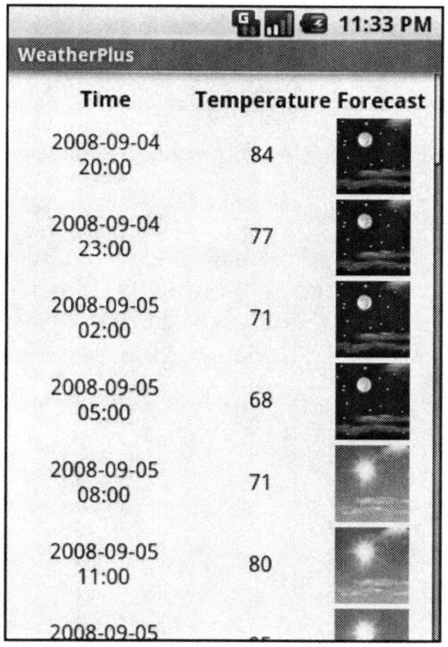

Figure 31-1. *The WeatherPlus service client*

The difference is that, as the emulator "moves", the weather forecast changes, based on updates provided by the service.

Bound for Success

To use a service, you first need to create an instance of your own ServiceConnection class. ServiceConnection, as the name suggests, represents your connection to the service for the purposes of making IPC calls. For example, here is the ServiceConnection from the WeatherPlus class in the WeatherPlus project:

```
private ServiceConnection svcConn=new ServiceConnection() {
  public void onServiceConnected(ComponentName className,
                    IBinder binder) {
    service=IWeather.Stub.asInterface(binder);

    browser.postDelayed(new Runnable() {
      public void run() {
        updateForecast();
      }
    }, 1000);
  }

  public void onServiceDisconnected(ComponentName className) {
    service=null;
  }
};
```

Your ServiceConnection subclass needs to implement two methods:

1. onServiceConnected(), which is called once your activity is bound to the service

2. onServiceDisconnected(), which is called if your connection ends normally, such as you unbinding your activity from the service

Each of those methods receives a ComponentName, which simply identifies the service you connected to. More importantly, onServiceConnected() receives an IBinder instance, which is your gateway to the IPC interface. You will want to convert the IBinder into an instance of your AIDL interface class, so you can use IPC as if you were calling regular methods on a regular Java class (IWeather.Stub.asInterface(binder)).

To actually hook your activity to the service, call bindService() on the activity:

```
bindService(serviceIntent, svcConn, BIND_AUTO_CREATE);
```

The bindService() method takes three parameters:

1. An Intent representing the service you wish to invoke—for your own service, it's easiest to use an intent referencing the service class directly (new Intent(this, WeatherPlusService.class))

2. Your ServiceConnection instance

3. A set of flags—most times, you will want to pass in BIND_AUTO_CREATE, which will start up the service if it is not already running

After your bindService() call, your onServiceConnected() callback in the ServiceConnection will eventually be invoked, at which time your connection is ready for use.

Request for Service

Once your service interface object is ready (IWeather.Stub.asInterface(binder)), you can start calling methods on it as you need to. In fact, if you disabled some widgets awaiting the connection, now is a fine time to re-enable them.

However, you will want to trap two exceptions. One is DeadObjectException—if this is raised, your service connection terminated unexpectedly. In this case, you should unwind your use of the service, perhaps by calling onServiceDisconnected() manually, as shown previously. The other is RemoteException, which is a more general-purpose exception indicating a cross-process communications problem. Again, you should probably cease your use of the service.

Prometheus Unbound

When you are done with the IPC interface, call unbindService(), passing in the ServiceConnection. Eventually, your connection's onServiceDisconnected() callback will be invoked, at which point you should null out your interface object, disable relevant widgets, or otherwise flag yourself as no longer being able to use the service.

For example, in the WeatherPlus implementation of onServiceDisconnected() shown previously, we null out the IWeather service object.

You can always reconnect to the service, via bindService(), if you need to use it again.

Manual Transmission

In addition to binding to the service for the purposes of IPC, you can manually start and stop the service. This is particularly useful in cases where you want the service to keep running independently of your activities—otherwise, once you unbind the service, your service could well be closed down.

To start a service, simply call startService(), providing two parameters:

1. The Intent specifying the service to start (again, the easiest way is probably to specify the service class, if it's your own service)

2. A Bundle providing configuration data, which eventually gets passed to the service's onStart() method

Conversely, to stop the service, call stopService() with the Intent you used in the corresponding startService() call.

Catching the Lob

In Chapter 31, we showed how the service sends a broadcast to let the WeatherPlus activity know a change was made to the forecast based on movement. Now, we can see how the activity receives and uses that broadcast.

Here are the implementations of onResume() and onPause() for WeatherPlus:

```java
@Override
public void onResume() {
  super.onResume();

  registerReceiver(receiver,
      new IntentFilter(WeatherPlusService.BROADCAST_ACTION));
}

@Override
public void onPause() {
  super.onPause();

  unregisterReceiver(receiver);
}
```

In onResume(), we register a static BroadcastReceiver to receive Intents matching the action declared by the service. In onPause(), we disable that BroadcastReceiver, since we will not be receiving any such Intents while paused, anyway.

The BroadcastReceiver, in turn, simply arranges to update the forecast on the UI thread:

```java
private BroadcastReceiver receiver=new BroadcastReceiver() {
  public void onReceive(Context context, Intent intent) {
    runOnUiThread(new Runnable() {
      public void run() {
        updateForecast();
      }
    });
  }
};
```

And updateForecast() uses the interface stub to call into the service and retrieve the latest forecast page, also handling the case where the forecast is not yet ready (null):

```java
private void updateForecast() {
  try {
    String page=service.getForecastPage();

    if (page==null) {
      browser.postDelayed(new Runnable() {
        public void run() {
          updateForecast();
        }
      }, 4000);

      Toast
        .makeText(this, "No forecast available", 2500)
        .show();
    }
```

```
        else {
          browser.loadDataWithBaseURL(null, page, "text/html",
                                      "UTF-8", null);
        }
      }
    }
    catch (final Throwable t) {
      svcConn.onServiceDisconnected(null);

      runOnUiThread(new Runnable() {
        public void run() {
          goBlooey(t);
        }
      });
    }
  }
}
```

■ ■ ■

CHAPTER 32

Alerting Users via Notifications

Pop-up messages. Tray icons and their associated "bubble" messages. Bouncing dock icons. You are no doubt used to programs trying to get your attention, sometimes for good reason. Your phone also probably chirps at you for more than just incoming calls: low battery, alarm clocks, appointment notifications, incoming text message or email, etc.

Not surprisingly, Android has a whole framework for dealing with these sorts of things, collectively called *notifications*.

Types of Pestering

A service, running in the background, needs a way to let users know something of interest has occurred, such as when email has been received. Moreover, the service may need some way to steer the user to an activity where they can act upon the event—reading a received message, for example. For this, Android supplies status-bar icons, flashing lights, and other indicators collectively known as *notifications*.

Your current phone may well have such icons, to indicate battery life, signal strength, whether Bluetooth is enabled, and the like. With Android, applications can add their own status-bar icons, with an eye towards having them appear only when needed (e.g., when a message has arrived).

In Android, you can raise notifications via the NotificationManager. The NotificationManager is a system service. To use it, you need to get the service object via getSystemService (NOTIFICATION_SERVICE) from your activity. The NotificationManager gives you three methods: one to pester (notify()) and two to stop pestering (cancel() and cancelAll()).

The notify() method takes a Notification, which is a data structure that spells out what form your pestering should take. The following sections describe all the public fields at your disposal (but bear in mind that not all devices will necessarily support all of these).

Hardware Notifications

You can flash LEDs on the device by setting lights to true, also specifying the color (as an #ARGB value in ledARGB) and what pattern the light should blink in (by providing off/on durations in milliseconds for the light via ledOnMS and ledOffMS).

You can play a sound, using a Uri to a piece of content held, perhaps, by a ContentManager (sound). Think of this as a ringtone for your application.

You can vibrate the device, controlled via a long[] indicating the on/off patterns (in milliseconds) for the vibration (vibrate). You might do this by default, or you might make it an option the user can choose when circumstances require a more subtle notification than an actual ringtone.

Icons

While the flashing lights, sounds, and vibrations are aimed at getting somebody to look at the device, icons are designed to take them the next step and tell them what's so important.

To set up an icon for a Notification, you need to set two public fields: icon, where you provide the identifier of a Drawable resource representing the icon, and contentIntent, where you supply a PendingIntent to be raised when the icon is clicked. You should be sure the PendingIntent will be caught by something, perhaps your own application code, to take appropriate steps to let the user deal with the event triggering the notification.

You can also supply a text blurb to appear when the icon is put on the status bar (tickerText).

If you want all three, the simpler approach is to call setLatestEventInfo(), which wraps all three of those in a single call.

Seeing Pestering in Action

Let us now take a peek at the Notifications/Notify1 sample project (available in the Source Code section at http://apress.com), in particular the NotifyDemo class:

```
public class NotifyDemo extends Activity {
  private static final int NOTIFY_ME_ID=1337;
  private Timer timer=new Timer();
  private int count=0;

  @Override
  public void onCreate(Bundle savedInstanceState) {
    super.onCreate(savedInstanceState);
    setContentView(R.layout.main);

    Button btn=(Button)findViewById(R.id.notify);
```

```
    btn.setOnClickListener(new View.OnClickListener() {
      public void onClick(View view) {
        TimerTask task=new TimerTask() {
          public void run() {
            notifyMe();
          }
        };

        timer.schedule(task, 5000);
      }
    });

    btn=(Button)findViewById(R.id.cancel);

    btn.setOnClickListener(new View.OnClickListener() {
      public void onClick(View view) {
        NotificationManager mgr=
          (NotificationManager)getSystemService(NOTIFICATION_SERVICE);

        mgr.cancel(NOTIFY_ME_ID);
      }
    });
  }

  private void notifyMe() {
    final NotificationManager mgr=
      (NotificationManager)getSystemService(NOTIFICATION_SERVICE);
    Notification note=new Notification(R.drawable.red_ball,
                                       "Status message!",
                                       System.currentTimeMillis());
    PendingIntent i=PendingIntent.getActivity(this, 0,
                        new Intent(this, NotifyMessage.class),
                                          0);

    note.setLatestEventInfo(this, "Notification Title",
                        "This is the notification message", i);
    note.number=++count;

    mgr.notify(NOTIFY_ME_ID, note);
```

This activity sports two large buttons, one to kick off a notification after a five-second delay, and one to cancel that notification (if it is active). See Figure 32-1.

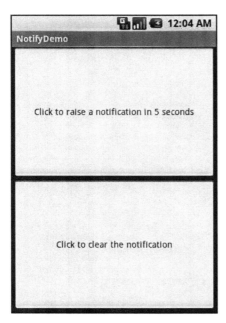

Figure 32-1. *The NotifyDemo activity main view*

Creating the notification, in notifyMe(), is accomplished in five steps:

1. Get access to the NotificationManager instance.

2. Create a Notification object with our icon (red ball), a message to flash on the status bar as the notification is raised, and the time associated with this event.

3. Create a PendingIntent that will trigger the display of another activity (NotifyMessage).

4. Use setLatestEventInfo() to specify that, when the notification is clicked on, we are to display a certain title and message, and if that is clicked on, we launch the PendingIntent.

5. Tell the NotificationManager to display the notification.

Hence, if we click the top button, after five seconds our red ball icon will appear in the status bar. Our status message will also appear briefly, as shown in Figure 32-2.

If you click on the red ball, a drawer will appear beneath the status bar. Drag that drawer all the way to the bottom of the screen to show the outstanding notifications, including our own, as shown in Figure 32-3.

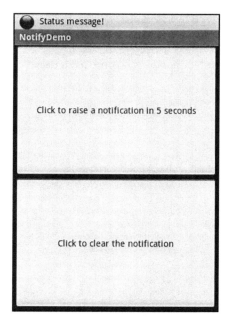

Figure 32-2. *Our notification as it appears on the status bar, with our status message*

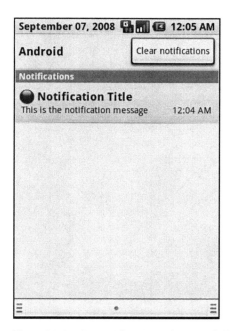

Figure 32-3. *The notifications drawer, fully expanded, with our notification*

If you click on the notification entry in the drawer, you'll be taken to a trivial activity displaying a message—though in a real application this activity would do something useful based upon the event that occurred (e.g., take users to the newly arrived mail messages).

Clicking on the cancel button, or clicking on the Clear Notifications button in the drawer, will remove the red ball from the status bar.

PART 6

Other Android Capabilities

CHAPTER 33

■■■

Accessing Location-Based Services

Apopular feature on current-era mobile devices is GPS capability, so the device can tell you where you are at any point in time. While the most popular use of GPS service is mapping and directions, there are other things you can do if you know your location. For example, you might set up a dynamic chat application where the people you can chat with are based on physical location, so you're chatting with those you are nearest. Or you could automatically geotag posts to Twitter or similar services.

GPS is not the only way a mobile device can identify your location. Alternatives include the following:

- The European equivalent to GPS, called Galileo, which is still under development at the time of this writing

- Cell-tower triangulation, where your position is determined based on signal strength to nearby cell towers

- Proximity to public WiFi "hotspots" that have known geographic locations

Android devices may have one or more of these services available to them. You, as a developer, can ask the device for your location, plus details on what providers are available. There are even ways for you to simulate your location in the emulator, for use in testing your location-enabled applications.

Location Providers: They Know Where You're Hiding

Android devices can have access to several different means of determining your location. Some will have better accuracy than others. Some may be free, while others may have a cost associated with them. Some may be able to tell you more than just your current position, such as your elevation over sea level, or your current speed.

Android, therefore, has abstracted all this out into a set of LocationProvider objects. Your Android environment will have zero or more LocationProvider instances, one for each distinct locating service that is available on the device. Providers know not only your location, but their own characteristics, in terms of accuracy, cost, etc.

You, as a developer, will use a LocationManager, which holds the LocationProvider set, to figure out which LocationProvider is right for your particular circumstance. You will also need the ACCESS_LOCATION permission in your application, or the various location APIs will fail due to a security violation. Depending on which location providers you wish to use, you may need other permissions as well, such as ACCESS_COARSE_LOCATION or ACCESS_FINE_LOCATION.

Finding Yourself

The obvious thing to do with a location service is to figure out where you are right now.

To do that, you need to get a LocationManager—call getSystemService(LOCATION_SERVICE) from your activity or service and cast it to be a LocationManager.

The next step to find out where you are is to get the name of the LocationProvider you want to use. Here, you have two main options:

- Ask the user to pick a provider.

- Find the best-match provider based on a set of criteria.

If you want the user to pick a provider, calling getProviders() on the LocationManager will give you a List of providers, which you can then present to the user for selection.

Or, you can create and populate a Criteria object, stating the particulars of what you want out of a LocationProvider, such as the following:

- setAltitudeRequired() to indicate if you need the current altitude or not

- setAccuracy() to set a minimum level of accuracy, in meters, for the position

- setCostAllowed() to control if the provider must be free or not (i.e., if it can incur a cost on behalf of the device user)

Given a filled-in Criteria object, call getBestProvider() on your LocationManager, and Android will sift through the criteria and give you the best answer. Note that not all of your criteria may be met—all but the monetary-cost criterion might be relaxed if nothing matches.

You are also welcome to hard-wire in a LocationProvider name (e.g., gps), perhaps just for testing purposes.

Once you know the name of the LocationProvider, you can call getLastKnownPosition() to find out where you were recently. Note, however, that "recently" might be fairly out-of-date (e.g., if the phone was turned off) or even null if there has been no location recorded for that provider yet. On the other hand, getLastKnownPosition() incurs no monetary or power cost, since the provider does not need to be activated to get the value.

These methods return a Location object, which can give you the latitude and longitude of the device in degrees as a Java double. If the particular location provider offers other data, you can get at that as well:

- For altitude, hasAltitude() will tell you if there is an altitude value, and getAltitude() will return the altitude in meters.

- For bearing (i.e., compass-style direction), hasBearing() will tell you if there is a bearing available, and getBearing() will return it as degrees east of true north.

- For speed, hasSpeed() will tell you if the speed is known, and getSpeed() will return the speed in meters per second.

A more likely approach to getting the Location from a LocationProvider, though, is to register for updates, as described in the next section.

On the Move

Not all location providers are necessarily immediately responsive. GPS, for example, requires activating a radio and getting a fix from the satellites before you get a location. That is why Android does not offer a getMeMyCurrentLocationNow() method. Combine that with the fact that your users may well want their movements to be reflected in your application, and you are probably best off registering for location updates and using that as your means of getting the current location.

The Weather and WeatherPlus sample applications (available in the Source Code area at http://apress.com) show how to register for updates—call requestLocationUpdates() on your LocationManager instance. This takes four parameters:

1. The name of the location provider you wish to use

2. How long, in milliseconds, must have elapsed before we might get a location update

3. How far, in meters, the device must have moved before we might get a location update

4. A LocationListener that will be notified of key location-related events, as shown in the following code:

```
LocationListener onLocationChange=new LocationListener() {
  public void onLocationChanged(Location location) {
    updateForecast(location);
  }

  public void onProviderDisabled(String provider) {
    // required for interface, not used
  }

  public void onProviderEnabled(String provider) {
    // required for interface, not used
  }
```

```
    public void onStatusChanged(String provider, int status,
                                 Bundle extras) {
      // required for interface, not used
    }
  };
```

Here, all we do is call updateForecast() with the Location supplied to the onLocationChanged() callback method. The updateForecast() implementation, as shown in Chapter 30, builds a Web page with the current forecast for the location and sends a broadcast so the activity knows an update is available.

When you no longer need the updates, call removeUpdates() with the LocationListener you registered.

Are We There Yet? Are We There Yet? Are We There Yet?

Sometimes you want to know not where you are now, or even when you move, but when you get to where you're going. This could be an end destination, or it could be getting to the next step on a set of directions so you can give the user the next turn.

To accomplish this, LocationManager offers addProximityAlert(). This registers a PendingIntent, which will be fired off when the device gets within a certain distance of a certain location. The addProximityAlert() method takes the following as parameters:

- The latitude and longitude of the position that you are interested in.

- A radius, specifying how close you should be to that position for the Intent to be raised.

- A duration for the registration, in milliseconds—after this period, the registration automatically lapses. A value of -1 means the registration lasts until you manually remove it via removeProximityAlert().

- The PendingIntent to be raised when the device is within the "target zone" expressed by the position and radius.

Note that it is not guaranteed that you will actually receive an Intent if there is an interruption in location services or if the device is not in the target zone during the period of time the proximity alert is active. For example, if the position is off by a bit and the radius is a little too tight, the device might only skirt the edge of the target zone, or go by so quickly that the device's location isn't sampled while in the target zone.

It is up to you to arrange for an activity or intent receiver to respond to the Intent you register with the proximity alert. What you then do when the Intent arrives is up to you: set up a notification (e.g., vibrate the device), log the information to a content provider, post a message to a Web site, etc. Note that you will receive the Intent whenever the position is sampled and you are within the target zone—not just upon entering the zone. Hence, you will get the Intent several times, perhaps quite a few times depending on the size of the target zone and the speed of the device's movement.

Testing...Testing...

The Android emulator does not have the ability to get a fix from GPS, triangulate your position from cell towers, or identify your location by some nearby WiFi signal. So, if you want to simulate a moving device, you will need to have some means of providing mock location data to the emulator.

For whatever reason, this particular area has undergone significant changes as Android itself has evolved. It used to be that you could provide mock location data within your application, which was very handy for demonstration purposes. Alas, those options have all been removed as of Android 1.0.

One likely option for supplying mock location data is the Dalvik Debug Monitor Service (DDMS). This is an external program, separate from the emulator, which can feed the emulator single location points or full routes to traverse, in a few different formats. DDMS is described in greater detail in Chapter 37.

■ ■ ■

CHAPTER 34

Mapping with MapView and MapActivity

One of Google's most popular services—after search, of course—is Google Maps, where you can find everything from the nearest pizza parlor to directions from New York City to San Francisco (only 2,905 miles!) to street views and satellite imagery.

Android, not surprisingly, integrates Google Maps. There is a mapping activity available to users straight off the main Android launcher. More relevant to you, as a developer, are `MapView` and `MapActivity`, which allow you to integrate maps into your own applications. Not only can you display maps, control the zoom level, and allow people to pan around, but you can tie in Android's location-based services to show where the device is and where it is going.

Fortunately, integrating basic mapping features into your Android project is fairly easy. However, there is a fair bit of power available to you, if you want to get fancy.

Terms, Not of Endearment

Google Maps, particularly when integrated into third party applications, requires agreeing to a fairly lengthy set of legal terms. These terms include clauses that you may find unpalatable.

If you are considering Google Maps, please review these terms closely to determine if your intended use will not run afoul of any clauses. You are strongly recommended to seek professional legal counsel if there are any potential areas of conflict.

Also, keep your eyes peeled for other mapping options, based off of other sources of map data, such as OpenStreetMap.[1]

The Bare Bones

Far and away the simplest way to get a map into your application is to create your own subclass of `MapActivity`. Like `ListActivity`, which wraps up some of the smarts behind having an activity dominated by a `ListView`, `MapActivity` handles some of the nuances of setting up an activity dominated by a `MapView`.

---

1. http://www.openstreetmap.org/

In your layout for the MapActivity subclass, you need to add an element named, at the time of this writing, com.google.android.maps.MapView. This is the "longhand" way to spell out the names of widget classes, by including the full package name along with the class name. This is necessary because MapView is not in the com.google.android.widget namespace. You can give the MapView widget whatever android:id attribute value you want, plus handle all the layout details to have it render properly alongside your other widgets.

However, you do need to have:

- android:apiKey, which in production will need to be a Google Maps API key—more on this here

- android:clickable = "true", if you want users to be able to click and pan through your map

For example, from the Maps/NooYawk sample application, here is the main layout:

```xml
<?xml version="1.0" encoding="utf-8"?>
<RelativeLayout xmlns:android="http://schemas.android.com/apk/res/android"
  android:layout_width="fill_parent"
  android:layout_height="fill_parent">
  <com.google.android.maps.MapView android:id="@+id/map"
    android:layout_width="fill_parent"
    android:layout_height="fill_parent"
    android:apiKey="<YOUR_API_KEY>"
    android:clickable="true" />
  <LinearLayout android:id="@+id/zoom"
    android:layout_width="wrap_content"
    android:layout_height="wrap_content"
    android:layout_alignParentBottom="true"
    android:layout_alignParentLeft="true" />
</RelativeLayout>
```

We'll cover that mysterious zoom LinearLayout and the apiKey in later sections of this chapter. In addition, you will need a couple of extra things in your AndroidManifest.xml file:

- The INTERNET and ACCESS_COARSE_LOCATION permissions

- Inside your <application>, a <uses-library> element with android:name = "com.google.android.maps", to indicate you are using one of the optional Android APIs

Here is the AndroidManifest.xml file for NooYawk:

```xml
<?xml version="1.0" encoding="utf-8"?>
<manifest xmlns:android="http://schemas.android.com/apk/res/android"
  package="com.commonsware.android.maps">
  <uses-permission android:name="android.permission.INTERNET" />
  <uses-permission android:name="android.permission.ACCESS_COARSE_LOCATION" />
```

```
    <application android:label="@string/app_name">
      <uses-library android:name="com.google.android.maps" />
      <activity android:name=".NooYawk" android:label="@string/app_name">
        <intent-filter>
          <action android:name="android.intent.action.MAIN" />
          <category android:name="android.intent.category.LAUNCHER" />
        </intent-filter>
      </activity>
    </application>
</manifest>
```

That is pretty much all you need for starters, plus to subclass your activity from MapActivity. If you were to do nothing else, and built that project and tossed it in the emulator, you'd get a nice map of the world. Note, however, that MapActivity is abstract— you need to implement isRouteDisplayed() to indicate if you are supplying some sort of driving directions or not.

In theory, the user could pan around the map using the directional pad. However, that's not terribly useful when the user has the whole world in her hands.

Since a map of the world is not much good by itself, we need to add a few things . . .

Exercising Your Control

You can find your MapView widget by findViewById(), no different than any other widget. The widget itself then offers a getMapController() method. Between the MapView and MapController, you have a fair bit of capability to determine what the map shows and how it behaves. The following sections cover zoom and center, the features you will most likely want to use.

Zoom

The map of the world you start with is rather broad. Usually, people looking at a map on a phone will be expecting something a bit narrower in scope, such as a few city blocks.

You can control the zoom level directly via the setZoom() method on the MapController. This takes an integer representing the level of zoom, where 1 is the world view and 21 is the tightest zoom you can get. Each level is a doubling of the effective resolution: 1 has the equator measuring 256 pixels wide, while 21 has the equator measuring 268,435,456 pixels wide. Since the phone's display probably doesn't have 268,435,456 pixels in either dimension, the user sees a small map focused on one tiny corner of the globe. A level of 16 will show you several city blocks in each dimension and is probably a reasonable starting point for you to experiment with.

If you wish to allow users to change the zoom level, you will need to do a few things:

- First, pick a spot on the screen where you want the zoom controls to appear. These are not huge, and they only appear when being used, so they can overlay the actual map itself if you choose. In the layout previously shown, for example, the zoom controls are placed over the map, in the lower-left corner of the screen. You should use a LinearLayout or other simple container for the zoom controls' position in your layout.

- In your activity's onCreate() method, get your zoom controls' container via findViewById().

- Add the result of map.getZoomControls() to that container.

For example, here are the lines from the NooYawk activity's onCreate() method that accomplish the latter points:

```
ViewGroup zoom=(ViewGroup)findViewById(R.id.zoom);
```

```
zoom.addView(map.getZoomControls());
```

Then, you can manually get the zoom controls to appear by calling displayZoomControls() on your MapView, or they will automatically appear when the user pans the map as seen in Figure 34-1.

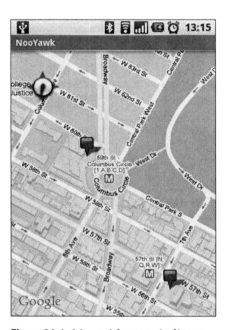

Figure 34-1. *Map with zoom indicator and compass rose*

Center

Typically, you will need to control what the map is showing, beyond the zoom level, such as the user's current location, or a location saved with some data in your activity. To change the map's position, call setCenter() on the MapController.

This takes a GeoPoint as a parameter. A GeoPoint represents a location, via latitude and longitude. The catch is that the GeoPoint stores latitude and longitude as integers representing the actual latitude and longitude multiplied by 1E6. This saves a bit of memory versus storing a float or double, and it probably speeds up some internal calculations Android needs to do to convert the GeoPoint into a map position. However, it does mean you have to remember to multiply the "real world" latitude and longitude by 1E6.

Rugged Terrain

Just as the Google Maps you use on your full-size computer can display satellite imagery, so too can Android maps.

MapView offers toggleSatellite(), which, as the names suggest, toggles on and off the satellite perspective on the area being viewed. You can have the user trigger these via an options menu or, in the case of NooYawk, via keypresses:

```
@Override
  public boolean onKeyDown(int keyCode, KeyEvent event) {
    if (keyCode == KeyEvent.KEYCODE_S) {
      map.setSatellite(!map.isSatellite());
      return(true);
    }
    else if (keyCode == KeyEvent.KEYCODE_Z) {
      map.displayZoomControls(true);
      return(true);
    }

    return(super.onKeyDown(keyCode, event));
  }
```

Layers Upon Layers

If you have ever used the full-size edition of Google Maps, you are probably used to seeing things overlaid atop the map itself, such as "push-pins" indicating businesses near the location being searched. In map parlance—and, for that matter, in many serious graphic editors—the push-pins are on a separate layer than the map itself, and what you are seeing is the composition of the push-pin layer atop the map layer.

Android's mapping allows you to create layers as well, so you can mark up the maps as you need to based on user input and your application's purpose. For example, NooYawk uses a layer to show where select buildings are located in the island of Manhattan.

Overlay Classes

Any overlay you want to add to your map needs to be implemented as a subclass of Overlay. There is an ItemizedOverlay subclass available if you are looking to add push-pins or the like; ItemizedOverlay simplifies this process.

To attach an overlay class to your map, just call getOverlays() on your MapView and add() your Overlay instance to it:

```
marker.setBounds(0, 0, marker.getIntrinsicWidth(),
                       marker.getIntrinsicHeight());


map.getOverlays().add(new SitesOverlay(marker));
```

We will explain that marker in just a bit.

Drawing the ItemizedOverlay

As the name suggests, ItemizedOverlay allows you to supply a list of points of interest to be displayed on the map—specifically, instances of OverlayItem. The overlay, then, handles much of the drawing logic for you. Here are the minimum steps to make this work:

- First, override ItemizedOverlay<OverlayItem> as your own subclass (in this example, SitesOverlay)

- In the constructor, build your roster of OverlayItem instances, and call populate() when they are ready for use by the overlay

- Implement size() to return the number of items to be handled by the overlay

- Override createItem() to return OverlayItem instances given an index

- When you instantiate your ItemizedOverlay subclass, provide it with a Drawable that represents the default icon (e.g., push-pin) to display for each item

The marker from the NooYawk constructor is the Drawable used for the last bullet—it shows a push-pin, as illustrated in Figure 34-1 earlier in this chapter.

You may also wish to override draw() to do a better job of handling the shadow for your markers. While the map will handle casting a shadow for you, it appears you need to provide a bit of assistance for it to know where the "bottom" of your icon is, so it can draw the shadow appropriately.

For example, here is SitesOverlay:

```
private class SitesOverlay extends ItemizedOverlay<OverlayItem> {
  private List<OverlayItem> items=new ArrayList<OverlayItem>();
  private Drawable marker=null;

  public SitesOverlay(Drawable marker) {
    super(marker);
    this.marker=marker;

    items.add(new OverlayItem(getPoint(40.748963847316034,
                                       -73.96807193756104),
                              "UN", "United Nations"));
    items.add(new OverlayItem(getPoint(40.76866299974387,
                                       -73.98268461227417),
                              "Lincoln Center",
                              "Home of Jazz at Lincoln Center"));
    items.add(new OverlayItem(getPoint(40.765136435316755,
                                       -73.97989511489868),
                              "Carnegie Hall",
          "Where you go with practice, practice, practice"));
    items.add(new OverlayItem(getPoint(40.70686417491799,
                                       -74.01572942733765),
                              "The Downtown Club",
                  "Original home of the Heisman Trophy"));
```

```
      populate();
    }

    @Override
    protected OverlayItem createItem(int i) {
      return(items.get(i));
    }

    @Override
    public void draw(Canvas canvas, MapView mapView,
                     boolean shadow) {
      super.draw(canvas, mapView, shadow);

      boundCenterBottom(marker);
    }

    @Override
    protected boolean onTap(int i) {
      Toast.makeText(NooYawk.this,
                     items.get(i).getSnippet(),
                     Toast.LENGTH_SHORT).show();

      return(true);
    }

    @Override
    public int size() {
      return(items.size());
    }
}
```

Handling Screen Taps

An Overlay subclass can also implement onTap(), to be notified when the user taps on the map, so the overlay can adjust what it draws. For example, in full-size Google Maps, clicking on a push-pin pops up a bubble with information about the business at that pin's location. With onTap(), you can do much the same in Android.

The onTap() method for ItemizedOverlay receives the index of the OverlayItem that was clicked. It is up to you to do something worthwhile with this event.

In the case of SitesOverlay, as previously shown, onTap() looks like this:

```
@Override
protected boolean onTap(int i) {
  Toast.makeText(NooYawk.this,
                 items.get(i).getSnippet(),
                 Toast.LENGTH_SHORT).show();

  return(true);
}
```

Here, we just toss up a short Toast with the "snippet" from the OverlayItem, returning true to indicate we handled the tap.

My, Myself, and MyLocationOverlay

Android has a built-in overlay to handle two common scenarios:

- Showing where you are on the map, based on GPS or other location-providing logic

- Showing where you are pointed, based on the built-in compass sensor, where available

All you need to do is create a MyLocationOverlay instance, add it to your MapView's list of overlays, and enable and disable the desired features at appropriate times.

The "at appropriate times" notion is for maximizing battery life. There is no sense in updating locations or directions when the activity is paused, so it is recommended that you enable these features in onResume() and disable them in onPause().

For example, NooYawk will display a compass rose using MyLocationOverlay. To do this, we first need to create the overlay and add it to the list of overlays:

```
me=new MyLocationOverlay(this, map);
map.getOverlays().add(me);
```

Then, we enable and disable the compass rose as appropriate:

```
@Override
public void onResume() {
  super.onResume();

  me.enableCompass();
}

@Override
public void onPause() {
  super.onPause();

  me.disableCompass();
}
```

The Key to It All

If you actually download the source code for the book, compile the NooYawk project, install it in your emulator, and run it, you will probably see a screen with a grid and a couple of push-pins, but no actual maps.

That's because the API key in the source code is invalid for your development machine. Instead, you will need to generate your own API key(s) for use with your application.

Full instructions for generating API keys, for development and production use, can be found on the Android Web site.[2] In the interest of brevity, let's focus on the narrow case of getting NooYawk running in your emulator. Doing this requires the following steps:

1. Visit the API key signup page and review the terms of service.

2. Re-read those terms of service and make really, really sure you want to agree to them.

3. Find the MD5 digest of the certificate used for signing your debug-mode applications (described in detail in the following).

4. On the API key signup page, paste in that MD5 signature and submit the form.

5. On the resulting page, copy the API key and paste it as the value of apiKey in your MapView-using layout.

The trickiest part is finding the MD5 signature of the certificate used for signing your debug-mode applications . . . and much of the complexity is merely in making sense of the concept.

All Android applications are signed using a digital signature generated from a certificate. You are automatically given a debug certificate when you set up the SDK, and there is a separate process for creating a self-signed certificate for use in your production applications. This signature process involves the use of the Java keytool and jarsigner utilities. For the purposes of getting your API key, you only need to worry about keytool.

To get your MD5 digest of your debug certificate, if you are on OS X or Linux, use the following command:

```
keytool -list -alias androiddebugkey -keystore ~/.android/debug.keystore -storepass
android -keypass android
```

On other development platforms, you will need to replace the value of the -keystore switch with the location for your platform and user account:

- Windows XP: C:\Documents and Settings\<user>\Local Settings\Application Data\Android\debug.keystore

- Windows Vista: C:\Users\<user>\AppData\Local\Android\debug.keystore

(where <user> is your account name)

The second line of the output contains your MD5 digest, as a series of pairs of hex digits separated by colons.

---

2. http://code.google.com/android/toolbox/apis/mapkey.html

CHAPTER 35

■ ■ ■

Handling Telephone Calls

Many, if not most, Android devices will be phones. As such, not only will users be expecting to place and receive calls using Android, but you will have the opportunity to help them place calls, if you wish.

Why might you want to?

- Maybe you are writing an Android interface to a sales management application (a la Salesforce.com) and you want to offer users the ability to call prospects with a single button click, and without them having to keep those contacts both in your application and in the phone's contacts application

- Maybe you are writing a social networking application, and the roster of phone numbers that you can access shifts constantly, so rather than try to "sync" the social network contacts with the phone's contact database, you let people place calls directly from your application

- Maybe you are creating an alternative interface to the existing contacts system, perhaps for users with reduced motor control (e.g., the elderly), sporting big buttons and the like to make it easier for them to place calls

Whatever the reason, Android has the means to let you manipulate the phone just like any other piece of the Android system.

Report to the Manager

To get at much of the phone API, you use the TelephonyManager. That class lets you do things like:

- Determine if the phone is in use via getCallState(), with return values of CALL_STATE_IDLE (phone not in use), CALL_STATE_RINGING (call requested but still being connected), and CALL_STATE_OFFHOOK (call in progress)

- Find out the SIM ID (IMSI) via getSubscriberId()

- Find out the phone type (e.g., GSM) via getPhoneType() or find out the data connection type (e.g., GPRS, EDGE) via getNetworkType()

You Make the Call!

You can also initiate a call from your application, such as from a phone number you obtained through your own Web service. To do this, simply craft an ACTION_DIAL Intent with a Uri of the form tel:NNNNN (where NNNNN is the phone number to dial) and use that Intent with startActivity(). This will not actually dial the phone; rather, it activates the dialer activity, from which the user can then press a button to place the call.

For example, let's look at the Phone/Dialer sample application. Here's the crude-but-effective layout:

```xml
<?xml version="1.0" encoding="utf-8"?>
<LinearLayout xmlns:android="http://schemas.android.com/apk/res/android"
    android:orientation="vertical"
    android:layout_width="fill_parent"
    android:layout_height="fill_parent"
    >
  <LinearLayout
    android:orientation="horizontal"
    android:layout_width="fill_parent"
    android:layout_height="wrap_content"
    >
    <TextView
      android:layout_width="wrap_content"
      android:layout_height="wrap_content"
      android:text="Number to dial:"
      />
    <EditText android:id="@+id/number"
      android:layout_width="fill_parent"
      android:layout_height="wrap_content"
      android:cursorVisible="true"
      android:editable="true"
      android:singleLine="true"
    />
  </LinearLayout>
  <Button android:id="@+id/dial"
    android:layout_width="fill_parent"
    android:layout_height="wrap_content"
    android:layout_weight="1"
    android:text="Dial It!"
  />
</LinearLayout>
```

We have a labeled field for typing in a phone number, plus a button for dialing said number. The Java code simply launches the dialer using the phone number from the field:

```java
package com.commonsware.android.dialer;

import android.app.Activity;
import android.content.Intent;
import android.net.Uri;
import android.os.Bundle;
import android.view.View;
import android.widget.Button;
import android.widget.EditText;

public class DialerDemo extends Activity {
  @Override
  public void onCreate(Bundle icicle) {
    super.onCreate(icicle);
    setContentView(R.layout.main);

    final EditText number=(EditText)findViewById(R.id.number);
    Button dial=(Button)findViewById(R.id.dial);

    dial.setOnClickListener(new Button.OnClickListener() {
      public void onClick(View v) {
        String toDial="tel:"+number.getText().toString();

        startActivity(new Intent(Intent.ACTION_DIAL,
                          Uri.parse(toDial)));
      }
    });
  }
}
```

The activity's own UI is not that impressive as shown in Figure 35-1.

Figure 35-1. *The DialerDemo sample application, as initially launched*

However, the dialer you get from clicking the dial button is better, showing you the number you are about to dial in Figure 35-2.

Figure 35-2. *The Android Dialer activity, as launched from DialerDemo*

CHAPTER 36

■ ■ ■

Searching with SearchManager

One of the firms behind the Open Handset Alliance—Google—has a teeny-weeny Web search service, one you might have heard of in passing. Given that, it's not surprising that Android has some built-in search capabilities. Specifically, Android has baked in the notion of searching not only on the device for data, but over the air to Internet sources of data. Your applications can participate in the search process by triggering searches or perhaps by allowing your application's data to be searched.

Note that this is fairly new to the Android platform, and so some shifting in the APIs is likely.

Hunting Season

There are two types of search in Android: local and global. Local search searches within the current application; global search searches the Web via Google's search engine. You can initiate either type of search in a variety of ways, including the following:

- You can call onSearchRequested() from a button or menu choice, which will initiate a local search (unless you override this method in your activity).

- You can directly call startSearch() to initiate a local or global search, including optionally supplying a search string to use as a starting point.

- You can elect to have keyboard entry kick off a search via setDefaultKeyMode(), for either local search (setDefaultKeyMode(DEFAULT_KEYS_SEARCH_LOCAL)) or global search (setDefaultKeyMode(DEFAULT_KEYS_SEARCH_GLOBAL)).

In either case, the search appears as a set of UI components across the top of the screen, with your activity blurred underneath it (see Figures 36-1 and 36-2).

Figure 36-1. *The Android local search pop-up*

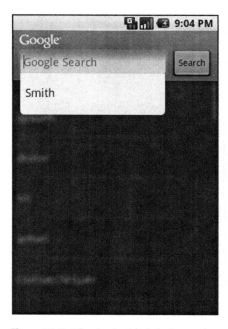

Figure 36-2. *The Android global search pop-up, showing a drop-down with previous searches*

Search Yourself

Over the long haul, there will be two flavors of search available via the Android search system:

- Query-style search, where the user's search string is passed to an activity that is responsible for conducting the search and displaying the results

- Filter-style search, where the user's search string is passed to an activity on every key press, and the activity is responsible for updating a displayed list of matches

Since the latter approach is under heavy development right now by the Android team, let's focus on the first one.

Craft the Search Activity

The first thing you'll want to do if you want to support query-style search in your application is to create a search activity. While it might be possible to have a single activity be both opened from the launcher and opened from a search, that might prove somewhat confusing to users. Certainly, for the purposes of learning the techniques, having a separate activity is cleaner.

The search activity can have any look you want. In fact, other than watching for queries, a search activity looks, walks, and talks like any other activity in your system.

All the search activity needs to do differently is check the intents supplied to onCreate() (via getIntent()) and onNewIntent() to see if one is a search, and, if so, to do the search and display the results.

For example, let's look at the Search/Lorem sample application (available in the Source Code section of http://apress.com). This starts off as a clone of the list-of-lorem-ipsum-words application that we first built back when showing off the ListView container in Chapter 8, then with XML resources in Chapter 19. Now we update it to support searching the list of words for ones containing the search string.

The main activity and the search activity share a common layout: a ListView plus a TextView showing the selected entry:

```xml
<?xml version="1.0" encoding="utf-8"?>
<LinearLayout xmlns:android="http://schemas.android.com/apk/res/android"
  android:orientation="vertical"
  android:layout_width="fill_parent"
  android:layout_height="fill_parent" >
  <TextView
    android:id="@+id/selection"
    android:layout_width="fill_parent"
    android:layout_height="wrap_content"
  />
  <ListView
    android:id="@android:id/list"
    android:layout_width="fill_parent"
    android:layout_height="fill_parent"
    android:drawSelectorOnTop="false"
  />
</LinearLayout>
```

In terms of Java code, most of the guts of the activities are poured into an abstract
LoremBase class:

```java
abstract public class LoremBase extends ListActivity {
  abstract ListAdapter makeMeAnAdapter(Intent intent);

  private static final int LOCAL_SEARCH_ID = Menu.FIRST+1;
  private static final int GLOBAL_SEARCH_ID = Menu.FIRST+2;
  private static final int CLOSE_ID = Menu.FIRST+3;
  TextView selection;
  ArrayList<String> items=new ArrayList<String>();

  @Override
  public void onCreate(Bundle icicle) {
    super.onCreate(icicle);
    setContentView(R.layout.main);
    selection=(TextView)findViewById(R.id.selection);

    try {
      XmlPullParser xpp=getResources().getXml(R.xml.words);

      while (xpp.getEventType()!=XmlPullParser.END_DOCUMENT) {
        if (xpp.getEventType()==XmlPullParser.START_TAG) {
          if (xpp.getName().equals("word")) {
            items.add(xpp.getAttributeValue(0));
          }
        }

        xpp.next();
      }
    }
    catch (Throwable t) {
      Toast
        .makeText(this, "Request failed: "+t.toString(), 4000)
        .show();
    }

    setDefaultKeyMode(DEFAULT_KEYS_SEARCH_LOCAL);

    onNewIntent(getIntent());
  }

  @Override
  public void onNewIntent(Intent intent) {
    ListAdapter adapter=makeMeAnAdapter(intent);
```

```java
    if (adapter==null) {
      finish();
    }
    else {
      setListAdapter(adapter);
    }
  }

  public void onListItemClick(ListView parent, View v, int position,
                long id) {
    selection.setText(items.get(position).toString());
  }

  @Override
  public boolean onCreateOptionsMenu(Menu menu) {
    menu.add(Menu.NONE, LOCAL_SEARCH_ID, Menu.NONE, "Local Search")
          .setIcon(android.R.drawable.ic_search_category_default);
    menu.add(Menu.NONE, GLOBAL_SEARCH_ID, Menu.NONE, "Global Search")
          .setIcon(R.drawable.search)
          .setAlphabeticShortcut(SearchManager.MENU_KEY);
    menu.add(Menu.NONE, CLOSE_ID, Menu.NONE, "Close")
          .setIcon(R.drawable.eject)
          .setAlphabeticShortcut('c');

    return(super.onCreateOptionsMenu(menu));
  }

  @Override
  public boolean onOptionsItemSelected(MenuItem item) {
    switch (item.getItemId()) {
      case LOCAL_SEARCH_ID:
        onSearchRequested();
        return(true);

      case GLOBAL_SEARCH_ID:
        startSearch(null, false, null, true);
        return(true);

      case CLOSE_ID:
        finish();
        return(true);
    }

    return(super.onOptionsItemSelected(item));
  }
}
```

This activity takes care of everything related to showing a list of words, even loading the words out of the XML resource. What it does not do is come up with the ListAdapter to put into the ListView—that is delegated to the subclasses.

The main activity—LoremDemo—just uses a ListAdapter for the whole word list:

```
package com.commonsware.android.search;

import android.content.Intent;
import android.widget.ArrayAdapter;
import android.widget.ListAdapter;

public class LoremDemo extends LoremBase {
  @Override
  ListAdapter makeMeAnAdapter(Intent intent) {
    return(new ArrayAdapter<String>(this,
                      android.R.layout.simple_list_item_1,
                      items));
  }
}
```

The search activity, though, does things a bit differently. First, it inspects the Intent supplied to the abstract makeMeAnAdapter() method. That Intent comes from either onCreate() or onNewIntent(). If the intent is an ACTION_SEARCH, then we know this is a search. We can get the search query and, in the case of this silly demo, spin through the loaded list of words and find only those containing the search string. That list then gets wrapped in a ListAdapter and returned for display:

```
package com.commonsware.android.search;

import android.app.SearchManager;
import android.content.Intent;
import android.widget.ArrayAdapter;
import android.widget.ListAdapter;
import java.util.ArrayList;
import java.util.List;

public class LoremSearch extends LoremBase {
  @Override
  ListAdapter makeMeAnAdapter(Intent intent) {
    ListAdapter adapter=null;

    if (intent.getAction().equals(Intent.ACTION_SEARCH)) {
      String query=intent.getStringExtra(SearchManager.QUERY);
      List<String> results=searchItems(query);
```

```
      adapter=new ArrayAdapter<String>(this,
                    android.R.layout.simple_list_item_1,
                    results);
      setTitle("LoremSearch for: "+query);
    }

    return(adapter);
  }

  private List<String> searchItems(String query) {
    List<String> results=new ArrayList<String>();

    for (String item : items) {
      if (item.indexOf(query)>-1) {
        results.add(item);
      }
    }

    return(results);
  }
}
```

Update the Manifest

While this implements search, it doesn't tie it into the Android search system. That requires a few changes to the auto-generated AndroidManifest.xml file:

```xml
<manifest xmlns:android="http://schemas.android.com/apk/res/android"
  package="com.commonsware.android.search">
  <application>
    <activity android:name=".LoremDemo" android:label="LoremDemo">
      <intent-filter>
        <action android:name="android.intent.action.MAIN" />
        <category android:name="android.intent.category.LAUNCHER" />
      </intent-filter>
      <meta-data android:name="android.app.default_searchable"
            android:value=".LoremSearch" />
    </activity>
    <activity
      android:name=".LoremSearch"
      android:label="LoremSearch"
      android:launchMode="singleTop">
      <intent-filter>
        <action android:name="android.intent.action.SEARCH" />
        <category android:name="android.intent.category.DEFAULT" />
      </intent-filter>
```

```
        <meta-data android:name="android.app.searchable"
                android:resource="@xml/searchable" />
      </activity>
    </application>
  </manifest>
```

The changes needed are as follows:

1. The LoremDemo main activity gets a meta-data element, with an android:name of android. app.default_searchable and a android:value of the search implementation class (.LoremSearch).

2. The LoremSearch activity gets an intent filter for android.intent.action.SEARCH, so search intents will be picked up.

3. The LoremSearch activity is set to have android:launchMode = "singleTop", which means at most one instance of this activity will be open at any time so we don't wind up with a whole bunch of little search activities cluttering up the activity stack.

4. The LoremSearch activity gets a meta-data element, with an android:name of android. app.searchable and a android:value of an XML resource containing more information about the search facility offered by this activity (@xml/searchable).

```
<searchable xmlns:android="http://schemas.android.com/apk/res/android"
      android:label="@string/searchLabel"
      android:hint="@string/searchHint" />
```

That XML resource provides two bits of information today:

- What name should appear in the search domain button to the right of the search field, identifying to the user where they are searching (android:label)

- What hint text should appear in the search field, to give the user a clue as to what they should be typing in (android:hint)

Searching for Meaning in Randomness

Given all that, search is now available—Android knows your application is searchable and what search domain to use when searching from the main activity, and the activity knows how to do the search.

The options menu for this application has both local and global search options. In the case of local search, we just call onSearchRequested(); in the case of global search, we call startSearch() with true in the last parameter, indicating the scope is global.

Typing in a letter or two then clicking Search, will bring up the search activity and the subset of words containing what you typed, with your search query in the activity title bar. You can get the same effect if you just start typing in the main activity, since it is set up for triggering a local search.

■ ■ ■

CHAPTER 37

Development Tools

The Android SDK is more than a library of Java classes and API calls. It also includes a number of tools to assist in application development.

Much of the focus has been on the Eclipse plug-in, to integrate Android development with that IDE. Secondary emphasis has been placed on the plug-in's equivalents for use in other IDEs or without an IDE, such as adb for communicating with a running emulator.

This chapter will cover other tools beyond those two groups.

Hierarchical Management

Android comes with a Hierarchy Viewer tool, designed to help you visualize your layouts as they are seen in a running activity in a running emulator. For example, you can determine how much space a certain widget is taking up, or try to find where a widget is hiding that does not appear on the screen.

To use the Hierarchy Viewer, you first need to fire up your emulator, install your application, launch your activity, and navigate to the spot you wish to examine. As you can see from Figure 37-1, for illustration purposes, we'll use the ReadWrite demo application we introduced back in Chapter 18.

You can launch the Hierarchy Viewer via the hierarchyviewer program, found in the tools/ directory in your Android SDK installation. This brings up the main Hierarchy Viewer window shown in Figure 37-2.

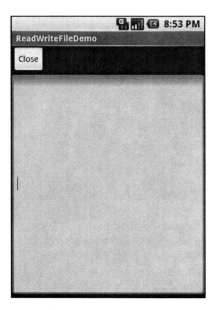

Figure 37-1. *ReadWrite demo application*

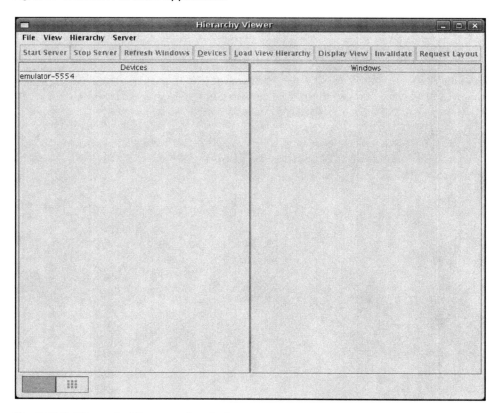

Figure 37-2. *Hierarchy Viewer main window*

The list on the left shows the various emulators you have opened. The number after the hyphen should line up with the number in parentheses in your emulator's title bar.

Clicking on an emulator shows, on the right, the list of windows available for examination as you can see in Figure 37-3.

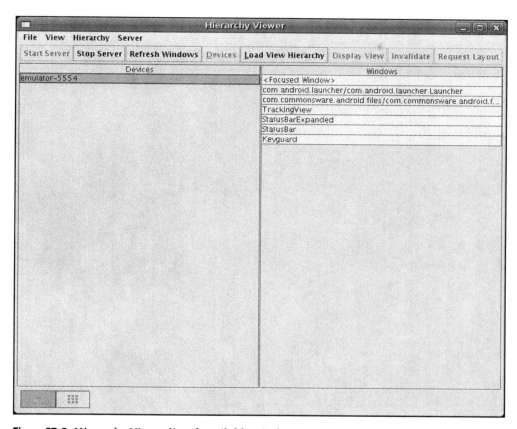

Figure 37-3. *Hierarchy Viewer list of available windows*

Note how there are many other windows besides our open activity, including the Launcher (i.e., the home screen), the Keyguard (i.e., the "Press Menu to Unlock" black screen you get when first opening the emulator), and so on. Your activity will be identified by application package and class (e.g., com.commonsware.android.files/...).

Where things get interesting, though, is when you choose a window and click Load View Hierarchy. After a few seconds, the details spring into view, in a perspective called the Layout View (see Figure 37-4).

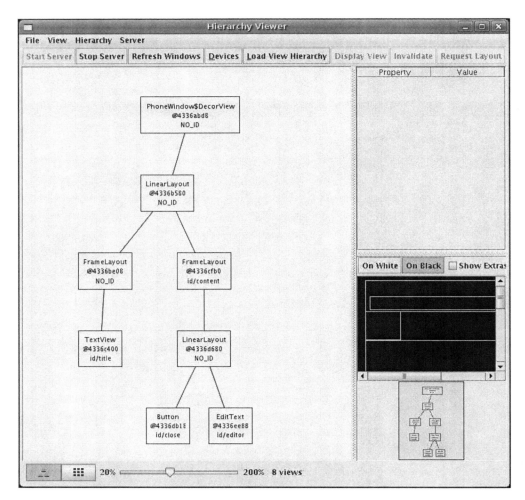

Figure 37-4. *Hierarchy Viewer Layout View*

The main area of the Layout View shows a tree of the various Views that make up your activity, starting from the overall system window and driving down into the individual UI widgets that users are supposed to interact with. You will see, on the lower-right branch of the tree, the LinearLayout, Button, and EditText shown in the previous code listing. The remaining Views are all supplied by the system, including the title bar.

Clicking on one of the views adds more information to this perspective and can be seen in Figure 37-5.

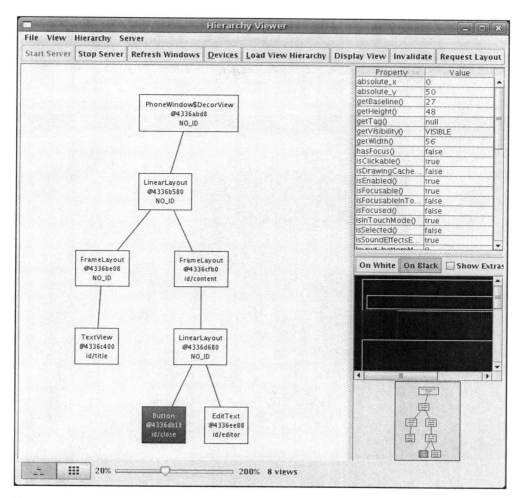

Figure 37-5. *Hierarchy Viewer View properties*

Now, in the upper-right region of the viewer, we see properties of the selected widget—in this case, the Button. Alas, these properties do not appear to be editable.

Also, the widget is highlighted in red in the wireframe of the activity, shown beneath the properties (by default, views are shown as white outlines on a black background). This can help you ensure you have selected the right widget, if, say, you have several buttons and cannot readily tell from the tree what is what.

If you double-click on a View in the tree, you are given a pop-up pane showing just that View (and its children), isolated from the rest of your activity.

Down in the lower-left corner, you will see two toggle buttons, with the tree button initially selected. Clicking on the grid button puts the viewer in a whole new perspective, called the Pixel Perfect View (see Figure 37-6).

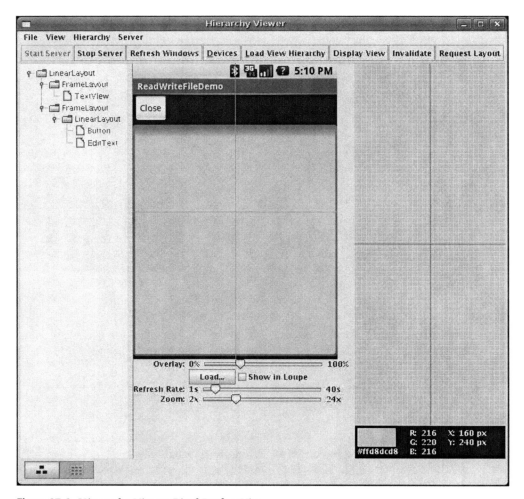

Figure 37-6. *Hierarchy Viewer Pixel Perfect View*

On the left, you see a tree representing the widgets and other Views in your activity. In the middle, you see your activity (the Normal View), and on the right, you see a zoomed edition of your activity (the Loupe View).

What may not be initially obvious is that this imagery is live. Your activity is polled every so often, controlled by the Refresh Rate slider. Anything you do in the activity will then be reflected in the Pixel Perfect View's Normal and Loupe Views.

The hairlines (cyan) overlaying the activity show the position being zoomed upon—just click on a new area to change where the Loupe View is inspecting. Of course, there is another slider to adjust how much the Loupe View is zoomed.

Delightful Dalvik Debugging Detailed, Demoed

Another tool in the Android developer's arsenal is the Dalvik Debug Monitor Service (DDMS). This is a "Swiss Army knife," allowing you to do everything from browse log files, update the GPS location provided by emulator, simulate incoming calls and messages, and browse the on-emulator storage to push and pull files.

DDMS has a wide range of uses, so this section will not try to cover them all, rather it will cover the most useful at the time of writing.

To launch DDMS, run the ddms program inside the tools/ directory in your Android SDK distribution. It will initially display just a tree of emulators and running programs on the left (see Figure 37-7).

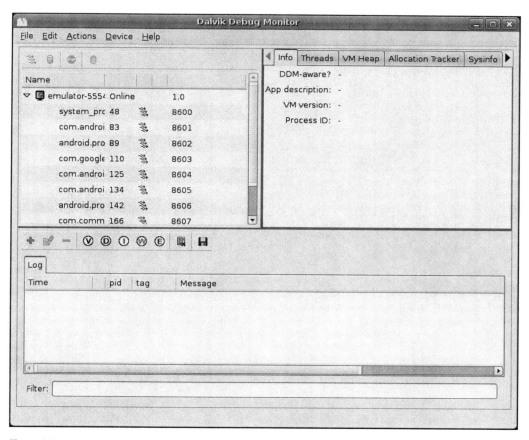

Figure 37-7. *DDMS initial view*

Clicking on an emulator allows you to browse the event log on the bottom and manipulate the emulator via the tabs on the right as shown in Figure 37-8.

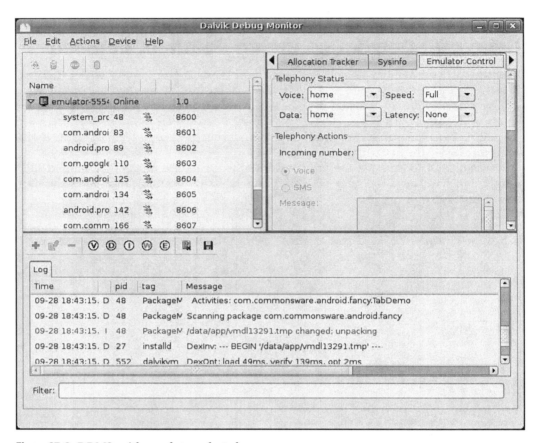

Figure 37-8. *DDMS, with emulator selected*

Logging

Rather than use `adb logcat`, DDMS lets you view your logging information in a scrollable table. Just highlight the emulator or device you want to monitor, and the bottom half of the screen shows the logs (see Figure 37-9).

In addition, you can:

- Filter the Log tab by any of the five logging levels, shown as the V through E toolbar buttons.

- Create a custom filter, so you can view only those tagged with your application's tag, by pressing the + toolbar button and completing the form. The name you enter in the form will be used as the name of another logging output tab in the bottom portion of the DDMS main window.

- Save the log information to a text file for later perusal, or for searching.

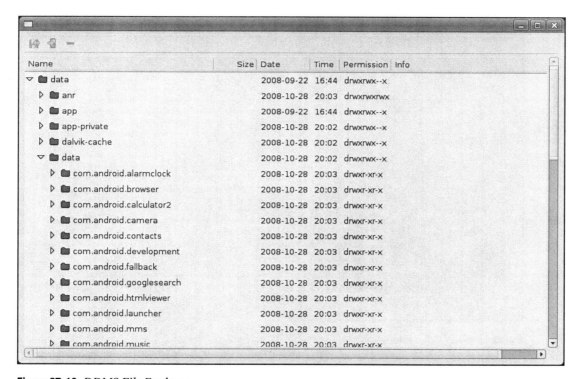

Figure 37-9. *DDMS logging filter*

File Push and Pull

While you can use adb pull and adb push to get files to and from an emulator or device, DDMS lets you do that visually. Just highlight the emulator or device you wish to work with, then choose **Device ➤ File Explorer...** from the main menu. That will bring up the typical directory browser seen in Figure 37-10.

Name	Size	Date	Time	Permission	Info
▽ ▪ data		2008-09-22	16:44	drwxrwx--x	
▷ ▪ anr		2008-10-28	20:03	drwxrwxrwx	
▷ ▪ app		2008-09-22	16:44	drwxrwx--x	
▷ ▪ app-private		2008-10-28	20:02	drwxrwx--x	
▷ ▪ dalvik-cache		2008-10-28	20:02	drwxrwx--x	
▽ ▪ data		2008-10-28	20:02	drwxrwx--x	
▷ ▪ com.android.alarmclock		2008-10-28	20:03	drwxr-xr-x	
▷ ▪ com.android.browser		2008-10-28	20:03	drwxr-xr-x	
▷ ▪ com.android.calculator2		2008-10-28	20:03	drwxr-xr-x	
▷ ▪ com.android.camera		2008-10-28	20:03	drwxr-xr-x	
▷ ▪ com.android.contacts		2008-10-28	20:03	drwxr-xr-x	
▷ ▪ com.android.development		2008-10-28	20:03	drwxr-xr-x	
▷ ▪ com.android.fallback		2008-10-28	20:03	drwxr-xr-x	
▷ ▪ com.android.googlesearch		2008-10-28	20:03	drwxr-xr-x	
▷ ▪ com.android.htmlviewer		2008-10-28	20:03	drwxr-xr-x	
▷ ▪ com.android.launcher		2008-10-28	20:03	drwxr-xr-x	
▷ ▪ com.android.mms		2008-10-28	20:03	drwxr-xr-x	
▷ ▪ com.android.music		2008-10-28	20:03	drwxr-xr-x	

Figure 37-10. *DDMS File Explorer*

Just browse to the file you want and click either the pull (left-most) or push (middle) toolbar button to transfer the file to/from your development machine. Or, click the delete (right-most) toolbar button to delete the file.

There are a few caveats to this:

- You cannot create directories through this tool. You will either need to use adb shell or create them from within your application.

- While you can putter through most of the files on an emulator, you can access very little outside of /sdcard on an actual device, due to Android security restrictions.

Screenshots

To take a screenshot of the Android emulator or device, simply press <Ctrl>-<S> or choose **Device ➤ Screen capture...** from the main menu. This will bring up a dialog box containing an image of the current screen shown in Figure 37-11.

Figure 37-11. *DDMS screen capture*

From here, you can click **Save** to save the image as a PNG file somewhere on your development machine, **Refresh** to update the image based on the current state of the emulator or device, or **Done** to close the dialog.

Location Updates

To use DDMS to supply location updates to your application, the first thing you must do is have your application use the gps LocationProvider, as that is the one that DDMS is set to update.

Then, click on the Emulator Control tab and scroll down to the Location Controls section. Here, you will find a smaller tabbed pane with three options for specifying locations: Manual, GPX, and KML (see Figure 37-12).

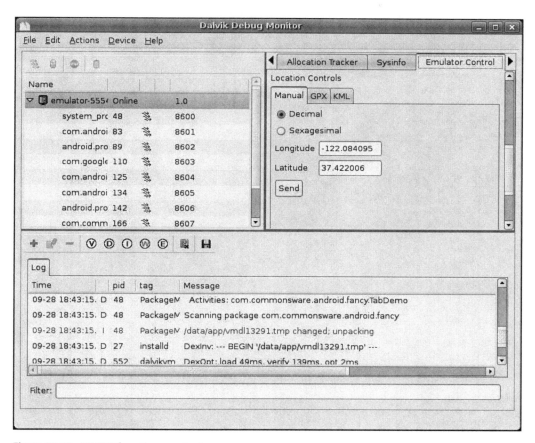

Figure 37-12. *DDMS location controls*

The Manual tab is fairly self-explanatory: provide a latitude and longitude and click the Send button to submit that location to the emulator. The emulator, in turn will notify any location listeners of the new position.

Discussion of the GPX and KML options is beyond the scope of this book.

Placing Calls and Messages

If you want to simulate incoming calls or SMS messages to the Android emulator, DDMS can handle that as well.

On the Emulator Control tab, above the Location Controls group, is the Telephony Actions group (see Figure 37-13).

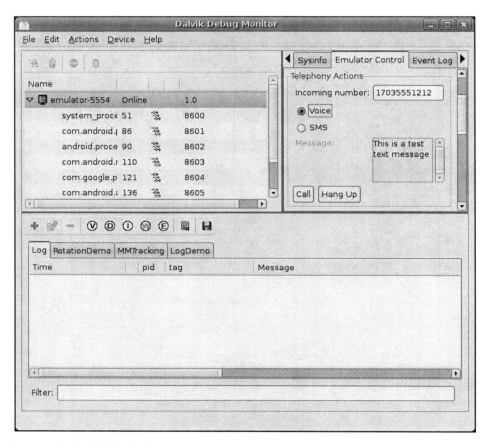

Figure 37-13. *DDMS telephony controls*

To simulate an incoming call, fill in a phone number, choose the Voice radio button, and click Call. At that point, the emulator will show the incoming call, allowing you to accept it (via the green phone button) or reject it (via the red phone button) seen in Figure 37-14.

To simulate an incoming text message, fill in a phone number, choose the SMS radio button, enter a message in the provided text area, and click Send. The text message will then appear as a notification as shown in Figure 37-15.

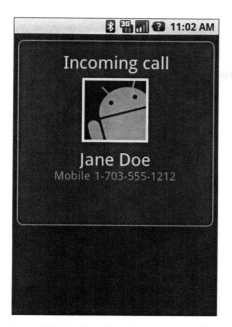

Figure 37-14. *Simulated incoming call*

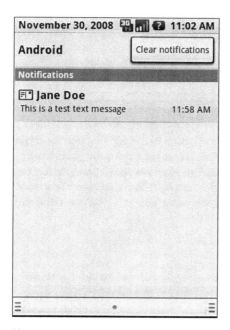

Figure 37-15. *Simulated text message*

Of course, you can click on the notification to view the message in the full-fledged Messaging application as you can see in Figure 37-16.

Figure 37-16. *Simulated text message, in Messaging application*

Put it On My Card

The T-Mobile G1 has a microSD card slot. Many other Android devices are likely to have similar forms of removable storage, which the Android platform refers to generically as an "SD card".

SD cards are strongly recommended to be used by developers as the holding pen for large data sets: images, movie clips, audio files, etc. The T-Mobile G1, in particular, has a relatively paltry amount of on-board flash memory, so the more you can store on an SD card, the better.

Of course, the challenge is that, while the G1 has an SD card by default, the emulator does not. To make the emulator work like the G1, you need to create and "insert" an SD card into the emulator.

Creating a Card Image

Rather than require emulators to somehow have access to an actual SD card reader and use actual SD cards, Android is set up to use card images. An image is simply a file that the emulator will treat as if it were an SD card volume. If you are used to disk images used with virtualization tools (e.g., VirtualBox), the concept is the same: Android uses a disk image representing the SD card contents.

To create such an image, use the mksdcard utility, provided in the tools/ directory of your SDK installation. This takes two main parameters:

1. The size of the image, and hence the size of the resulting "card." If you just supply a number, it is interpreted as a size in bytes. Alternatively, you can append K or M to the number to indicate a size in kilobytes or megabytes, respectively.

2. The filename under which to store the image.

For example, to create a 1GB SD card image, to simulate the G1's SD card in the emulator, you could run:

```
mksdcard 1024M sdcard.img
```

Inserting the Card

To have your emulator use this SD card image, start the emulator with the -sdcard switch, containing a fully-qualified path to the image file you created using mksdcard. While there will be no visible impact—there is no icon or anything in Android showing that you have a card mounted—the /sdcard path will now be available for reading and writing.

To put files on the /sdcard, either use the File Explorer in DDMS or adb push and adb pull from the console.

■ ■ ■

CHAPTER 38

Where Do We Go from Here?

Obviously, this book does not cover everything. And while your number-one resource (besides the book) is going to be the Android SDK documentation, you are likely to need information beyond what's covered in either of those places.

Searching online for "android" and a class name is a good way to turn up tutorials that reference a given Android class. However, bear in mind that tutorials written before late August 2008 are probably written for the M5 SDK and, therefore, will require considerable adjustment to work properly in current SDKs.

Beyond randomly hunting around for tutorials, though, this chapter outlines some resources to keep in mind.

Questions. Sometimes with Answers.

The official places to get assistance with Android are the Android Google Groups. With respect to the SDK, there are three to consider following:

- Android Beginners,[1] a great place to ask entry-level questions

- Android Developers,[2] best suited for more-complicated questions or ones that delve into less-used portions of the SDK

- Android Discuss,[3] designed for free-form discussion of anything Android-related, not necessarily for programming questions and answers

You might also consider these:

- The Android tutorials and programming forums at anddev.org[4]

- The #android IRC channel on freenode

---

1. http://groups.google.com/group/android-beginners
2. http://groups.google.com/group/android-developers
3. http://groups.google.com/group/android-discuss
4. http://anddev.org/

Heading to the Source

The source code to Android is now available. Mostly this is for people looking to enhance, improve, or otherwise fuss with the insides of the Android operating system. But, it is possible that you will find the answers you seek in that code, particularly if you want to see how some built-in Android component does its thing.

The source code and related resources can be found at the Android Open Source Project Web site.[5] Here, you can

- Download[6] or browse[7] the source code

- File bug reports[8] against the operating system itself

- Submit patches[9] and learn about the process for how such patches get evaluated and approved

- Join a separate set of Google Groups[10] for Android platform development

Getting Your News Fix

Ed Burnette, a nice guy who happened to write his own Android book, is also the manager of Planet Android,[11] a feed aggregator for a number of Android-related blogs. Subscribing to the planet's feed will let you monitor quite a few Android-related blog posts, though not exclusively related to programming.

Now to focus more on programming-related Android-referencing blog posts; you can search DZone for "android" and subscribe to a feed[12] based on that search.

You might also consider keeping tabs on those mentioning Android in Twitter messages, such as by using a Summize feed.[13]

---

5. http://source.android.com
6. http://source.android.com/download
7. http://git.source.android.com/
8. http://source.android.com/report-bugs
9. http://source.android.com/submit-patches
10. http://source.android.com/discuss
11. http://www.planetandroid.com/
12. http://www.dzone.com/links/feed/search/android/rss.xml
13. http://summize.com/search.atom?lang=en&q=android

Introducing Android 1.5

Android is a continuously changing product. In fact, while this book was being put into production Google and the Open Handset Alliance released Android 1.5.

This was great for you, the developer, because Android 1.5 adds in quite a bit more to the product.

On the other hand, the timing left a bit to be desired in terms of getting this book into print. The vast majority of what you have read so far is accurate for Android 1.1 and Android 1.5. This Appendix will point out the exceptions—the places where Android changed and so the advice for Android 1.1 is no longer correct. Those changes are few in number, so the bulk of this Appendix is spent covering what is new and how, in basic terms, you can make use of the new material as a developer. This material is nowhere near the depth that you will find in the rest of the book, because Android 1.5 has been available for only a few weeks, and it will take months to write up everything that is new and exciting.

Getting Started, Virtually

Android 1.5 introduced the Android Virtual Device (AVD) system. This allows you to have multiple Android emulator images available, targeting different device profiles. Each image can vary in terms of Android API version (e.g., 1.1 versus 1.5), available add-ons (e.g., whether or not Google Maps are included), and hardware capabilities (e.g., does it have a touch screen?).

To create an AVD, you must first choose a "target". Targets represent a combination of an API version and a set of available add-ons. You can find out the available targets for your environment by executing the following command:

```
android list targets
```

For example, at the time of this writing, three targets are available:

- 1, indicating the Android 1.1 SDK with no add-ons

- 2, indicating the Android 1.5 SDK with no add-ons

- 3, indicating the Android 1.5 SDK with the Google Maps add-on

Then, once you have a target in mind, to create the AVD itself, execute the following command:

```
android create avd -n ... -t ...
```

The first ellipsis indicates where you specify your own name for this AVD; the second ellipsis is where you fill in the target you wish from the available targets in your environment.

If you choose a target that represents a "standard system image" (i.e., no add-ons), you will be prompted to optionally configure the hardware profile. If you go through that process, you will be able to determine how much RAM is in your emulated device, whether or not it has a touchscreen, etc.

Creation, Yes. Myth, No.

With the new AVD system comes a new way of creating and updating projects for use with the Ant build system.

To create a new project, run `android create project`. This will require a few additional parameters, notably:

- `-k` to supply the package name to use with your application (e.g., `-k com.commonsware. android.sample`)

- `-n` to supply the name of the project, which will determine the name of the APK file (e.g., `-n MyProject`)

- `-a` to supply the name of the activity class (e.g., `-a MyMainActivity`)

- `-t` to supply the target ID for use with this project, following the same target system used when creating AVDs, described in the preceding section "Getting Started, Virtually" (e.g., `-t 3`)

- `-p` to indicate where the project files should be generated (e.g., `-n MyProject`)

To update an existing project, run `android update project`. This will replace your build.xml file and do a few other odds and ends to convert a project to be built using the Android 1.5 build system. As with `android create project`, you will want to provide a few additional parameters on the command, including:

- `-t` to supply the target ID for use with this project, following the same target system used when creating AVDs, described in the preceding section "Getting Started, Virtually" (e.g., `-t 3`)

- `-p` to indicate where the project files should be generated (e.g., `-n MyProject`)

Make Your Demands Heard

In addition to using the target ID system to indicate what level of device your project is targeting, you can use a new `AndroidManifest.xml` element to specify hardware that is required for your application to run properly.

You can add one or more `<uses-configuration>` elements inside the `<manifest>` element. Each `<uses-configuration>` element specifies one valid configuration of hardware that your application will work with.

At the present time, there are five possible hardware requirements you can specify this way:

- `android:reqFiveWayNav` to indicate you need a 5-way navigation pointing device of some form (e.g., `android:reqFiveWayNav="true"`)

- `android:reqNavigation` to restrict the 5-way navigation pointing device to a specific type (e.g., `android:reqNavigation="trackball"`)

- `android:reqHardKeyboard` to specify if a hardware (physical) keyboard is required (e.g., `android:reqHardKeyboard="true"`)

- `android:reqKeyboardType`, probably used in conjunction with `android:reqHardKeyboard`, to indicate a specific type of hardware keyboard that is required (e.g., `android:reqKeyboardType="qwerty"`)

- `android:reqTouchScreen` to indicate what type of touchscreen is required, if any (e.g., `android:reqTouchScreen="finger"`)

Add and Subtract

Since the Android M5 SDK in the summer of 2008, Google Maps has been available to application developers willing to agree to the terms and conditions. However, since Google Maps is not part of the open source Android project, there was always the possibility that some Android devices would not have Google Maps on them. For example, anyone porting Android via the open source project to existing hardware on a "homebrew" basis would unlikely be in a position to license Google Maps.

To accommodate this and similar scenarios with other possible technology, Android 1.5 has introduced a more formal add-on mechanism. You can see this with the target ID system, whereby some targets have Google Maps and others do not. If a device manufacturer decides to add some APIs to their devices that are unique to them, presumably they could use this same add-on system to help developers target their devices. This also opens up the possibility for other platform-level optional components, particularly ones that might need to be licensed, such as the oft-rumored Adobe Flash add-on.

Slide and Scroll

Android 1.5 introduces some new widgets, notably `SlidingDrawer` and `HorizontalScrollView`.

`SlidingDrawer` introduces a container akin to the one on the home screen used to hold the application icons. You control the image to use for the drawer "handle" and the contents to go in the drawer. You can also control the orientation, to determine if the drawer opens from the bottom or the side. Then, you can add listeners to monitor the state of the drawer, or toggle the state yourself, if desired.

As the name suggests, `HorizontalScrollView` works just like the original `ScrollView` except that it scrolls horizontally, not vertically.

Squeezably Soft

With the May 2009 debut of the HTC Magic, we now have Android phones lacking hardware keyboards. This makes text entry rather difficult . . . except that Android 1.5 added in support for soft keyboards. Soft keyboards also help for internationalization, as the user is not limited to the particulars of whatever hardware keyboard their device may actually have.

Soft keyboards take effect automatically, for basic functionality. The EditText widgets in your layout will cause the soft keyboard to spring up, assuming the device either does not have a QWERTY keyboard (e.g., HTC Magic) or is being held with the keyboard closed (e.g., T-Mobile G1 in portrait mode) as seen in Figure A-1.

Figure A-1. *Android 1.5's Input Method Editor (a.k.a., soft keyboard)*

You can tailor the behavior of the soft keyboard in your layouts or via Java code. For example, in the screenshot shown previously, you will see a "Next" button in the lower-right corner. By default, Android will take a guess as what to use this "action button" for—in this case, it moves you to the next field. You can add attributes to your layout to control what the caption is for this button, and what actually occurs when the action button is tapped. So, for example, if you are allowing people to enter a URL to visit in a Web browser, you might rename the action button to "Go" and have it launch the Browser application upon the typed-in URL.

You can also provide light control over what sort of keyboard is displayed by indicating what sort of text entry is supposed to occur in the EditText. For example, you can indicate that the android:inputType is textEmailAddress, which will ensure an @ key is available without having to use a soft shift key.

You can also control what happens to your activity layout when the soft keyboard is displayed. Your activity can either scroll out of the way to support the keyboard, or it can be resized to accommodate the keyboard, or have the keyboard appear full-screen, eclipsing your activity until the text entry is complete. Android will attempt to determine the best answer automatically, but via the `android:windowSoftInputMode` on your `<activity>` element in your manifest, you can override the default behavior.

This Input Method Framework (IMF) is extensible, should you wish to create your own customized soft keyboard (a.k.a., input method editor, or IME) for use in your application or by other applications. A sample IME is provided with the SDK to serve as a basis for your own custom keyboards.

Sprucing Up Your Home

Android 1.5 lets you do more with the built-in home screen application, notably by adding "app widgets" and "live folders". As an application developer, you can choose to offer app widgets and/or live folders from your own applications for users to add to their home screens.

App widgets are simply user interface elements added to the home screen. Previous Android editions had some of these (the analog clock, the Google search bar), but they were fixed in type and number. Now, not only does Android add in a couple of more app widgets (e.g., media player, picture frame), but users can add and remove app widgets, and developers can create their own (see Figure A-2).

Figure A-2. *Some stock Android 1.5 app widgets*

App widgets are built not using ordinary layouts, but rather with a layout subset known as `RemoteViews`. You cannot use arbitrary widgets with `RemoteViews`, though it supports many common ones. The term "remote views" comes from the fact that while the UI is defined by your application, the UI (in the form of the "app widget") runs in the context of another application, in this case the home screen.

Implementing an app widget involves creating some XML metadata, associating that metadata with a `<receiver>` element in your manifest, and implementing that receiver as an `AppWidgetProvider`. Most likely in conjunction with a service that will handle any time-consuming work (e.g., network lookups), your provider will create and push out `RemoteViews` when requested by the home screen. Note that app widgets are designed for infrequent update, since frequent polling for new widget contents can rapidly drain the device battery.

Live folders are, in essence, a simplified home-screen-launched look into the contents published by a `ContentProvider`. In the screenshot shown previously, you see a "Phones" icon. Tapping that brings up a dialog over the home screen containing a list of all contacts containing phone numbers as you can see in Figure A-3.

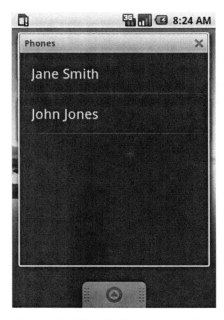

Figure A-3. *A Live Folder in Android 1.5*

Tapping an individual contact, of course, brings up the detail screen for that contact.

To create your own live folders for your users to offer, you can add an intent filter watching for a `CREATE_LIVE_FOLDER` `Intent` on an activity in your application. That activity, in turn, simply calls `setResult()` with another `Intent` object, this one describing the live folder, such as its icon, name, and display mode (e.g., `LiveFolders.DISPLAY_MODE_LIST`). This `Intent` also contains the `Uri` pointing to the `ContentProvider` whose information you are trying to display. That `ContentProvider` should be updated to recognize the live folder `Uri` and, on `query()`, return an ID, title, and description of each piece of content in the provider (or a subset if appropriate). Android will take care of the rest, in terms of formatting the data in the live folder convention (large font title, small font description), pouring the query results into a list, etc.

Tying Up Loose Threads

A common pattern in Android is to perform some work on a background thread, then update something on the UI thread when the background work is complete. A simple way to handle this is to fork a background thread and use a Handler or runOnUiThread() to accomplish the UI thread work. However, the danger here is in forking too many threads—the user might do something that causes you to fork many threads in short order, bogging down the device at best. And while there are classes that can help you manage a work pool (e.g., LinkedBlockingQueue), their use can be mildly tedious.

Enter AsyncTask.

AsyncTask manages a work queue with a thread pool, so you do not need to implement that yourself. Moreover, all of the communication between foreground and background threads are handled for you. All you need to do is override a few methods to describe what you want done in the background or in the foreground.

To create an AsyncTask, simply extend one anonymously, like you might do to create a Runnable. You can then override whatever methods you need to for the pattern you want:

- Override onPreExecute() to specify something that should be done on the UI thread when the task is started

- Override doInBackground() to indicate the work that should be done in the background thread

- Override onProgressUpdate() to update your progress on the UI thread when doInBackground() calls publishProgrss() (e.g., update a ProgressBar)

- Override onPostExecute() to do whatever work needs to be done on the UI thread after the background work is complete

Using your custom AsyncTask is then a matter of calling execute() on one of its instances, such as one might call run() on a Runnable.

Now, the Rest of the Story

Of course, there are many, many more things added to Android 1.5 beyond what is covered earlier. Here is a quick recap of other capabilities you will be able to take advantage of in Android 1.5.

Speech Recognition

Android 1.1 debuted Google Voice Search, where you could tap on a microphone icon text to the search field on the home screen, speak your search request, and have the search conducted on what you said.

Android 1.5 opens this up to be available to all applications. You can start an activity using an Intent using the RecognizerIntent.ACTION_RECOGNIZE_SPEECH action and have the converted text supplied to you in response via onActivityResult().

IntentService

A common pattern, particularly when using AlarmManager for scheduling periodic background work, is to have a service that implements onStart() and forks a background thread to do the desired work. This runs the risk of forking too many threads, though, and managing your own work queue and thread pool can be annoying.

The IntentService class wraps that pattern up for you. All you do is implement onHandleIntent(), and Android will process all inbound Intents via a work queue on a background thread. Android will also automatically stop the service when the work queue becomes empty, to help minimize the memory footprint of your application.

Audio Playback Options

The SoundPool class, largely undocumented in Android 1.1, is now ready for widespread use in Android 1.5. The SoundPool is designed to play back multiple overlapping sounds, particularly useful for games. Moreover, you can specify priorities for these audio streams and a maximum number of streams, so your application can simply play back clips as needed (e.g., based on game events), and Android will ensure the maximum number of streams is not exceeded. That way, you can minimize the amount of CPU power audio playback requires.

Android 1.5 also offers AudioTrack, whereby the device can play back audio that your code converts, perhaps from a streaming source, into PCM data. So, for example, should you want to implement a Voice-Over-IP (VOIP) application, you might use AudioTrack to handle playback of the audio coming off of, say, the SIP connection.

Android 1.5 also introduces the JetPlayer, designed to play back JET interactive music filesJET interactive music files.

Media Recording

Android 1.1 offered a MediaRecorder class, but it would only record audio. Now, with Android 1.5, you can record video as well. You control the frame rate and size, along with the encoding (e.g., H.264) and output format (e.g., MP4). Android will then, on demand, record video off of the device's camera to a file you specify.

Index

Breinigsville, PA USA
30 June 2010
240876BV00008B/25/P